To Gail:

Thanks for all your
support through
all my changes

love,
Anna

7-28-90

Anne, the White Woman in Contemporary African-American Fiction

Recent Titles in
Contributions in Afro-American and African Studies

Visible Now: Blacks in Private Schools
Diana T. Slaughter and Deborah J. Johnson, editors

Feel the Spirit: Studies in Nineteenth-Century Afro-American Music
George R. Keck and Sherrill V. Martin, editors

From a Caste to a Minority:
Changing Attitudes of American Sociologists Toward Afro-Americans, 1896–1945
Vernon J. Williams, Jr.

African-American Principals: School Leadership and Success
Kofi Lomotey

Class and Consciousness: The Black Petty Bourgeoisie in South Africa, 1924 to 1950
Alan Gregor Cobley

Black Novelist as White Racist:
The Myth of Black Inferiority in the Novels of Oscar Micheaux
Joseph A. Young

Capital and the State in Nigeria
John F. E. Ohiorhenuan

Famine in East Africa: Food Production and Food Policies
Ronald E. Seavoy

Archetypes, Imprecators, and Victims of Fate:
Origins and Developments of Satire in Black Drama
Femi Euba

Black and White Racial Identity: Theory, Research, and Practice
Janet E. Helms, editor

Black Students and School Failure: Policies, Practices, and Prescriptions
Jacqueline Jordan Irvine

Anne, the White Woman in Contemporary African-American Fiction

ARCHETYPES, STEREOTYPES, AND CHARACTERIZATIONS

Anna Maria Chupa

CONTRIBUTIONS IN AFRO-AMERICAN AND AFRICAN STUDIES, NUMBER 133
John W. Blassingame and Henry Louis Gates, Jr.,
Series Editors

GREENWOOD PRESS
New York • Westport, Connecticut • London

Library of Congress Cataloging-in-Publication Data

Chupa, Anna Maria.
    Anne, the white woman in contemporary African-American fiction :
archetypes, stereotypes, and characterizations / Anna Maria Chupa.
      p. cm. — (Contributions in Afro-American and African
studies, ISSN 0069–9624 ; no. 133)
    Includes bibliographical references.
    ISBN 0–313–25447–8 (lib. bdg. : alk. paper)
    1. American fiction—Afro-American authors—History and criticism.
2. American fiction—20th century—History and criticism. 3. White
women in literature.   4. Race relations in literature. 5. Whites in
literature. I. Title. II. Series.
PS374.W45C48 1990
813′.509352042—dc20   89-25919

British Library Cataloguing in Publication Data is available.

Library of Congress Catalog Card Number: 89–25919
ISBN: 0–313–25447–8
ISSN: 0069–9624

First published in 1990

Greenwood Press, Inc.
88 Post Road West, Westport, Connecticut 06881

Printed in the United States of America

∞

The paper used in this book complies with the
Permanent Paper Standard issued by the National
Information Standards Organization (Z39.48–1984).

10 9 8 7 6 5 4 3 2 1

For I am the first and the last.
I am the honored one and the scorned one.
I am the whore and the holy one.
I am the wife and the virgin.
I am the mother and the daughter.
I am the members of my mother.
I am the barren one
     and many are her sons.
I am she whose wedding is great,
     and I have not taken a husband.
I am the midwife and she who does not bear.

. . . .

Why, you who hate me, do you love me,
     and you hate those who love me?
You who deny me, confess me,
     and you who confess me, deny me.

. . . .

I am control and the uncontrollable.
I am the union and the dissolution.
I am the abiding and the dissolving.
I am the one below,
     and they come up to me.
I am the judgement and the acquittal.
I, I am sinless,
     and the root of sin derives from me.

. . . .

For many are the pleasant forms which exist in
     numerous sins,
     and incontinencies,
     and disgraceful passions,
     and fleeting pleasures,
          which men embrace until they become sober
          and go up to their resting place.
And they will find me there,
     and they will live,
     and they will not die again.

The Thunder, Perfect Mind
Gnostic text

Contents

Preface

I encountered my first serious study of African and African-American art and literature at Dartmouth College while preparing the research material for a performance art piece examining the images of women and goddesses in Celtic, Haitian, African and contemporary American contexts. Beginning with the survival of archaic myths as they appear in contemporary American culture, I developed a preliminary paper on contemporary African-American fiction exploring the image of white women from a Jungian perspective. This volume developed as a Jungian analysis of specific characters as they relate to European and African symbolic representations of feminine archetypes.

Accordingly, I proceed with the following assumptions culled from African religious thought and Jungian psychology.

- An archetype is a primordial mental image or pattern "inherent in the human psyche,"[1] and therefore universally recognizable, from which all particular representations are derived.

- Myth is a necessity of human life. The specific manifestations of archetypes within a geographical or cultural context make up the local mythos through which the universal patterns are alternately revealed to the initiates and concealed from outsiders.

- Individual pathologies occur as a result of alienation from the local mythos into which one is born.

- A society's pathologies occur as consequences of the failure of the local mythos to encompass and resolve new experiences and conflicts.

The pathologies evident in African-American fictional characterizations represent the result of tragic circumstances that severed the continuity between human experience and spiritual order. Healing these injuries depends upon the exposure of the oppression and injustice that brought about the current state of spiritual collapse, and the vital transformation of the local mythos that will bring the individual and the community to spiritual balance. Through a selection of fictional works by James Baldwin, Toni Cade Bambara, Cecil Brown, Alice Childress, Eldridge Cleaver, Ralph Ellison, Chester Himes, LeRoi Jones/Amiri Baraka, Paule Marshall, Toni Morrison, Ishmael Reed, Jean Toomer, Alice Walker, John A. Williams, Richard Wright, and Al Young, and two novels by Japanese-American John Okada and Native American Leslie Silko, issues of fragmentation and depersonalization in contemporary society are addressed, revealing a spiritual void within the images of men and women disinherited from myth.

A mythological orientation to reality is presupposed in Jungian psychology and in the West African religious traditions that inform the inherited Africanisms of the New World. Among the Yoruba of Nigeria, the soul selects an *ori*, or destiny, before birth. In the state before birth, one is free from temporal considerations and is in harmony with the patterns of the cosmological order. One's personal *ori* determines what social, sexual, political and spiritual alignments the individual will make as he enters the world of oppositions (male/female, good/evil). His *ase*, or spiritual vitality, is the force that will empower his choices, but it is his vital connection to primordial mythic images "behind the veil" of the *ori* that keeps the individual balanced between polarized forces. This connection is reinforced by the community through ritual imagery. Occupying the position of intermediary, the "Trickster" figure in African and African-American religion provides a connection between the spiritual and physical planes while maintaining a fundamental balance between oppositions. In this way the vital link between the *ori* and the *ase* is retained.

In the works of Ishmael Reed and Toni Cade Bambara, Jung's theory that a patterning force is "inherent in the human psyche" is reaffirmed. A "body of Africanisms . . . survived in the New World," despite deliberate attempts (by slaveowners) to undermine tribal ties through cultural and linguistic dispersals.[2] New mythologies formed, synthesizing the experiences of isolated groups emerging from a history of white oppression, each with varying degrees of absorption of local cultural influences. Thus it is shown that even when "traditions were cut off, . . . [a] whole mythology and the whole history of religion [will] start all over again with the next generation."[3] The evolution of African-American fiction embodies this transformation of African mythos in the New World.

According to Carl Jung, archetypes exist *a priori* but are recognized as they manifest themselves *a posteriori*, through specific cultural images. The instinctive recognition of an archetype is a genetic inheritance of the human species. The imagery through which the archetype appears to a specific society belongs to a cultural inheritance. Although they appear and are apprehensible through the respective masks of individual cultures, archetypes "are inherently expressive neither of local social circumstance nor of any individual's singular experience but of common human needs, instincts and potentials."[4] Specific cultural traditions provide the imagery through which an archetype is manifest and can be perceived. Basic archetypal images of African religion remain intact in varying degrees in the New World; however, the vehicle for expression was transformed by the new social context.

The presence of a connecting principle that provides a link between disparate entities—the human and the divine, the corporeal and the supernatural, culture and nature, the known and the unknown, the waters above and the waters below—performs an ordering function within society. Symbolic retentions of African religion in the New World provide links between the dichotomies of sacred and profane, good and evil, man and nature. Social and spiritual continuity are assisted by the intermediary position of the ancestors and the *orisha/Vodun* (respectively, Yoruba deities and Fon mysteries) between human experience and a supreme impersonal god. Transformed in the New World with considerable variation in rituals and in the names of principal figures, the fundamental tenets of an African world view that remain constant in the New World are animism, spirit possession and belief in a sacred continuity between all events and entities. The relationship between African religious philosophy and animism is limited to the belief that although a *loa* (the African-Haitian intermediary god or goddess) may reside in a rock, tree or stream, it is not equated with the spiritual essence of the natural phenomena in which it resides. A specific entity is not the *god of* lightning; rather, he may be *associated with* the forces of lightning. New *loa* emerge in changing contexts. Their relationship with natural phenomena is dynamic not static. Spiritual forces pervade the natural world and the *loa* have affinities with certain environments and natural phenomena. Damballah, the harbinger of change and the *loa* of cosmological order, is associated with springs and marshes, lightning, rainbows and serpents. He is the principal *loa* of Toni Cade Bambara's *The Salt Eaters*. The *loa* actively participate in the community through spirit possession. If they are properly "fed" (i.e., if they receive sufficient devotion) the *loa*'s benevolence may be entreated to assist the community. Minnie Ransom appeals to the *loa* for aid (*The*

Salt Eaters) to heal Velma. In Ishmael Reed's *Mumbo Jumbo*, Papa LaBas and Black Herman feed the traditional *loa* and enlist the aid of new *loa* to fight the enemies of a new age. As priests of an emerging global mythos, they have learned to interpret signs in events that appear to be insignificant to the uninitiated. They perceive underlying connections between seemingly disparate phenomena. Continuity in all facets of human experience increases as one's spiritual affinity with the external world reveals the interconnectedness of nature, humanity and the divine. No single event exists independently without effects on the world order. An individual who becomes estranged from myth can set several disruptive forces into motion. For this reason, a ritual healing is perceived as a benefit for the community, not just the individual. The principle of continuity assumes that an affinity exists between the patterns of nature, world order and individual growth.

Connection to myth is a basic necessity for human health. The individual "who thinks he can live without myth, or outside it is an exception. He is like one uprooted, having no true link with the past, or with the ancestral life which continues within him, or yet with contemporary human society."[5] A community operating with its mythic images and ceremonies intact facilitates the aberrant individual's return to a state of harmony with spiritual laws. Although crises of growth may threaten an individual's complacency, severe crises may impair the fundamental connection between the individual and myth. "If the manner of life and thought of an individual so departs" from myth that a "pathological state of imbalance ensues, . . . dreams and fantasies analogous to fragmented myths will appear."[6] A trained healer or medicine man recognizes the individual's dreams and fantasies as analogous to myth and creates ceremonies specifically designed to realign the individual with his spiritual center.

As a result of my studies under Ishmael Reed and William Cook at Dartmouth College during the summer of 1981, as well as subsequent conversations thereafter, I have selected a list of approximately thirty fictional works in which aspects of the African-American folklore stereotype "Miss Anne" appear. Miss Anne is mentioned directly by name only in Cecil Brown's *The Life and Times of Mr. Jiveass Nigger* and Ishmael Reed's *Reckless Eyeballing*; however, the stereotype of a woman who exerts her power over the lives of black men and women to secure a measure for her own self-worth appears frequently throughout African-American fiction. Both the Miss Anne figure and the characters she affects are analogous to fragmented myths.

The cause of their pathological behavior lies in the oppressive and tragic circumstances experienced in the context of peoples forcibly uprooted from their ancestral connections and made to endure the long-term effects of racism. These pathologies are "best interpreted, not by reference backward to repressed infantile memories [as in traditional psychoanalysis], but by comparison outward with the analogous mythic forms . . . so that the disturbed individual may learn to see himself . . . in the mirror of the human spirit and discover by analogy the way to his own larger fulfillment."[7] The African necromancer incarnate in Minnie Ransom (*The Salt Eaters*) approaches healing with the attitude that conflict and pain are resolved by realigning the individual with the patterns of a spiritual order. Minnie Ransom draws on a broad multicultural pool of imagery in order to reconnect with Velma, her patient. Similarly, the Native American medicine man of Leslie Silko's *Ceremony* recognizes that the world has expanded and an ethnocentric frame of reference is no longer relevant in addressing the broader issues of a growing society. Therefore, he expands his ceremonies to include the phenomena of a larger world. The psychic duress experienced by his patient, Tayo, is treated by analogy to this expanded perspective of an integrated universal mythos.

I use analogy to mythic forms instead of taking a biographical approach to determining the motives behind the pathological murders committed by Lula in *Dutchman*, Bigger in *Native Son*, and Jesse in *The Primitive*; or Rufus's suicide in *Another Country* and Velma's breakdown in *The Salt Eaters*; or the pitiful characterizations of white women: Margie in *The Salt Eaters*, Leona in *Another Country* and Lynne in *Meridian*. By viewing the behaviors of characters through reference to archetypes, I use the Jungian and/or ceremonial healing approach that interprets these fragmented lives in relation to a larger perspective of myth.

To assume a defensive posture regarding white society in an exploration into the degraded image of white women in minority literature is to miss the point. The "Anne" of African-American literature is a negative stereotype; however, the genesis of the type is within the configuration of an oppressive social structure. To interpret these images of white women as products of reversed racism is not only overly simplistic but also another example of blaming the victim. Exposing the results of oppression through the maimed personalities of white women (and black men, black women and white men) neither accepts nor denies the validity of stereotyped images. Exaggerated characterizations of soulless beauties (Vivian in *Flight to Canada*), or the bitterness of aging blondes who once believed in the power of their beauty (Madge in *The Primitive*), reveal the forceful anti-aesthetic of white materialism as it is reflected in the vacuous billboard Aphrodites. The respective struggles of Jesse (*The Primitive*), Clay (*Dutchman*) and Lillian (*The Man Who Cried I Am*), reveal the conflict shared by black men and women between the will to identify with middle-class values (and thereby deny personal injustice) or choose a road of self-discovery to confront injustice, to move beyond fragmentation, disillusionment and billboard seductions to reconnect with myth. Recognizing these misaligned characters as symptoms of contemporary depersonalization leads one to an honest assessment of the need to repair a damaged world. Exposure is the first step for healing.

When I began this book, I was confronted by a hypothesis extant in criticism of minority literature: The characterizations of white women in African-American fiction are an attempt by a minority group to seek revenge on an oppressive society by attacking the female image of White America. I believe the intent of these novels transcends reversed racism. Although novels placed within an historical context do not escape the tendency toward social commentary, they tend to expose symptoms rather than prescribe cures for the social realities they reveal. There is a basic consistency between African-American social commentary in literature and West African rituals for social healing. These ceremonies begin with a process of ridicule from which no one is exempt. Once this exposure of social ills is underway, the process toward correcting community problems can begin. The artists and necromancers of modern society are the contemporary priests who initiate us back to a cosmological order through confrontation. The approach taken toward reestablishing spiritual connections within a fragmented society is consistent with the Jungian model for individual integration of unconscious projections. Jung departs from African systems when he focuses less on the specific cultural phenomena that create unique manifestations of archetypes and more on the individual psyche. The social organism and its growth is dynamically involved with the individual self-realization in traditional African societies. Continuity of mythic forms following the African diaspora depended upon an extraordinary capacity for absorbing outside influences within the umbrella of a constantly transforming mythic structure.

Promoting the restoration of spiritual vitality, artist Romare Bearden and novelist Ishmael Reed exemplify the modern shamans who sustain the connection to myth through image transformation. Bearden's collages include fragments of African funerary masks, textile and scarification patterns with a heritage of American imagery (trains, cats, ironwork grilles and city blocks) to synthesize and perhaps memorialize African-American experience. Reed employs the outrageous aesthetic of African social ridicule in his scathing satires of vacuous lifestyles in American society, equating contemporary Americans with the stage of development, the "Terrible Twos," in which children feel entitled to anything they desire and accept no responsibility for their behavior. Depersonalization and detachment from the vitality of life is personified in the "Wallflower Order" (*Mumbo Jumbo*), whereas the aesthetic of an ancestral memory and celebrative ritual is consolidated in the lifeforce of "Jes Grew."[8]

Leslie Silko's *Ceremony* provides us with an example of a contemporary Native American necromancer, Betonie, who assists the organic growth of ceremonies by blending tradition with symbols of an expanding mythos. Along with his bundles of herbs and pollens, Betonie collects telephone books and calendars to form stories that evolve with the fragility of a changing world. This process of transforming mythic symbols in art and literature is called *ethno-aesthetics*.

Ethno-aesthetics is the study of the cosmological beliefs and aesthetic values that contribute to the formation of symbolic imagery particular to a geographical area or culture. The ethno-aesthetic process in art entails constant transformation of the symbols that refer to primordial images. In his introduction to *The Portable Jung*, Joseph Campbell describes the local mythos as the cultural structure that enables archetypes to be manifest specifically through symbols that will be readily recognizable by members within the context of a cultural group. The raw archetype has no material form and is only recognizable as it becomes manifest through physical symbols. Whereas the archetype belongs to a collective unconscious, its manifestation belongs to a specific set of local circumstances wherein symbols are created from early tribal roots and variously transformed throughout history.

Symbols, like living organisms, die when they cease to grow. Ancient symbols survive through time only when they continue to be relevant to current needs. To satisfy the criterion of current relevance, the symbol is transformed through the synthesis of old forms and new experiences. In West Africa, the Gelede mask survived the transition of European influences by expanding the visual imagery represented in the superstructure. The helmet remains constant as the serene face of the Great Mother bearing the superstructure of the world, which may be represented in images ranging from a traditional council of elders and blacksmiths to airplanes and motorcycles.

I have examined Celtic and West African ethno-aesthetic systems to compare manifestations of particular archetypes: the Terrible Goddess, the sensual unbound feminine figure (the Virgin), the Seductress/Initiator, the transcendent Wise Woman, and the Nurturing Mother. Recurrent motifs include horses, birds, rivers, oceans and curvilinear patterns as manifestations of the Feminine. I am also interested in the archetypal crossroads figure that stands as guardian and guide between the physical and spiritual worlds. This figure may be represented as a harlequin, Trickster, buffoon, saviour, warrior or harbinger of change. Damballah, the primary *loa* of *The Salt Eaters*, is an example of a figure representing cosmological order. Legba, the crossroads figure of life, and Ghede, his underworld counterpart, both ridicule social ills and are the primary *loa* in Ishmael Reed's novels. The specific imagery common to African and Celtic connecting principles are the world tree, rainbow and serpent.

These are some of the themes I have examined through the study of ethno-aesthetics as part of my involvement in the movement of the visual arts toward content and away from the purely formal concerns of minimalism and abstraction. Art forms and preliterate oral traditions that emerged from a spirito-religious milieu inform my pursuits in visual productions. These productions attempt to create a ritual context through which the symbols of the Feminine and the crossroads figure can be manifest.

The all-encompassing questions that connect my undertakings in art with the study of the survival of archaic forms in contemporary culture and the current investigation of archetypes as they appear in African-American literature are:

- How does the individual become disengaged from myth?
- What happens to the individual and the society that lives outside of myth?
- Once estranged, how does one return to the mythological orientation of the psyche?

A disruption in personal life can be the springboard for growth (providing the individual adapts), just as cataclysmic events in a cultural context force myth to expand for the symbols to survive. When these crises are too overwhelming to be healed by the traditions that support myth in a specific society, the growth process becomes impaired and pathology develops. An active mythos transforms itself through crises. A crisis can be the introduction of a new, albeit intrinsically neutral, influence such as the airplane. The Yoruba aesthetic system which informs Gelede symbolism was able to encompass new imagery.

If the Mother-Of-Us-All who appears in the substructure of the Gelede mask is the creative agent responsible for the existence of traditional technologies, then her wisdom also incorporates the new technologies brought to Africa by foreigners. Similarly, the Yoruba mythos absorbed additional Western influences attributing a causal connection beyond imperialism to the creative force of the gods. Thus, in the shrines to Ogun, the *orisha* of war and of the traditional technologies associated with iron and fire, the automobile spark plug is added. In this way, the mythos assumes ownership of an image by evolving within its own continuum (thereby maintaining autonomy), instead of simply assimilating the imagery of popular Western culture (and forfeiting a unique cultural heritage to the "melting pot").

At the other extreme, crises can be life threatening. Threats to one's physical well-being and self-esteem present obstacles that are detrimental to normal growth. When an individual's experience departs so radically from the mythos that informs his reality, splitting occurs within. The modern individual develops separate personae to cope with the antithetical fragments of his society. In *The Salt Eaters*, Velma "found a home amongst" both those who considered themselves to be politically oriented and those who thought of themselves as " 'psychically adept,' . . . but somehow she'd fallen into the chasm that divided the two camps," and somehow she had to find her way back to seeing the world pattern where the two camps were interconnected.[9]

My position builds upon that of Chester Himes;[10] if it is true that African-American literature is laden with pathological, fractured personalities, then this is but the result of a series of crises brought about through racism that were threatening to life and the nurturance of an ethno-aesthetic milieu. Instead of hiding the injury or pretending that an inner fragmentation does not exist, the pathology must be exposed.

The function of the artist as a necromancer is to provide creative analogies so that, as members of a beleaguered society, we may see our own pathologies through the mirrors of art and find the will to confront corruption. Swille (*Flight to Canada*), as the bigoted white robber baron and Ms. Anne, the white woman, parody the forces who "are running things" and perpetuating racist policy in American society.[11] Here, Reed functions as the provocative *loa*, Ghede, by exposing the ills of society in seemingly outrageous satire. Exposure of deep wounds within the fabric of American society calls for honesty on the part of the author and the reader. Honesty is necessary before any real change can be effected.

These books are more than sociological statements—they are novels. A sociological study has to prove that a problem exists, as well as define the problem within the appropriate context of historical development and contemporary setting. The authority of the sociologist is often based on field studies and statistics. The novelist also defines and exposes social problems but the "proof" that the problem exists is generated through the human experience of the characters and the credibility of the novel does not need to rely on statistics. The social problems addressed in novels speak to the heart of the reader and, in this way, jostle old prejudices.

Sociologists run the risk of having their work criticized for its bias; the novelist doesn't have to assume this position of omniscient objectivity in order to get the point across. These are stories. Often minority literature is criticized for being overly political in content; however, I suspect that this is because the message that may come through makes readers uncomfortable because of their own participation in the perpetuation of destructive social patterns. In taking the risk to seriously read these novels as potential analogies to one's own split behaviors, individuals may see themselves revealed in the mirrors of mythic images and conflicts and find guidance through spiritual darkness to light. Seeing one's experiences within the larger context of myth is the second step toward healing the rift between individual isolation and society.

The most profound connection I feel with the material is with the despair that lurks beneath the many facades of characters caught in a society that likewise aches for healing. Beneath the superficial Anne of African-American fiction, who is as obsessed with control as she is with trying to emulate the fashion magazine aesthetic, is an empty figure we can sympathize with once we overcome the disdain we feel for her apathetic, bitter, brittle, beaten, cold or sexless defenses that belie a critical emptiness. Because she is supposed to embody an ideal, her failings evoke even greater disgust. Because she exposes the fissures in society, she is an object of derision. Because she mirrors the poverty in any reader's self-esteem, she represents a threat that we may also succumb to the despair that lurks beneath a fragmented world. For all the pain she may cause others and the destruction she may represent, the irretrievably lost soul of the despairing woman is still pitiable. Although at first we may despise the vulnerability the Despairing Goddess awakens within our own hearts, we are inevitably drawn to comfort the embodiment of the Tragic Mistress so aptly described in Maya Deren's encounter with the African-Haitian *loa*, Erzulie.

Out of the context of poverty, Erzulie embodies luxury, representing man's "capacity to conceive beyond reality, to desire beyond adequacy, to create beyond need." She embodies "all the excessive pitch with which the dreams of men soar, when, momentarily, they can shake loose the flat weight, the dreary, reiterative demands of necessity."[12] Man will expend "his every resource" for her, yet, in the midst of this promise of fulfillment, "she will inexplicably recall, . . . some old, minor disappointment." She will notice "the one inadequate detail" among all the luxuries lavished upon her. Erzulie, "who suddenly seemed so very close, so real, so warm, is suddenly of another world, beyond this reality, this reason. It is as if below the gaiety a pool had been lying, . . . and now its dark despair surfaces and engulfs her beyond succor." Although she is the most loved of all *loa*, the weeping Erzulie "is convinced, by some curious inversion, that [she has been] betrayed." It is because of her grief that men are moved to give even more and "women, who might otherwise resent her, are so gentle."[13]

From our own dark pools we can find a source for the empathy that moves us to comfort the abject grief of the lost women characterized in these novels. The rage and disgust characters such as Leona in *Another Country* or Lynne in *Meridian* invoke should be directed at the social circumstances that created their condition. To the black men represented in fiction, the white woman embodies luxury beyond attainment. Similarly, Erzulie is the *loa* who embodies all that is unattainable and irretrievably lost. Perhaps we, like the men and women of Haiti, may be moved to comfort the lost soul instead of despising the Tragic Goddess as she appears in the stereotyped image of white woman, the Anne of African-American folklore. The Tragic Mistress and Erzulie Red Eyes are manifestations of a *loa* who has not been fed. If her rites are remembered, her rage can be appeased. The poverty of the billboard image of white women is a symptom of an excessive imbalance toward patriarchal values. Persistent denial and repression of the efficacy of the feminine side of life will invoke chaotic eruptions that appear in the form of shattered entities. If we seek to avoid the tendency to deny, repress or annihilate the truth beneath the image we might learn to confront fragmentation in the mirror of broken symbols and find a means to revitalize our spiritual milieu.

The single thread uniting all mythologies, religions and "great poems" is the capacity "to point infallibly through things and events to the ubiquity of a 'presence' or 'eternity' that is whole and entire in each. . . . The first condition, therefore, that any mythology must fulfill . . . is that of cleansing the doors of perception to the wonder at once terrible and fascinating, of ourselves and the universe."[14] Affirmation, rather than denial, is the means by which we can recapture mythic symbols. And through these mythic symbols we "can learn to know and come to terms with the greater horizon of our own deeper and wiser, inward self." Through the maintenance of an open channel connecting "contemporary life" with the patterns of "inherited myths" we can join forces to revitalize the sacred canopy of our world.[15]

Acknowledgments

I am very grateful to Ishmael Reed, who was a visiting writer-professor at Dartmouth College while I studied in the M.A.L.S. program from 1979 to 1981, and to Professor William Cook, head of the African-American Studies Department at Dartmouth College, for their assistance throughout the development of this volume. In addition to the inspiration he has given through his writing, Ishmael Reed has initiated the publishing process for many of his students. As my professor, he suggested a project that fit my interdisciplinary background and opened the door to publishing opportunities. The generous gift of his time and the inspiration he provides as an advocate for writers who might not otherwise gain visibility is truly appreciated. William Cook also did numerous readings of the manuscript and has advised me during the last eight years regarding contacts and resources for multi-cultural interdisciplinary education.

For their readings of the manuscript, editing and the help I received in tracking down the final details and permissions, I want to thank the editors, reviewers and the highly professional staff at Greenwood Press. In particular, I want to thank Marilyn Brownstein, Meg Fergusson and Maureen Melino.

Finally, for emotional support and patience with the frustrations I projected as I moved from the visual to the verbal medium, I am deeply grateful to my son Zachary and my husband Michael. Mike nurtured me through the process of computerizing my writing (from the first typed version to the final version, I changed word processing programs six times) and his proofreading was invaluable. To the friends, colleagues and family along the way who have all shown me pieces of the transcendent archetype, I thank you for the initiations and the healing you have given.

Anne, the White Woman
in Contemporary
African-American
Fiction

Introduction

In European and African myth, the death figure responsible for despair is inextricably joined to the Mother and giver of life. The *orisha* of the sea, Yemoja, is the mother of Mothers and queen of the Witches. Like the Indo-European Kali, she is associated with death and the subsequent rebirth out of the abysmal sea. Instead of turning against her as a symbol of slave ships, Africans in the New World remembered Yemoja as a symbol of the return to the land across the ocean. Like Kali, she is "the Ferry Across the Ocean of Existence."[1] Life is a feminine deity and her counterpart is death. In Nigeria, Yoruba Gelede ceremonies celebrate the Mothers—the origin of everything—and appease their *aje* (negative aspect) in order to call forth their blessings.

In Haiti, the ritual reclamation of the deceased spirit from the land beneath the waters of the abyss is known as the third birth of man. First, individuals enter the physical world as little more than animals. Through initiation, individuals become fully human. When they die, individuals are lost to the physical world. Through the ceremony of *retirer d'en bas de l'eau*, the soul that "was lost to the visible world is brought back into it once more."[2] After generations, this ancestor may undergo a final transfiguration and emerge as a *loa*. Through temporary possession of a living host, the *loa* becomes an active participant in the community. "The power of the loa to become manifest in living matter marks their final mastery over matter."[3] Every individual partakes of this cycle of birth, initiation, death and rebirth. Instead of rejecting despair and death, African-American literature reaffirms death as the means by which the hero takes his leap of surrender toward the eternal cycle of the living dead, the ancestors and the gods. Macon Dead of *The Song of Solomon* takes his leap toward the metaphysical Africa to reunite with the invisible world of the ancestors. His death is a paradox of affirmation and despair. Toni Morrison leaves us with the question: Did he jump to his death or did he fly?

Neither resignation nor sentimental grief explain the individual's final act of affirmation when he encounters death. Both Macon Dead and Max (*The Man Who Cried I Am*) undergo a transformation similar to initiation before they die. Macon Dead completes a journey that is initiated through some very significant women in his life, Circe and Pilate. Max takes his flight into the nightmare territory of semiconscious release from physical pain, where he encounters his Initiator. In this flight, Max reconstructs his past and banters with Sammie (an internal Trickster figure) about the meaning of his life, "Why remember more than most . . . the gift of that raving bitch, evolution, nature, now made gentle with the title, Mother, and keep crying I Am?"[4] Sammie urges Max's flight to transformation through ridiculing Max's ceaseless search for purpose. In spite of apparent meaninglessness, Max takes the existential leap toward self-affirmation. At the threshold of death, Max recapitulates evolution, remembers "warm, ancient seas," and, through "the vast labouring distance so filled with internecine horror and commonplace death,"[5] he is still compelled to cry "I Am." Whereas Max's worldly circumstances bar him from any feeling of integration between self, society and an archetypal structure, he regains an approximate connection to primordial beginnings through delirium. The modern hospitals have no ritual healing for body and spirit. Through the medium of pain, Max finds release from the bondage to an oppressive society that impinged upon his marriage to a white woman. At the moment of his death, freed from the contradictions of temporal boundaries, Max reconnects with the archetypal element he recognizes in Maggie and calls out to her. He returns to the Mother and releases himself from the concrete images that bind him.

Joseph Campbell maintains that archetypes cease to function for us when they become concretized into specific personalities and events. Maggie becomes the archetype for Max only when the concrete world fades away. Throughout their time together, Maggie is a fixed image, only a reified fragment of the Goddess who Max cannot kiss publicly because of social sanctions against interracial marriages. Max cannot help but yearn for the image of "whitey Aphrodite" that promises warmth and reprieve yet delivers punitive consequences.[6] In his dreams, he encounters only incomplete images of the myth and is disillusioned.

The fragmentation and disillusionment in the Western world is echoed in the manifestos of Dada and Existentialism. The conclusion inherent in these philosophies and in Sammie's barbs is that reason cannot resolve chaos; there is no hidden cause to be identified; life is absurd and one must make a leap of faith to resolve the experience of disconnection. Furthermore, there is no guarantee of resolution. Although the horrors in Max's experience would suggest that life is absurd, his questioning throughout the course of his illness leads to inward understanding. His internal purgation reveals the true cause of disintegration. The image of white women is not a cause but a symptom of the fragmented mythos that operates in American society. Likewise, images of embittered black men are symbolic characterizations of a split in the human psyche between the conscious (reason) and the unconscious (chaos) mind, which generates a series of unreconcilable dichotomies: culture versus nature, materialism versus spiritualism, oppressor versus oppressed, masculine versus feminine, black versus white.

Whether it be Jungian psychology or the old medicine of Sophie in *The Salt Eaters* and Betonie in *Ceremony*, once a crisis point is reached, the return to wholeness includes the acceptance of a sick world and an internal reconciliation with the paradox of pain and release. The path of the necromancer is one of wholeness and balance. Inherent in the teachings of West African religion is the respect for paradox reconciled through a spiritual journey rather than reason. Centering on the concept of balance, West African philosophy recognizes that the invisible world behind the veil of material illusion has no oppositions. When individual souls select an *ori*, they determine their own way of resolving polarities. Individuals are assisted by "the invisibles," who will intervene on one's behalf and provide a connection between the corporeal and the metaphysical planes.

Pre-Christian Celtic mythology held a similar concept regarding the resolution of polarities. Mist was used as a metaphor for shifting from one plane of experience to another wherein different laws operated. Long after its link with the mystery schools was lost to the masses, Christian doctrine imposed dualism on the pagan world. To undermine and banish the local gods of the British Isles, Christian fanatics likened Celtic gods to Satan; in this way, the old god of the witches lost its benevolence and became equivocated with evil. Instead of being the spiritual instructor, administering tests of fire for purification, the horned Trickster god became a figure to be loathed and feared. In this way, the Roman Empire secured greater control over the masses. Similarly, the crossroads figure (Legba/Ghede) so central to New and Old World *Vodun* became Satan in Western cosmology when, contrarily, he is more closely aligned with medieval manuscript paintings of Christ as the *axis mundi*. The fact that Ghede is associated with death does not make him evil, yet Christian fanatics in Haiti liken him to the devil.

Reed's Papa LaBas (*Mumbo Jumbo*) is a *houngan* (priest) who maintains the balance between polarities while fighting the oppression of the "Wallflower Order." In his poem "why i often allude to osiris,"[7] Reed contrasts the will for power with the desire for balance. Under the guise of seeking a unified concept of god, Iknaton (portrayed by Reed as a dictator/son of Aton) destroys all images and references to the pantheon of deities under Amen-Ra. He "brought re/ligious fascism to egypt." Like the Christian conquerors, colonists and slaveholders, Iknaton sought to solidify his power over Egypt by undermining the religious expression of his subjects. Iknaton wanted to rule, whereas Osiris, "he'd rather dance than rule."[8]

The healer of *The Salt Eaters*, Mrs. Heywood, counsels her followers, "There is a world to be redeemed. . . . And it'll take the cooperation of all righteous folks."[9] Bambara and Silko describe a world view in which one individual's struggle between wholeness and disintegration is a vital link to the community's well-being. Ku'oosh tells World War II veteran Tayo that his health and return to the mythic structure "is important to all of us. Not only for your sake, but for this fragile world."[10] The problems faced by American minorities go beyond the pain of social injustice to the spiritual chasms pervading contemporary human experience. A split in human experience between the intellect and the heart, the spiritual and the commonplace, nature and culture has yielded "a Babel of paths, of plans."[11] In search of ways to bridge the gap between spirit and intellect, since the 1930s European and American artists have sought the imagery of child art, tribal art and the world of the unconscious, where boundaries are constantly shifting. Transcendentalism promised the dissolution of boundaries to the Western psyche. Disappointed with the promises of politically separatist groups surrounding Berkeley, Al Young's Angelina (*Who Is Angelina?*) turns to meditation to establish her own center. True transformation of mythic vitality goes beyond adaptation of styles and non-Western motifs. Adorning assemblages of multicultural accoutrements, a youth disillusioned with American society in the 1970s awaited transformation and revolution.

The key to any revival of the wisdom inherent in the mystery schools and African-American *Neo-Hoodoo* is the dissolution of limits through the expansion of awareness. Instead of seeing life as real and illusory, sane and insane, one may begin to interpret experiences phenomenologically as they relate to growth. Our experiences make up our choices for consequent actions. "Personal action can either open out possibilities of enriched experience or it can shut off possibilities."[12] In *The Man Who Cried I Am*, Margrit unconsciously invalidates Max's experience of racism in America and consequently shuts off the means to effectively address the tension between them. She does not experience his discomfort, thus Margrit assumes that Max's perception of racist attitudes is exaggerated. Without maligned intention, Margrit denies the legitimacy of Max's pain. She responds destructively instead of creatively supporting Max; she is incapable of informed response because her sensibilities are attuned to a more tolerant, European milieu.

The more exacting our sensibilities become with experience, the more informed our choices become. In the mythic context, every action (or inaction) is significant to cosmological order. Small decisions become related to a larger context and the individual becomes aware of a broader spiritual responsibility, recognizing that life depends on the individual's search for spirit, "that initiation [is] the beginning of transformation and that the ecology of the self, the tribe, the species, the earth depend[s] on just that."[13] The individual's responsibility lies in opening oneself to wholeness, to the awareness of choices and decisions, to one's place in the "karmic law" and in "becoming available to the spirits summoned to regenerate the life of the world."[14]

In order that individuals may become available to the forces of regeneration, they must be willing to relinquish painful attachments; however, if personal identity is entangled in painful memories, then individuals face not only emptiness but a loss of identity if they disencumber themselves from pain. They may be desperate for reprieve but the eyes that hold the memory of ancient pain "will not let [them] let it go."[15] The bondage of rage, grief and despair is abandoned only when a powerful good of equal strength is present to replace the emptiness filled by pain. In *The Salt Eaters*, Minnie coaxes Velma to release the hurt in order to "make room for lovely things to rush in and fill [her] full." Before she can break through the narrowness of painful memory and release her spirit to the healing forces that promote wholeness and connection with the universe, Velma must exhaust, and therefore neutralize, the energies that urge her absorption in the "mud puddle."[16]

Velma's reconciliation of obstacles to her growth represents a categorically different approach than the pursuit of the American Dream summarized in the cliché of pulling oneself up by the bootstraps. Velma's struggle for self-healing is part of the regeneration of a living mythos, whereas the Protestant work ethic promises material and spiritual reward for hard work and conformity to a rigid mythos. In this way, a child is encouraged to conform to a system of behavior with the promise of a "Someday" which will bring him happiness. The disheartened employee is encouraged to work harder for a future payoff. A society can thus deny any responsibility for unhappiness of its constituents by implying that failure is not the result of a faulty system but of laziness and inadequacy on the part of the individual.

The "Someday" of white, middle-class America promises a pay-off of happiness and well-being in return for leading a good life. This reward is a different concept than the spiritual healing that Minnie espouses. Healing restores balance but never guarantees freedom from future conflict. The necromancer does not mislead the patient with promises of an easier road ahead. Instead, the healer provides a vehicle for healthier alignment with beneficent forces. The Protestant ethic promises conformers that they will earn a respected place in the status quo if they work hard enough. Furthermore, this Someday is expected to guarantee happiness and faith in self-worth. In *Ceremony*, Tayo thought he could earn a secure place in American society through his enlistment as a soldier in World War II, but returned to find his social status unchanged and his spiritual life askew. Tayo was diverted from an awareness of his essential link to myth by the assumption that hard work, good intentions and faithful adherence to American values will secure happiness. A growing awareness of the emptiness inherent in this Someday became evident in the social upheavals of the 1960s and the 1970s. A search to rediscover and establish a spiritual foundation spread throughout the not-so-solid foundations of the white community. Many individuals, artists and writers took a leap of faith out of the disillusionment of white middle-class society toward spiritual evolution. Surpassing mere castigation of white society and its evils, Bambara, Silko and Reed call upon us to both confront and move beyond pain, as well as to work collectively toward spiritual renewal.

Before one can discard the attachment to injury, anger and hate, one must become aware of the cost that energy levies on the psyche. Reluctant to take a leap of faith without guarantees, the Western psyche relinquishes attachments only when something better is immediately available. Accustomed to immediate gratification, those who strive for membership in the American mainstream become unwilling to undergo purgation or swallow prescribed doses of empty ritual to relieve their angst; the billboard aesthetic does not promote an existence of self-denial. Finally, after rebounding from one easy solution to the next, modern men encounter the "dark night of the soul" (St. John of the Cross) in which they are truly alone and escape through denial is impossible. Through acceptance of the shadow self, individuals can integrate all that has hitherto been repressed.

By acknowledging the existence of negative traits in themselves, they can proceed to fully actualize their choices. The idea of primeval mitosis, the original split of the inner universe, suggests that before salvation can be reached, the fragmented self must be rejoined. Jung called this reconciliation of the opposing aspects of the psyche the *syzygy*. Reconciliation of oppositions does not imply an ultimate evolution toward an absolute. Through seeking the balance of the syzygy, in the process of self-individuation, individuals discover their role in the world ceremony. The ceremonies must grow and transform and the stories must expand to regenerate the essential truths of the past and bring them forward into the context of the present.

Traditional philosophies attribute to the Feminine such traits as negativity, passivity, emotionalism and irrationality. At the same time reason, aggression and depersonalization may be attributed to masculine experience. Reconciliation of opposites generates both turmoil and transcendence. Pain can create the movement of energy necessary to break the inertia of complacency and apathy. On the spiritual plane, there is a paradoxical relationship between chaos and order where contradicting forces simultaneously find definition and resolution. "The white European and North American in particular, commonly has a sense not of renewal, but of being at an end."[17] Out of an experience of essential alienation one might find a beginning rather than an end. The evolving spirit in the European-American psyche turns to its shadow and anima for a mirror. Within vast differences of cultural accoutrements is mirrored opposition. Geographic and cultural groups will find their points of correspondence and opposition; and contradictions may be resolved, but not without conflict.

The is the raison d'être for the White Bitch. The Bitch Goddess is yet another test of fire for the purgation of spirit through the violence of conflict. Only through struggle are the rough spots and aberrations of our spirits made smooth. The turbulent encounter of rigidly defined oppositions is instigated to bring about greater harmony, not disharmony. Like the quiet center within the hurricane, and Velma shedding her cocoon amid the violent clash of psychic and physical elements (*The Salt Eaters*), the magician holds his position of stillness within the chaos, acting as catalyst to healing forces. The spirit who creates order out of chaos and acts as a messenger to the gods also controls the storm. Damballah is the *loa* of order in African-Haitian cosmology whose symbols are the rainbow and the bridge, images of paradox and connection. Like Legba, he creates havoc to instigate change. He is the vital bridge between the spiritual and material worlds whose symbol is the rainbow. A rainbow can only be seen when the contradictory forces of sun and rain are present. Contained within Damballah's storm is the paradox of reconciliation, the vibrant center of the inner self, like Velma shedding her cocoon or Tayo driving out the bad magic in Laguna.

In Jungian psychology, the final reconciliation of the self comes in the recognition and integration of the syzygy: shadow, anima/animus and transcendent self. The shadow is only recognized via projection of similar traits onto another person of the same sex. The shadow requires a mirror to be self-cognizant. Initial awareness of the shadow occurs when criticizing another individual's intolerable behavior. What we are most loathe to accept in others are often the traits that we cannot accept in ourselves. The anima/animus is recognized via projection onto a person of the opposite sex. Again, it is often the most oppressive traits that we cannot tolerate in ourselves that are projected onto a partner or mate. The feminine quality in men is known as the *anima*; conversely, the masculine quality in women is known as the *animus*. Beneath the surface of a battle between a black man and a white woman, Jesse and Kriss (*The Primitive*) are waging war with one another's projections; thus, they encounter, in each other, the archetypal anima/animus, feminine/masculine unconscious. Finally, the third level of the syzygy is the recognition of the archetypal Wise Woman or Wise Man respectively in women and men. Full consciousness of the forces within us requires the presence of mirrors, often uncomfortable ones, in order that the integration of selves be complete. This study of the image of white women in contemporary African-American fiction attempts to hold up a mirror. The process begins with an attempt to understand through empathy. Once individuals can honestly see themselves in the white women (however they are portrayed), and in the aesthetic of any given culture, they can retrieve their projections, integrate them into their beings and begin to see the images from a broader perspective. Once individuals honestly confront the paradoxes of their own world, they can begin to reconcile internal conflict. The process is aided by the healers and artists who have opened themselves to the forces of renewal. These guides use analogy to myth to enable individuals to see themselves in the mirror of human experience.

Once individuals become the objective observers of their own psyche, it becomes easier to move beyond stereotypical ways of perceiving others. In her process of self-growth, Cora (Childress, *A Short Walk*) moves past her own misconceptions to see into the world of a white woman who hired Cora and Looli to serve at an expensive party. The white woman's boyfriend "skipped town" leaving Cora's employer to pay for the bills. "Poor soul cried herself sick, but did try to do right." Cora thought that "white women always got treated nice." She learns through opening her heart to May that white women also suffer.[18] The experience of the white woman exceeds the image she represents of privileged ease and cool detachment from suffering.

The image of white women in contemporary African-American fiction is multilayered. Personality traits entwine with layers of environment: socioeconomic status, political and educational background, friends, lovers, family. In short, a character cannot be studied in isolation; experience dictates growth from childhood to adulthood. Through each character's response to experience, we gain insight into her total personality; however, the phenomena of individual experience should not be isolated from the conceptual type each character represents.

Within the types there are more layers. A stereotype is defined within a limited frame of reference, whereas an archetype is universal. The sloppy white woman with sagging breasts, "slumming" with black men, is a stereotype. Add the fear and taboo that surround her relations with black men and one begins to approach a similarity with the archetypal Goddess. Increase her appearance as a hag, add a nasty temperament and she again corresponds with the Terrible Goddess. Describe her as beautiful and elusive with long, streaming hair and a diaphanous gown and she becomes the unattainable Femme Fatale. If she dies, she is Edgar Allen Poe's vision of the ultimate object of poetry, that melancholy and transient Beauty.[19]

In each character, the layers of the outer (cultural) experience and the inner psyche may be seen in relationship to a universal, archetypal world to which we can all respond. Whatever is lacking in experience, either personally or culturally, is apprehensible on a more universal, subliminal level. Therefore, each character may be viewed as a reexperiencing of the White Goddess in local costume, not as a reinterpretation of an archaic image. As such, each character becomes (in the moment of closest resemblance to the archetypal woman, i.e., full possession) the living embodiment of the Goddess (instead of a mere likeness, as would be seen in a lifeless portrait). When the individual transcends the passive state of possession and finds the part of the inner self that is aligned with the primeval Feminine, she becomes a self-possessed participant in the archetypal mysteries. None of the white women in books considered here are portrayed as self-realized. Instead, aspects of the Goddess are manifest occasionally in the behavior of these women as fractured mythic remnants.

A true portrait is one in which we recognize both a likeness of the individual portrayed and her participation in the universal qualities as perceived by the artist. Each of these characters may be seen both as an individual and as a manifestation of the archetype. Before the archetypal soul of a character may be glimpsed we must first be introduced. For the sake of continuity, the characters will be introduced in categories. As is the problem with all methods of classification and analysis, the characters may overlap categories and the categories themselves have areas of commonality.

I begin with those women who bear closest resemblance to the "Terrible Goddess," because I think it is this form out of which the others generate. This Goddess is the combination of all that is desired and despised; she is the Mother of life and the Goddess of death. The characters introduced in this category represent her many faces: the Destructive/Seductive Bitch, the Benevolent (yet inevitably destructive) Witch, the Mad Woman in the Attic, the Slob-Bitch and the Whores, Mothers and Virgins.

The next category falls within the realm of sociological constructs: Low-class Ignorant, Upper-class Snob, Slummer/Thrill Seeker, Dumb Blonde, White-Negro Woman. The following classification, discussed in the same context as the social stereotypes, is the political type. The sexual-political objects are nameless white women desired purely for the payback for racism they represent. They are seen as vehicles of upward mobility but are held in contempt because they are actually unable to elevate the status of the oppressed. Also in this category are the Political Do-Gooders Without Insight, who try to fight oppression and attempt to help others before they have freed themselves. Many of these stereotyped women suffer a profound emptiness; nevertheless, they must maintain absolute control. They too can be loosely related to the Devouring Goddess.

In addition, there are the women who are simply nice though empty and innocuous. They are described by Meridian and her mother as bland, odorless creatures,[20] the counterpart to the sensuality that characterizes the sexual stereotypes of black men and women. They may possess a trapped reserve of passion (as with Jo in *Blues For Mister Charlie*) or a contemptible mediocrity (as with Mrs. Pribby in *Cane*). Unlike the Confidant, the Nice Girl does not have the experience to be an understanding listener. There is a deep strength within the Confidant's vulnerability, unlike the china-doll Nice Girl who lives inside a glass case.

Viewed from a Jungian perspective, the fact that most of these women are portrayed negatively means that they refer more to shadow and animus projection than to the archetype of the infinite Wise Woman. The syzygy is completed in the characterization of the indomitable spirit of black women in *The Color Purple* (Celie), *Meridian* (Meridian), *Song of Solomon* (Pilate) and *The Salt Eaters* (Velma), which are all by female authors. Although reviews of the film version of *The Color Purple* accuse Alice Walker of promoting negative stereotypes of black men and romanticizing the stereotype of an indomitable matriarchal image of black women, I think these reviews succumb to the same problems that arise when black authors are accused of presenting only negative images of white women and men. Although it is true that several of these authors exploit stereotypes, the basic impetus behind the use of negative stereotypes is the exposure of oppressive sociocultural circumstances that interfere with the full realization of human potential. Character pathologies appear as fragments of primordial images that, when finally acknowledged as a mirror of ourselves, can be integrated to complete the syzygy.

CHAPTER 1

The Terrible Goddess

And her slim body, white as the ash of black flesh after flame.
                                        Toomer, *Cane*

The White Goddess, giver and taker of life, has many faces; the most formidable being that of the destroyer, the Terrible Goddess of death. The same mother who engenders and nourishes all of life is also the woman "who takes them back into herself, who pursues her victims. . . . Disease, hunger, hardship, war above all, are her helpers." As "the hungry earth, [she] devours [her] own children and fattens on their corpses."[1] Jean Toomer's "Portrait in Georgia" (*Cane*) describes a White Goddess specific to black American life, with hair that is associated with the "lyncher's rope" and breath that evokes the olfactory memory "of cane."[2] Toomer symbolically connects her vital energy with an image of human bondage and exile. She is banished like the biblical Cain for her association with black men while remaining a symbol of slavery on sugar plantations. She is the archetypal Femme Fatale reified in an African-American mythos. Similarly, Robert Graves describes the European White Goddess as "a lovely, slender woman" with "deathly pale" skin.[3] Toomer describes her eyes as "fagots,"[4] and Graves calls them "startlingly blue." She is always described with "long fair hair"[5] and, in *Meridian*, the children are fascinated by Lynne's long fine hair that Walker compares to horses' tails.[6]

Horse imagery is connected to a triad of river goddesses in Celtic mythology. One of these, Rhiannon, is the protector of horses; her symbol is three birds whose singing melodies "give sleep to the living and awaken the dead."[7] Among the Romans, the Celtic Epona was associated "with the journey of the soul after death."[8] Although the protecting goddess of horses usually possesses a positive matriarchal image, in *Meridian* the connotation refers to her opposite manifestation, the nightmare. "Epona was believed to preside over the mating of mares" and childbirth. Like many images of the Great Mother, "her relationship with children [is] ambivalent; sometimes a child is depicted crouching under the raised leg of the mare, a threatening pose."[9] The Indo-European mare is "symbolic of the evil mother, the dark mother, the erotic and devouring mother, the whore. . . . Instead of feeding her child . . . the mare eats her child. Moreover, like the female praying mantis, she devours her husband as well."[10] The erotic powers of the mare are dangerous "precisely because they [are] untamed; as raw forces of a Goddess." If the force of her power "flow[s] freely" and unthwarted, she will "bless and make fruitful." In contrast, the image of the "underwater mare" symbolizes "angry, thwarted sexuality" and "power blocked by authority." The "suppressed or repulsed eroticism" of a woman is "volatile and explosive" and "Hell hath no fury to match this."[11]

Bird motifs may also manifest the White Goddess's horrific form. In Yoruba symbolism, the Mothers or Witches are similarly associated with birds, who "favor the edge of the sea because they can fly freely along the beaches at night." The "liminality and uncertainty attach[ed] to this boundary between land and water and even life and death" epitomizes the ambivalence and the binary opposition inherent in the good and terrible manifestations of the Great Mother.[12] Negative aggression may be manifested in the image of the Witch appearing as a bird preying upon the eyes of a sleeping victim. "It is also believed the witch may eat the spirit of the individual or interfere with his sexuality, creating, for example, impotence."[13] On the other hand, she may obtain the "sympathy of her human followers because she has the power to give children and lengthen years."[14] By appealing to the Mothers with praise for their beneficence, the Yoruba invoke their nurturing power.

Retaining only the horrifying qualities of the Goddess, Reed's Vivian (*Flight to Canada*) is a transformation of both European and African archetypes. A parody of Poe's tragic Annabel Lee, she resides in her "sepulcher by the sea" where she is most powerful. Wearing a "white-death negligee," she is an apparition with a "hideous sardonic grin."[15] Although this Death Goddess may manifest herself as a beautiful woman, she may also physically transform herself (as in the shapeshifting world of Celtic mythos[16] or the Yoruba birds). Her ugliness and the evil she represents may be visible or internalized.

As death is part of life, so deadliness is vital to the Bitch Goddess's seduction. Despite the horror and ugliness of her negative aspect, this "loathsome hag"[17] is irresistible because her erratic nature mirrors the powerless anger so ingrained in the broken identities of the people around her (e.g., Jesse in *The Primitive*). She is self-hatred personified and romanticized as in the Femme Fatale paintings of Norwegian Expressionist Munch. African-American characterizations of the malevolent Death Goddess personified in white women are only fragments of the entirety of the feminine archetype. The promise of redemption offered by the Femme Fatale is most often a cruel illusion.

Whereas the regenerating qualities of Graves's White Goddess and the Yoruba Mothers may be redeemed once wrath is invoked, the African-American's White Goddess is primarily an image of despair. Poe similarly isolates the death aspect of Graves's Goddess. To Poe, the tragic woman is the epitome of beauty and loss, attaining her ultimate form of worship in death. Reed exaggerates Poe's notion of tragic beauty. The objectification of her brother's obsession with southern purity, Vivian is hideous yet irresistible. The diabolical nature that mocks Vivian's chastity is as seductive as her beauty.

Reed's parody of Poe's Annabel Lee[18] exposes the irony inherent in the chivalric image of the chaste, unattainable woman as the embodiment of the Holy Grail. Beautiful, yet unapproachable and therefore irretrievably lost, the mythical woman represents goals that can only bring despair to the man who seeks to possess her and to the human woman who attempts to fulfill the image. The conflict between sexuality and purity defined as chastity is largely due to the prevalent patriarchal definition of virginity as *virgo intacta*; however, as Nor Hall defined the Virgin Goddess, she is "one-in-herself; not maiden inviolate, but maiden alone, in-herself. To be virginal does not mean to be chaste, but rather to be true to nature and instinct."[19] The American Goddess, reified into a billboard seductress, has lost all connection to the earth.

If the essential freedom of the Feminine is denied, then as soon as a woman takes a lover (or, being consistent with the patriarchal definition, as soon as she is conquered), she can no longer transcend human consciousness, for her transcendence depends on upholding a misinterpreted idea of purity. She can be either Goddess or Whore; but, in the patriarchal dichotomy, she cannot be both, and so she is caught in the contradiction. Denied the freedom to determine her own worth, she is a dead image of times past, a sad, melancholy beauty.[20] The archetypal purity of the Virgin and the Whore lies in their fundamental freedom as women, "as opposed to the domesticated woman."[21] The Virgin "may give herself to many lovers but, like the moon, she can never be possessed." The archetypal prostitute "symbolizes the creative submission to the demands of instinct, to the chaos of nature."[22] By repressing the essential freedom of the archetypal Feminine, "one encourages a violent emergence," such as those represented by Poe's Annabel Lee and Reed's Vivian.[23]

The separation of the feminine archetype into opposing fragments produces degenerate versions of the Goddess. Poe's abbreviated image of the highest manifestation of Beauty (i.e., the death of a beautiful woman) is parodied by Reed in Swille's infatuation for his dead sister Vivian. "Standing over the coffin lid" with an erection, Swille violates Vivian's "chaste Southern belle upbringing."[24] The worship of the Death Goddess is expressed as incestuous necrophilia, and, as a result of the perversion of her image and the denial of her freedom, the Death Goddess's terrible image is invoked: "She will break the doors down and come in to individual or cultural consciousness in a negative, devouring (literally 'shit-eating'), stone-cold way."[25] The pervasive terror experienced by Poe's Roderick Usher is actualized when the enshrouded and bloodied sister falls "heavily inward upon the person of her brother, and in her violent and now final death agonies, [bears] him to the floor a corpse, and a victim to the terrors he had anticipated."[26] Ignoring the terror that obsessed Roderick Usher, Swille is devoured by his passion to possess his sister. When men attempt to ascend to the control and possession of the Goddess, instead of calling forth her beneficent presence with the praise she is due, they invoke the terrible descent of her fury.

Reed's parody of "The Fall of the House of Usher" exposes the extreme results of white patriarchal obsession with ownership of women and land. His allusion to incest also refers to the landowner's need to keep property rights within the family. In *Flight to Canada*, Reed calls Poe the "principal biographer" of the Civil War and of the demise of what "the planters called 'the fairest civilization the sun ever shone upon,' and the slaves called 'Satan's Kingdom.' "[27] Swille represents the decadence of a fallen empire, wherein tyrants seek to consolidate their power by expelling the old gods and converting the masses to a new religion that will reinforce baronial goals. The banished gods desert those who refuse to recognize them and inflict their wrath upon those who attempt to control and censor them. The exile of the old gods of Europe was hastened with feudalism and Papal imperialism. The descendants of King Arthur (described by Reed as the original ancestor of the Swille dynasty of Virginian plantation owners) repressed the heathens in favor of the Christian god and lost their connection with the Celtic mysteries. "His descendents came to his America and made war against the gods of 'Indians' and Africans."[28] Thus, the underlying theme of the Civil War was a "Spirit War" between "Satan's Kingdom" and the gods of the Old World.[29] As the principal Goddess of Satan's Kingdom, Vivian is the Queen of Death without resurrection.

In Jungian psychology, Vivian might be explained as a product of her brother's anima projection. The anima (the feminine side of the male psyche) is projected onto real women. If the individual possesses a negative or gloomy anima (and sometimes he will respond as though possessed by this feminine image), he will often project this image onto another woman, perceiving traits in her that are actually part of his own psychological makeup. The female archetype, experienced vis-à-vis anima projection, has varied manifestations. The mother-seeking anima manifests itself in a man who seeks a relationship that will envelop and devour him while offering nourishment and protection. This manifestation is both mother-protectress and lover-enchantress. Possessed of such an anima "the son is spouse and sleeping infant all in one."[30]

The Mother image may also manifest in a form of necrophilia when the anima emerges in needs for nourishment and fulfillment that exceed the individual's capacity to apply his own instinctive modes of knowledge to connect with the mysteries of the phenomenal world. When the individual denies his own capacities for creative conception, then a supernatural image of the Mother must suffice to meet his needs. Neither can a corporeal woman meet these needs. He moves beyond life and looks to the Death Goddess for the Mother who will give him ultimate and final unchanging love. In *Another Country*, Rufus seeks the finality of this love through suicide.

During the search for a transcendent equivalent for his anima, the individual may select a forbidden or inaccessible mate. The billboard aesthetic of a white woman provides this forbidden, transcendent figure who embodies the promise of fulfillment denied to black men in white society. Reed's parody of white men in search of ultimate purity (i.e., the Dead Virgin) and forbidden love (Swille's desire for his sister) shows the mother-seeking anima as it manifests itself in necrophilia. Swille's existence is proof of his mother's deviation from southern chastity. A domesticated woman is perceived as bound and conquered. She is no longer pure, therefore she is not desired and so she is sexless. The forbidden love is reconciled by joining the dichotomy of the seductive, virginal Sister with the sexless, nourishing Mother to create Reed's parody of the captive Goddess. To Swille, she is as irresistible as she is destructive. "Staring into his eyes" with hypnotic "skeleton sockets,"[31] she backs him into the fire, demonstrating the wrath that is invoked when one attempts to deny the Goddess her essential freedom.

Reed's satirical mode exaggerates themes that are apparent in the work of other black American novelists. The Goddess's irresistibility is expressed in Ralph Ellison's *Invisible Man* when a white woman dances for the "little shines" who are rounded up like cattle for the white men to observe.[32] This is Ellison's battle royal and, like Reed's parody of Swille, Ellison's victim at once abhors and is fascinated by the Goddess personified. He cannot escape looking at her, yet she possesses only the irresistibility, not the beauty, of the Death Goddess. Her blonde hair is "yellow like that of a circus kewpie doll," her face caked with makeup, "as though to form an abstract mask" and, like Toomer's white woman in "Portrait in Georgia" or Reed's Vivian, her eyes are "hollow." Ellison's "Invisible Man" experiences the same ambivalent feelings that characterize Freud's description of taboo in the Oedipus complex. He feels "a desire to spit upon her as [his] eyes [brush] slowly over her body."[33] He is unable to escape, yet he wants to run; he is captivated at the same time he is repulsed. The taboo surrounding her image is ritualized in this scene where the onlookers may be compared to a gladiator's audience.

In an interview on "The Art of Fiction," Ellison describes the ritual content in his work: "This is a vital behavior pattern in the South, which both Negroes and whites thoughtlessly accept. It is a ritual in preservation of caste lines, a keeping of taboo to appease the gods and ward off bad luck."[34] This perversion of the ritualistic dance, which has as its aim the encouragement of man's self-destruction, is similarly performed in *Ceremony* by a "witch." At the same time she is performing at a bar, the lover who scorned her is being trampled by his stampeding horses.[35] Aphrodite similarly "arranges to have [Hippolytus] torn apart by horses" after he denies her.[36] The Witch is actually a manifestation of the Goddess who appears when the world has need of her aid to balance the forces of darkness and light; however, when the world itself is fragmented and pathological, the manifestation of the Goddess is perverted into the only available image of the Feminine. Tayo and Josiah (who risk the dangers to welcome the Goddess into their world and give her due attention) witness the gradual emergence of the Feminine. Ellison's "little shines" are not only the victims of the dancing Goddess's captivation, they are also the victims of a society whose fractured image of the Goddess is imposed upon them. There is no benevolent image of the Goddess awaiting them as long as they are trapped within a culture that has created a rift between the Goddess and the phenomenal world and, furthermore, has imposed additional barriers upon the ability of the minority population to connect with its image of the forbidden Goddess.

THE DESTRUCTIVE BITCH

Whereas the Witch is supernaturally seductive, the unattainable Bitch is seductive because of society's taboos. Although social stereotypes are part of a localized set of prejudices and lack the universality of the archetypal Witch, the characters Madge (*If He Hollers Let Him Go*) and Kriss (*The Primitive*) produce the same destructive effect as the malevolent manifestation of the archetype. The fear and disgust felt toward white women like Himes's Madge increases their seductivity, and herein they approximate the Bitch Goddess. Robert is plagued with his ambivalence; he is both attracted and repulsed. When Madge finally allows him to see her in her apartment, Robert appraises her in a way in which Madge cannot afford to see herself. She is dressed in a "nubby maroon robe" with "worn-out play shoes" she wears as slippers. Her white ankles are "laced with blue veins, and dirty on the bone." Wearing "curlers tight to her head" Madge has "blond hair [that is] dark at the roots." Madge's mouth is "brutal" and "colorless." Her "popping" eyes have a "muddy look"; her breasts sag loosely and, "beneath her robe," the contours of her hips "lump out."[37] Convinced that his desire for her is a privilege he must earn, Madge challenges Robert's worthiness. Although she repeatedly deflates him psychologically or repulses him physically, Robert always comes back. Passionless and hating "her guts," Robert waits anyway.[38]

The black man is equally taboo to Madge. Madge's ambivalence is complicated by a need to think she is irresistible to black men and that they will risk being lynched just to have her body. Her real fear is not that they will rape her, but that they will not desire her. Although Madge has rape fantasies and enjoys teasing Robert, she (like Lula in Amiri Baraka's *Dutchman*) cannot reconcile her internal scenario with reality. Like Clay (*Dutchman*), Robert does not say the right things; he misses cues and is left with nothing to say. Robert's desire, his "determination" and "whole build-up" are drained by Madge's "thick" excited invective, "All right, rape me then, nigger!"[39] Even though he is aware of the consequences, Robert (like Swille in *Flight to Canada*, Clay in *Dutchman* and Jesse in *The Primitive*) is compelled to follow the elusive Bitch. He is allured by the destruction she represents in spite of occasional rational moments when he realizes his whole involvement with Madge is senseless.[40] He pursues her in spite of his awareness of her game and the way she uses her whiteness. Her look communicates both her desirous thoughts about black men and her epithet, "KEEP AWAY NIGGER, I'M WHITE." This same look elicits a response from white men, "feeling they ha[ve] to protect her from black rapists."[41] She teases black men, delighting in her power to keep them interested despite the rejection and the risk she represents. The perseverance of their lust is proof that she is sexually attractive; her "virtue" is protected by white men, which provides additional proof of her worthiness. Madge takes satisfaction in humiliating the men who take the dare. "Luring me with her body and daring me with her color. It ate into me, made me want her for her color, not her body."[42]

Madge is from Texas, where preachers told her that "niggers were full of sin."[43] Madge is also attracted to the aspects of Robert she perceives as destructive. Each is attracted to the myth perceived in the other. Madge's behavior makes Robert want to rape her; and thus, her myth-version of black men's secret desire to rape white women is supported in reality. Yet she is more excited at the prospect of teasing him and making him want her than she is prepared for the actuality. She wants to be raped (but cannot face the idea that her complicity in acting out the fantasy would mean that it was not rape) and Robert perceives the caprice immediately in her coy, frightened look. They maintain eye contact from the moment his way is blocked in the yard. Even though it is Madge who deliberately blocks Robert's way, she affects a "frightened, wide-eyed look," retreating as if it is Robert who has made the overt move, "as if she [i]s a naked virgin and [Robert] [i]s King Kong."[44] His fury at her pretense communicates his awareness of her seduction and Madge receives the thrill she is seeking. A subtle quirk in her expression and a fluttering of eyelashes draws his response: "It poured out of my eyes in a sticky rush and spurted over her." He imagines that the blush that has replaced her coy look is spreading down her "overripe breasts, . . . over her milk-white stomach."[45]

This last image leaves Robert feeling nauseated. Similarly, in *The Primitive*, Jesse experiences the urge to vomit whenever he drinks excessively and argues with white women, particularly Kriss. Himes provides the reader with insight into the motivation for Kriss's behavior. Kriss absolves herself from any responsibility for her actions with self-pity and bitterness. She does not have the strength of character to accept responsibility for her own unhappiness. Instead, Kriss prefers to blame her anguish on the injustice of the world, which has "given her a drunkard for a father and a wretch for her first lover, two abortions and the loss of fertility, [and] a homosexual for a husband." She begrudgingly accepts society's judgment of her worth, but even her self-hatred is blamed on "them." She perceives her involvement with men as situations in which "she ha[s] been required to satisfy [them] because of their importance, receiving no satisfaction in return."[46] This is Kriss's rationalization for her "bitch" behavior. Closely related to her sense of self-esteem, the rationalization for Kriss's attraction to black men has less accessible motives than her bitterness.

Kriss assumes the challenge of "solving the Negro problem in bed"[47] like the white women in Himes's *Pinktoes*. Her own life can become validated if she can uplift the plight of those who are on her level. What distinguishes Kriss from other white women (who becomes sexually intimate with black men in order to earn absolution) is that she feels not only elitist sympathy but empathy with the black man's despair. From Kriss's perspective, the same race that ruined them had ruined her: Only through sexual intimacy with black men "could she feel secure in the knowledge that she wasn't dirt."[48] Her low self-esteem makes Kriss an equal with Jesse and her struggle to elevate her self-concept results in confused alliances. She will call Jesse "nigger," assuming the superior role at his expense, or she will commiserate with his situation, assuming moral superiority over "them"—white men. Kriss's pattern is to get hurt, feel rage, enter into battle and win, thus alienating the men. As a result, she feels extremely lonely and continues the bitch cycle, making "them" pay for her loneliness (e.g., the scene with Dave when he comes to pick up his watch[49]). This battling is usually spread out over a time period when her lovers leave and then come back to her; Jesse gets immersed in the pattern and cannot escape.

An equally complicated character, Jesse is plagued with a failure identity and bad dreams. Jesse lives in a gay boarding house in hopes of seducing the landlady. He has not only failed to please his public with his writing, but has failed in his marriage to Becky as well. Both Jesse and Harold had failed Kriss by choosing black wives over her and she cannot let them forget it. Jesse has to have a few drinks before seeing Kriss. Anticipating his meeting with her, he realizes that Kriss will not tolerate his mood or his discomfort, nor does he wish to credit her with his lack of ease. Despite his resolve to be the "entertaining, ardent" stereotype of "frantic" sexual energy that Kriss expects, the company of white women reveals Jesse's own sense of "futility, . . . plung[ing him] in a mood of black despair, during which he [cannot] say a word, [cannot] smile. . . . Los[ing] his desire," Jesse ultimately withdraws "in sullen silence."[50] That she might be considered an implied party to his victimization infuriates Kriss, who prefers to be seen as the victim. This identification with the victimization of blacks is Kriss's only rationale for her involvement with others who are "ruined."

What begins as mutual mockery to relieve tension—Kriss's from past hurt, Jesse's from sexual frustration and rage at her power over him—becomes a battle to the death from which neither can withdraw. When Harold joins them, Kriss volleys her insults and seduction between the two men. Laughing maliciously, Kriss is instrumental in pushing Jesse to lucid moments when he approaches the answer he so desperately seeks, the answer he wanted to name in his book that was going to be a separate peace. Like the dreaded Muse, Graves's White Goddess, Kriss has pushed

Jesse to the edge; he is on the verge of finding his answer, "that one simple thing he never knew which in moments of extreme drunkenness was always so close."[51]

Just as Kriss never forgave Jesse for returning to his wife, she never forgave Harold for choosing a black streetwalker. Enraged by her memories of Harold's condescension toward her, and insensitive to Jesse's turmoil, Kriss pushes Harold to tears and refreshes Jesse's anger, screaming, "*Niggers! niggers! niggers!* . . . Ever since I've known you you've talked of nothing but *niggers!*"[52] Harold kneels before her crying, and Kriss's pleasure at hurting him after "all the years of his critical arrogance" is intensified to "orgiastic ecstasy."[53]

Before he falls asleep on the couch, Jesse types a letter revealing his insight into Kriss's character and the nature of their relationship as absolution for her and payment for him. Jesse's letter accuses Kriss of enjoying hatred because it absolves her from guilt and helps her to "bear defeat." Yet she feels she has to pay for adulation with her body: "Somebody tell you you're pretty. Pay. Tell you you're smart. Pay." Using her body as a "cheap dirty weapon," Kriss delights in her ability to unnerve Jesse by inviting Harold to join their private weekend.[54] Jesse is already beginning to lose face by acknowledging that Kriss disturbs him. Ignoring him most of the time and occasionally shouting her orders, Kriss startles Jesse out of his silence and "the cheesebits he [is] eating [fly] into the air like buckshot." Giggling, Kriss orders more drinks and demands that he participate in conversation. Jesse responds, "I'm listening to every word," and tries to counter, "Fascinating. Beats Rimbaud's *Season in Hell*. Beats *Macbeth*."[55] This "definitely mature, fat-jowled blonde . . . [with] a bloated stomach, and skin as white as a fish's belly," has him engaged in a cycle he cannot escape without killing her.[56] Despite admissions of being the fool, Jesse continues the battle.

Neither fears alcoholism as much as they fear being alone with their failures. Kriss encounters this fear when she wakes up alone in her apartment. "Aloneness [is] her greatest fear, . . . greater than her fear of becoming an alcoholic, or a slut." Alcoholism and promiscuity are only the symptoms of her debilitating loneliness. Kriss's actions are defenses against this fear of being alone, though in moments of honesty she has to admit that "she [can] not blame it all on men." She can cry at night, cover it up and lie in the daytime, "but morning [i]s the time for fear."[57] Morning, though sobering, likewise brings fear to Jesse who, accustomed to "the small bright cell of debauchery," cannot leave Kriss's apartment. His ability to cope has been so stretched in this "cell" that escape into the normality of the outside world is "too terrifying to be ventured." Kriss is a known, and therefore less threatening, evil; whereas "the *outside* ha[s] become the *unknown*."[58] Thus, Jesse is seduced to stay with the Lorelei and be swallowed into the world that drowns him. To avoid drowning he kills Kriss. When he finally absorbs his actions, Jesse's thoughts turn "inward and be[come] sealed within a sardonic self-lacerating humor, so that he" equates "the body of his victim" with the culmination "of his own whole life." In Jesse's twisted logic, Kriss's death summarizes the "impact of Americanism on one Jesse Robinson—black man." The only way for him to become a human being within his defined model of Americanism is to kill a white woman.[59]

Jesse's feelings of guilt over Becky, combined with his feelings of inadequacy concerning both his writing and his manhood, along with a series of dreams that reflect a tortured inner world, demonstrate his susceptibility to Kriss's seduction. Jesse also feels a need to pay, but it is his need to be paid back by a world that will not accept his writing that makes his psyche fit so well with Kriss, who feels more compelled to atone than to be paid back.

Unlike the poets described by Graves who seek to edify her, Jesse kills the Bitch Goddess personified. But, according to Graves, poets are gifted with divine insanity and Jesse the writer wishes instead to become part of the human race. In the dedication to *The White Goddess*, Graves begins a poem, "All saints revile her, and all sober men."[60] Jesse is no saint and he is not a sober man. He cannot stand her rebukes and rejection and he is not equipped to choose the road of the artists who curse her in code. Instead, he chooses the simple answer: *"Black man kills white woman."* He rationalizes his solution by calling it "natural" and "inevitable." It is behavior that is only "plausible" and "sociologically conclusive" from the unique pathological viewpoint of Jesse Robinson. His rite of passage from the ethical life of a "primitive" to the moral "expedien[ce]" of being "human" is the act of murder. Always searching for the simple answer, in Jesse's mind Othello had no choice but to kill Desdemona.[61] Jesse's simplistic reasoning is evident in his sullen monologues. Identifying with William Shakespeare's Moor, he reveals his dependency on Western myth, which informs his objectification of Kriss as a Bitch Goddess. Although her death gives him his answer, this act of murder—by Jesse's own definition—also removes the insanity that feeds his art. Opting for his twisted view of humanity and using the system as an excuse, Jesse loses his Muse. He has not conquered the Bitch Goddess because he does not recognize his own animus. What he "reviles" and kills is another pathetic victim much like himself. Remaining out of touch with his own mythos, Jesse is one of those maimed fragments of a local mythology that has lost its "text" and a means to find healing.[62] His pathetic victory is evident in his lament that Kriss is not there to witness his entry "into the human race,"[63] and he leans first on his identity as a "crazy nigger," then on his identification with the system, as a crutch for an unrestrained id.

Jesse's simple solution for his internal conflicts is to kill a white woman. Similarly, in *The Slave*, Walker's assertion that it is time to replace those who are on top with a new ruling class is an oversimplification of revolutionary change. Essential change entails a complete regeneration of a spiritual order, otherwise a fractured political system will perpetuate itself with new heirs. Jesse and Walker attack the symptoms rather than working to heal the causes of rupture within their worlds.

In *Ceremony*, Tayo takes the shaman's journey to play his role in the reinstatement of spiritual order. If he kills the pawns of witchery (Harley and friends), Tayo will continue the evil that has been set in motion. The whites, their mines and nuclear testing are only part of a pattern of witchery that undermines all racial groups. As long as the Laguna perceive the white world as a cause of witchery, they will only perpetuate a system patterned for destruction. Tayo halts the pattern by choosing to observe the evil play itself out while he remains consistent with the ritual of healing. By his refusal to be seduced into violence, Tayo has liberated himself from the vicious circle of reaction to imbalance. Tayo struggles for the healing that makes him his own master.

Walker and Jesse do not have an internal connection to a world mythos that will enable them to take a shaman's journey. They are caught in a pattern of reaction to external forces. The irony of *The Slave* is revealed in Walker's confession that he has no system to replace the corruption of white power, "but that it is simply someone else's turn."[64] Walker concedes that taking power simply because it is his turn is "ugly."[65] The significance of this admission shows that Walker "and his followers, like their white counterparts, are still enslaved by certain ideas and forces they do not understand."[66] When the taking of turns goes beyond replacing the political hierarchy and changes the value structure and aesthetic system by which the quality of life is determined, then a true revolution can emerge.

Demands for a similar revolutionary transformation in literature are made by black authors and critics. Baraka calls for a truly "independent black American literature," free from the tendencies of former writers to conform to the models and mythos of English literature.[67] In his essay on the "Dilemma of the Negro Novelist in the U.S.A.," Himes cautions the black writer to retain the honesty and the heritage of being a black person in America, instead of identifying with a system of white middle-class values that perpetuates racism. Furthermore, the unique experience of the black writer should not be reduced to a vague human problem with universal application.[68] Jesse is an example of an author who struggles between his need for inclusion in the white-dominated publishing world and the impulse to retain his individual experience. In *Dutchman,* Clay exemplifies the black bourgeois who plays out a middle-class role and identifies his internal despair with Charles Pierre Baudelaire, committing the error of generalizing his particular experience of racism into a vague universal despair. The error of vague representation tends to neutralize and reduce the reader's perception of the real damage that is wrought by oppressive circumstances. The writer who is committed to revolutionary change will not sacrifice truth for acceptance into the European-American mainstream of classic fiction.

"The history of Afro-American literature is abundant with examples of writers using other people's literary machinery and mythology in their work." Traditionally, black writers have worked within a Western aesthetic, writing "sonnets, iambic pentameter, ballads," and alluding to European myth.[69] The "Black Aesthetic" ranges from the works of the "modern writer who terms Egyptians 'villains,' or equates Babylon with America," to the classical styles of Richard Wright and Ellison or the mythic encounter with New World *Vodun* in Bambara's *The Salt Eaters* and Reed's *Mumbo Jumbo.* "What distinguishes the present crop of Afro-American and Black writers from their predecessors is a marked independence from Western form." The problem of portrayal is complicated when the images of characters must be created out of more than one aesthetic. The white feminine stereotype in black literature has roots in her own European-American "dark heathenism,"[70] which the novelist combines with his unique psychic heritage as an African-American.

Lula (*Dutchman*) is White America with her own mythological base, but she is also White America as seen by a black author. White America provides its own norms and supporting myths in which the archetypal Feminine is represented. The "normative" experience of the African-American includes oppression and hopelessness, giving birth to the distortion of the white mythos wherein a parody of the White Goddess, the antithesis of the ideal, becomes the common image. Therefore, her character formation must come from combined mythologies. This is the White Goddess absorbed and transformed in the African-American aesthetic. The Indo-European prototype for Lula is the Seductress who initiates men into knowledge of polarity. Eve and Ishtar represent an initiation out of an innocence (that apprehends the world as a peaceful unified whole) and into the knowledge of life with all its adversity. If knowledge of adversity ultimately leads to the transcendent return to wholeness, and if the Goddess is fundamentally connected to a process of transformation, growth and synthesis, then one can look at the prototypical Seductress as a positive force. Lula may be perceived as an Initiator who reacquaints Clay with the knowledge of oppression that he has repressed in order to maintain his place in middle-class life; however, the ultimate end of her "path" brings neither Clay nor Lula into final recognition of the transcendent self. The syzygy of the anima/animus conflict remains incomplete and Lula represents a stasis in which growth is halted at the stage of awareness of adversity. Baraka's imagery of the dark underworld, through which the potential initiate (Clay) must pass in order to gain enlightenment, is a subway universe with no exits beyond death. Furthermore, this death does not lead the hero toward reemergence into life. There is no ceremony of *retirer d'en bas de l'eau* for Clay. Unlike the Nigerian Egungun dances, the Dionysian cults, Osirian pantheon or Haitian *Vodun*, wherein the passage into a death state implies rebirth into a greater arena of spiritual knowledge, Lula's ritual reaches its conclusion in death. If we can equate Lula with the Terrible Mother, the man-killer, then Lula's subway is not a womb but a grave.

Whereas Robert's ordeal with Madge leads to his final emergence and Jesse's murder of Kriss reveals his collusion with the system he is trying to escape, Clay's revelations at the hands of the Destructive Goddess are aborted. Madge and Kriss are unaware of the roles they have played as mythic figures, whereas Lula's role is self-conscious. Madge and Kriss are motivated by unconscious ambivalence, whereas Lula's pendulation is deliberate. Her seduction and rejection of Clay has a predetermined pattern that will lead to Clay's destruction. Lula seduces Clay with mock advances. She feigns interest to draw his response then twists his words to make Clay look ridiculous. Clay is fascinated by Lula's strangeness and is baited by her apparent seduction. Although Lula's deliberate overtures are obvious, she immediately manipulates Clay's uneasiness by accusing him of "eyeballing" her. She makes Clay's interest in her a matter of fact before he has a chance to recover his own volition. Although it is true that Lula boarded the train just to search him out, she insinuates that Clay's sexual motives provoked her reaction. Although Clay continues to be uneasy with her accusations, he is relieved somewhat by her admission that she entered the train to find him. His response ("Really? That's pretty funny.") is simultaneously an attempt to dismiss Lula and disentangle himself from an uncomfortable stance while encouraging the seduction. Lula takes his ambivalence as an opportunity to humiliate Clay ("God, you're dull.") before he has a chance to absorb the situation and recover control.[71]

Despite the pattern of seduction and rejection, Clay is motivated to save face and regain lost ground from the attack on his ego. Clay's defensive role in the game is a weak counterattack (he would lose in Calypso, the dozens and any form of verbal contest) to Lula's insults and insinuations. She accuses Clay of trying to pick her up and tells him he looks like he's "been reading Chinese poetry and drinking lukewarm sugarless tea." Clay is manipulated to fulfill Lula's image of him as the black bourgeois who forfeited his essential connection with African-American experience for acceptance into middle-class innocuity. He parries inanely, "Really? I look like all that?"[72] Immersed in a battle with the Destructive Bitch, Clay's motivation (which at first is his sexual attraction to Lula) is survival.

The Destructive Bitch appears in a unique role to each man according to his personality. She is most effective where he is most vulnerable. For middle-class Clay from New Jersey, who has mellowed since college (when he "thought [he] was Baudelaire"[73]), her seduction has to appeal to his intellectual and physical curiosity, and to his Baudelairian fascination with evil and empathy for despair. She has to attack his deepset misgivings regarding his tenuous position within white society; therefore, her attack is public. On the surface, Clay has earned himself a more secure position in American society than either Jesse or Robert. The Death Goddess's apparition through Lula's psychosis reveals Clay's vulnerability. Those who appear to be most stable on the surface are frequently the individuals who feel most threatened in the presence of psychosis. It seems plausible, then, that a latent fear exists within such individuals that the security of their reality is not absolute.

Clay is unaware of the unconscious sources of fear that motivate his battle with the Death Goddess, whereas Jesse's daily conflict between preserving his individuality and conforming to the demands of the publishing world is more immediate. Jesse's sensitivity surfaces easily with Kriss, who mirrors his conflicts. Jesse is plagued with an internal battle evident in his monologues, whereas Clay gives the appearance of self-satisfaction until Lula penetrates his defenses. Kriss is the personification of Jesse's archetypal view of the white Bitch. She personifies his struggle. Kriss's abrupt flashes of anger are analogous to Jesse's mercurial moods. For Robert, whose immediate struggle is economic, the Goddess is a co-worker who poses a threat to his job. The anima projection for each man materializes in a woman who undermines his sense of control in the area where he is most vulnerable. Because she represents his worst fears, she assumes the proportion of the Death Goddess.

Aside from their existence as types, these women also have individual motivations for their actions. A husband who left her, a restricted life in

Texas, her fears of inadequacy, an aging body, her socioeconomic status, all contribute to the nourishment of Madge's fantasy of black men as being "full of sin" just waiting to rape her.[74] They represent the adulation she hungers for and the passion she fears does not exist. Kriss's self-esteem is a motivating factor as it is with Madge, but Kriss is further complicated by her fear of being alone. Whereas Madge and Kriss's fantasies surface in their actions or can be attributed to real life history, Lula's motivations approximate mythic proportions. Although Kriss and Madge may have archetypal roles, they do not perceive themselves as mythic figures. Lula is never realistic. Her behavior may be deranged; however, Lula is far more conscious of her mythic function as the Destructive Goddess.

Lula attempts to actualize her fantasy and reacts violently when her partner does not fulfill the role she had in mind. In her fantasy, Clay should respond to a formula. Because he cannot follow her internal script, Clay becomes one of a type, a type of man Lula cannot coerce into loving her freely and absolutely. She can avoid the disappointment of a partner who cannot conform to her needs by killing him. Lula's fantasy world becomes delusional when she bases her sense of control on the foreknowledge of Clay's failure to fulfill her ultimate fantasy. She knows Clay "like the palm of [her] hand" because, like all the others, he has failed her and "everything [he] say[s] is wrong."[75]

Like the Flying Dutchman, Lula can only find escape from her eternal cycle of destruction through a man who genuinely loves her. She describes how her fantasy ought to be staged (hoping he's the hero), leading Clay into traps where he will appear foolish, then punishing him for becoming the anti-hero. She seduces him, stripping away all of his defenses, until his most vulnerable spot is exposed. Guiding his fantasies of her "dark living room" where they will "talk endlessly," Lula tells Clay that they will discuss what they have been talking about all along, his "manhood."[76] She has revealed his vulnerability and he feels further exposed as more people come onto the subway. Lured by the seduction of her fantasy and distracted by Lula's bizarre behavior, Clay is initially oblivious to the people surrounding him and the real danger he faces. Robert, too, is shocked by his own vulnerability, thinking he is safe within a crowd who would surely see the absurdity of Madge's accusations. For both men, anxiety penetrates their realization that a crowd will empathize with a crazy white woman before they will support a black man. Lula preys on Clay's discomfort, asking if the crowd frightens him. Clay believes in the protection of middle-class upbringing. Ignoring the injuries of racism, Clay prefers to believe that he is on equal terms with Lula and he reacts defensively, "Frighten me? Why should they frighten me?" Lula counters, " 'Cause you're an escaped nigger."[77]

Clay is tenacious in his struggle to decode the arbitrary rules of her battle. Lula does not fit a pattern that Clay can comprehend. He cannot use logic because she is inconsistent. He cannot patronize her because the things that offend Lula are wholly unpredictable. Yet, typical to the psychosis, Lula does have ground rules (known only to herself); Clay, however, is defenseless. He finally loses control and becomes a fool in the process. Within Lula's pathological system, Clay has no option but a pathological response. If Clay reacts immediately with anger, he is punished for daring to break the rules of a system designed to undermine his self-control. If he swallows the injuries, he is emasculated. Instead of emulating the African model of controlled aggression, Shango, Clay hides his injuries to insure his acceptance in middle-class society. The lesson of Shango is not to pacify one's aggression but to hold the fire balanced until the need for action arises.[78] Clay waivers between accommodation and self-control. When he realizes the futility of his role in conflict with Lula, Clay's anger is impotent.

Clay's approach to battle is direct; however, he begins to realize that the survival of his identity as a black man depends upon the indirect expression of aggression. In his final monologue, Clay stresses the strength that lies in channeled aggression, in being a "crazy nigger." Diffusing his strength, Clay becomes the fool for having revealed the code to the uninitiated. The neurosis of being a black American is the struggle to "keep from being sane." According to Clay, this resistance to two-plus-two-equals-four rationality and linear thinking underlies the music of Bessie Smith and Charlie Parker. The full retention of one's heritage as an African-American entails the struggle to maintain a world mythos that supersedes a fractured world view as expressed in middle-class values. Without this struggle to remain as "crazy niggers" there would be no need for poetry. Like Jesse, Clay chooses to abandon the system he had adhered to through finding an easy cure. Clay shows that his final embracement of the regenerating powers of the spiritual order implied in African-American mythos (as described by Sophie and Minnie in *The Salt Eaters* or Jes Grew in *Mumbo Jumbo*) is incomplete in this statement: "And the only thing that would cure the neurosis would be your [Lula's] murder."[79]

In this murderous act of becoming human, a culture based on resisting a "two and two are four" ideology is weakened. As long as the Western world is "curse[d] . . . in code," according to Clay, it is safe. But as soon as "crazy niggers" want the money-power-luxury aesthetic that Jesse tried to buy, the first to be murdered will be the white woman.[80] She is not only the symbol of the unattainable archetypal woman of the white world but of everything that is beyond reach in the African-American's experience. Lula is a tool for Clay's revelation, a revelation that also defeats him. Clay is murdered after his speech; Jesse will be arrested for killing Kriss. Even in death, Clay is stripped of the integrity he tried to gain, "slump[ed] across her knees, his mouth working stupidly."[81] A metaphor for America and for death, the subway society will support Lula, who will not be caught. The persistence of attitudes that foster the image of blacks as subhuman allows behaviors like Lula's to continue. She will continue to roam the subways because the historical mechanism is there to justify her victimization of black men. Jesse (*The Primitive*) and Walker (*The Slave*) will be caught or, in some way, they will have to face the consequences of their actions. Lula's victim dies without dignity; Walker's victim, a white man, dies with a last word.

Lula exemplifies the extreme viciousness of the two-sided Goddess. Lula, Vivian (*Flight to Canada*) and the Night Swan (*Ceremony*) personify the enraged Femme Fatale who has not been worshiped enough. Of the three, only the Night Swan embodies the full complement of the archetypal Feminine. The Night Swan resembles Erzulie and Ishtar, manifestations of the Goddess who bestow beneficence on those who give appropriate attention in return and wreak havoc for those who refuse her. Lula and Vivian display only the fury and none of the warmth of the Goddess. They epitomize the anima of a culture that has ignored the presence of the Feminine, inadvertently invoking her wrath.

Apart from her fury, the element of the Goddess that is retained in these women is her despair. Like the water nymphs, mermaids and Lorelei, who lure men to their deaths, there is a tragic quality to these characters that, along with exceptional beauty, contributes to their appeal. According to Jung, this Femme Fatale is as much a part of the male psyche as it is integral to the psychological makeup of the female. Vivian, the Night Swan and Lula all inspire in their lovers the impulse to destroy the women who torment them with one exception: Joseph and Tayo are not destroyed by the Night Swan because they give unconditional love and respect worthy of her power. In return, she helps them with their quest. The Night Swan has a beneficent side. Lula and Vivian do not have a complementary side to their destructive functions. When the anger of Erzulie or Ishtar is provoked, their benevolent sides can be appeased. When the Feminine is denied in all its aspects, her positive manifestations are the first to disappear. Similarly, in Haiti, attempts to wipe out *Vodun* resulted in strengthening the violent, Petro side of the cult.

The negative form of the anima, attributed to a man's poor ties with his mother, manifests in "anima moods" characterized by a "dullness, a fear of disease, of impotence or of accidents." Life becomes "sad and oppressive . . . lur[ing] a man to suicide, in which case the anima becomes a death demon."[82] Rufus's suicide (*Another Country*) is the more obvious result of a negative anima. Clay's death is a form of suicide, in which he allows the projection of his anima to gradually take over and destroy him. The Femme Fatale is an analogous manifestation of the negative animus in women. The tragic loneliness of the European nymph (e.g., the German Lorelei, the Greek Siren) lies in the knowledge that her love will kill the men she cherishes. Still worse is the Femme Fatale's conviction that she has been betrayed by her lover. Madelaine (in "The Fall of the House of Usher") is betrayed by her brother; Vivian's dead but chaste body is desecrated by her brother; the Night Swan's former lover denies her because he is not strong enough to realize his love for her; Lula is locked into the tragic continuation of an obsessive pattern that makes her the true Dutchman of Baraka's play. The only way she can find finality and escape from lovers who change is to kill them. As the Dutchman is no longer self-possessed in his passion for the sea, Lula's pattern is beyond human control.

Lula has all the possible lines and responses memorized. She knows the men who come up to her room will respond in sympathy. They will expect her to pay for their sympathy by accepting sexual comfort. And because they are human, and realize that they, like all the others, will contribute to the darkness of her "tomb" by leaving her alone, they will convince themselves that they care for her. They will lie and tell her that they love her, "especially if [they] think it'll keep [her] alive."[83] In the image of the lonely, eternally unsatisfied woman, Lula is the Femme Fatale, kin to the Death Goddess.

John Williams's macabre description of Michelle places her within the same context of death imagery as Baraka's Lula (*The Man Who Cried I Am*). Dressed in black, the red-head at Harry's funeral gestures toward Max with an eeriness that startles him, while "her eyes [seem] to come through the veil."[84] An unwilling harbinger of doom, Michelle's benevolent nature is disguised behind a dark mask. Harry left behind a legacy of death to his red-haired mistress and to his best friend Max who, ironically, had always wanted a red-haired woman. The horrific vision of Michelle at the graveyard foretells the fate of Harry's friends and the grim sanctuary Max and Michelle will find hours before death. Under the guise of a crude remark about his desire for a redhead,[85] Max conveys his uneasiness to Michelle, who shares his fears and the two find refuge in a brief moment of tenderness. Max's ironic empathy with Michelle generates a surreal sense of clarity. Triggered by grief and loss, and by the amorphous fear and dread that accompany an anima mood, this clarity of fragmented myth images characterizes the works of surrealist artists. Similarly, in James Baldwin's *Another Country*, Cass's painful, though lucid, insight in the midst of her crisis with Richard reveals the failures and emptiness of her life. Cass describes her fatalistic conception of the world ethos to Eric, who encounters his own terrifying fears as he waits for the arrival of Yves.[86] Vivaldo and his friend Rufus face this mood of amorphous dread whenever they discuss their respective experiences with women.

Possessed by the foreboding of an animus mood, Vivaldo and Rufus fear that although the dream of an ultimate relationship with a woman might exist, for some reason the ideal may not be available to them. Rufus's negative identity is rooted in the conviction that he has become what the white world expects of black men, a failure who expresses his resentment and despair at the futility of his life by brutalizing his lover. Vivaldo intervenes in an argument between Rufus and Leona and accuses Rufus of wanting to destroy her. Rufus counters by asking Vivaldo to define what he wants from women. At first Vivaldo claims that he "just want[s] to get laid."[87] Ultimately, he discards his bravado and concedes that he simply wants to be loved. Rufus's incessant probing leaves Vivaldo questioning his partial and dismal encounters with women. Memories of awkward sex with "the dreadful Catholic girls"[88] are marked by half-felt satisfaction taken without mutual warmth.[89] Although sex with prostitutes may have been less clumsy, the experience was equally unsatisfying. His only remaining image of a lover is the combatant artist, Jane. Vivaldo is forced to conclude that either there is no partner who can share his notions of ideal love or he is inadequate. The negative anima in Vivaldo and Rufus promotes dreamy ideals of women while underscoring their inner sense of failure as men.

The negative anima becomes the devouring or smothering aspect of the Great Mother archetype. In Paule Marshall's *The Chosen Place, The Timeless People*, Harriet Shippen attempts to shape her husband's world with the rigid control she applies to her own life. This rigidity is evident in the extreme neatness of her clothing and the certainty reflected in Harriet's winter-grey eyes. She maintains a daily swim in the Bournehills ocean that is eventually the instrument of her suicide. Harriet is haunted by the "feelings of guilt and horror at herself which she had sought to flee by leaving" her former husband so she could avoid admitting her complicity with the destruction inherent in Andrew's research.[90] Saul recognizes Harriet's drive "to take over and manage everything and everybody on

[her] own terms."[91] Harriet is so consumed by her need for control and the fear of being useless that she is blind to the fact that her world view is quite limited and cannot extend to the Bournehills culture. A product of her upbringing (which interferes with any understanding of the people around her), Harriet cannot understand why the Bournehills people do not fix their teeth.[92] She cannot comprehend why her preparation of an omelette for Gwen's children (which she equates with the miracle of the "fishes and loaves"[93]) was a gross interference of the kind that Saul had cautioned her against. Merle readily recognizes a resemblance between her benefactor in England and Harriet.[94] Harriet and the English woman are possessed by an obsessive need to manage the lives of others, all the while "draining" the "very substance" of those people they attempt to manipulate.[95] Harriet's need for absolute control is driven by the encompassing "fear, with her from a child, that she would somehow end up like her mother, useless, alone, a slow suicide." Even more terrifying is her fear of succumbing to ultimate helplessness and numb hands incapable of useful action.[96] Despite the winter cold behind her eyes, Harriet is nonetheless powerful in her unconscious complicity with Bournehills's refusal to change. She is instrumental in keeping things the way they are. Just as Saul is beginning to feel he can make some significant changes in Bournehills, his dream is ironically aborted by Harriet's attempt to save their marriage. Harriet uses her connections to have Saul withdrawn from the project so they can return to Philadelphia where she can exert her influence to recover her strength and repair their marriage.

Throughout the book, Marshall contrasts the warmth of Merle's fey eyes with Harriet's steel cold eyes that are ultimately drained of all reserve. Yet in spite of all the contrast in personality, background and ideology, both women "had long been assailed by the sense of their uselessness." Neither woman had ever "found anything truly their own to do, no work that could have defined them." Each had "always had to look outside themselves to the person of a lover for definition, a sense of self and for the chance, in their relationship with him, in helping to shape his life, to exercise some small measure of power."[97] Harriet succeeds in hampering Saul's purpose with her smothering need for control. Saul is aware of Harriet's motives but he is not completely aware of the extent to which he is susceptible to her maneuvering and he is too naive to consider Harriet capable of undermining the whole project. The negative anima that makes Saul vulnerable to the devouring aspect of the Goddess operates unconsciously as a remnant of his own guilt and complicity with the events that led up to his first wife's death.

The positive anima, once the life-giving, fertile and nourishing facet of the Mother, was translated in chivalric mythos as the Virgin and her negative aspect "is often personified as a witch or a priestess."[98] The princess in the tower is the imprisoned anima of the patriarchal conscious-ness, and her negative counterpart is satirically represented by the hideous 'princess' of Reed's Camelot in *Flight to Canada*. Swille built his planta-tion and estate to be a replica of Camelot, and the accumulated guilt of southern white men over the atrocities of slavery is projected onto a woman who serves out his punishment in prison. Swille's princess in a tower, at once the image of atonement and of purity, is his embalmed sister Vivian; his negative anima manifests itself in a devouring, witchlike corpse.

The animus (or male element) in women "personifies a cocoon of dreamy thoughts, filled with desire and judgments about how things 'ought to be,' which cut a woman off from the reality of life."[99] The animus may manifest in the form of an outlaw. Toomer describes an ambivalent relationship between a white woman (Bona) and a black man (Paul) who go to the same school together. Despite the crowd of white college students who stare at them, Bona and Paul advance and retreat with the wax and wane of their attraction for one another. Bona's friend Helen attributes the seduction of "men like him" to an involuntary "fascination" white girls have for black men.[100] Bona thinks she is in love with Paul, yet she wants to stay in control by insisting that she has "never loved a man who did not first love" her.[101] She "flares to poise and security" when she finds him "critical"[102] and "cold."[103] Paul maintains his control over a situation that might entail some risk by intellectualizing his feelings, yet he is critical of the same behavior he sees in Bona. When Bona attempts to conquer Paul, he belittles her. Mutual contempt feeds their passion.[104] Thus, the white woman's attraction to the "outlawed" black man is a product of the male part of her psyche, the animus. It also follows that the white woman's rape fantasy is also the product of the negative animus in the female psyche.

The man who lives outside of society's laws governing human behavior is an outlaw or a "crazy nigger." The individual who lives outside a mythos develops a pathological disorder in which "dreams and fantasies analogous to fragmented myths will appear" and become indistinguishable from the outer reality.[105] The television entwines itself into Kriss and Jesse's battle when the monkey foretells the events of Kriss's murder (*The Primitive*). The South becomes a part of the mythos of the past that Lynne (*Meridian*) tries to recapture; and Lula's pathos extends to the subway, where riders become her accomplices.

In spite of psychological explanations for Lula's actions, it is still difficult for the reader to establish sufficient motives for her behavior. Lula is not merely a figure of uncomplicated evil like the cartoon sketch of

"Lena the Hyena,"[106] nor is she motivated out of an innocent or ignorant perception of her victims (as we might say with Harriet Shippen). She makes sense to us only through her similarity to an archetype and her self-conscious awareness of her role as the Destructive Bitch. The Death Goddess we might naturally abhor is also the Mother Goddess to whom we have loyalties. The back-to-the-womb experience so urgently sought by men possessed with a negative anima is simply the experience of the state before birth. Lula's chastisement of "Jewish poets from Yonkers" parodies this mother-seeking tendency.[107]

Assuming the prenatal state is identical to the afterlife, men are forever in pursuit of death at the same time they fear finality. This ambivalence is characteristic of the "divine insanity" attributed to poets and artists. Divine or not, the madness leads black men either to deify or destroy the white woman. As soon as she becomes a transcendent symbol, some form of destruction is inevitable. There are some women who escape the mold created by men. There are some men who escape the destruction that the transcendent symbol suggests. None, including Robert (who escapes to the army in *If He Hollers Let Him Go*), go away untouched. All men who enter Lula's apartment are destined to tell her they love her. She tells Clay that even he would say he loved her if he thought his lie would keep her alive and, when he does not understand, she answers "too shrilly, . . . 'It's the path I take, that's all.' "[108]

The laws of social taboo inhibit the natural, fluid movement of the psyche toward emergence out of the adversity of polarized images into the transcendent state of syzygy. The denial of the Feminine "encourages a violent emergence"[109] (whether it be through the fear of reprisals for forbidden interracial relationships, or the inhibition of the essential freedom of a woman to move toward full self-recognition without the limiting patriarchal definition of her essential self as *virgo intacta*). The regenerative powers of the Feminine denied in a patriarchal mythos concerned primarily with needs to define, control and possess, are only part of a greater, more pervasive disregard for the need to assist the nurturance of man's vital connection to myth. Modern man in the Western world reacts to the loss of an ability to function with ambiguity and the pendulation "of doubts and certainties" by striving for a rigid need to define the universe with logical, verifiable principles. Life becomes "one-sided and unbalanced" through "placing too much emphasis upon achievement and production" and upon "the excessive valuation of logical conclusions." By over-emphasizing "youth and beauty" and "pushing the environment for an ever-increasing energy yield, we set ourselves up for an invasion of the opposite side: cultural destruction, poverty, madness, death, ugliness, famine, and the depletion of natural resources."[110] In so-called primitive societies, the local mythos supports the shaman's rituals to reunite the afflicted with their essential inward paths toward individual syzygy in harmony with the universe. Lula may be considered as the quintessential representation of the Destructive Bitch. Although she explains her actions as deriving from an involuntary need to follow "the path" she takes, her path has become misdirected. In order to restore the social framework in which the individual can resolve and integrate internal destructive forces and find balance in the psyche, "it takes either a collective effort or an act of recollection to face the shadows of evil" and to renew the vital connection to myth.[111]

CHAPTER 2

The Benevolent Witch and Insanity

Insane white shameless wench, . . . taking their words,
they filled her, like a bubble rising—then she broke.

Toomer, *Cane*

The Benevolent Witch may be defined as a woman in a position of power (usually, but not necessarily, supernatural) with good intentions. Frequently, benevolent motives are directed with misguided vision. An overbearing mother who interferes with the lives of her children can be a negative influence. Missionaries may believe in the spiritual justification of their activities, but the ultimate rightness of their actions is not determined by the strength of their convictions. Many of the women mentioned in this chapter sincerely believe in the usefulness of their life choices; nevertheless, the results of their actions are often damaging to the people they encounter.

The Benevolent Witch, by her good intentions alone, appears to occupy a positive position; however, her nature is such that she functions in a neutral capacity. She may contribute to the arousal and growth of the "psychic life in a friend or companion" or she may "lure the other away from realistic adaptation to the world."[1] The former functions as an Initiator to greater insights that can only strengthen one's life, whereas the latter elicits madness. The well-intentioned political figures discussed in chapter 3 function primarily in a sociological context; however, the aim of this chapter is to explore the mythological function served by the medial white woman. Similarly, the Confidants of chapter 4 are discussed here in their roles as medial figures, whereas their role in the capacity of the positive Old Wise Woman archetype is the subject of discussion in chapter 4.

The medial feminine role takes on magical proportions when the extent of awakening or aberration resulting from her intervention initiates extreme consequences in the lives of her companions. In instances of interracial relationships the black man may project a negative anima onto a white woman. The results of a gloomy anima have been elaborated in chapter 1, which put forth that a negative anima projection may take the form of a search for unattainable ideals or a preoccupation with premonitions of disaster. If the white woman's image recalls the facts of oppression while promising liberation, then her capacity to assume magical proportions increases.

Some white female characters are described as witchlike (e.g., Mrs. Dalton in *Native Son*), whereas others (Vivian in *Flight to Canada* and Becky in *Cane*) may actually be ghosts. Pathologically disturbed women may also occupy a medial position because they (like the Yoruba Witches who reside at the edge of the sea) occupy the borders of consciousness. Unlike the normal person, the insane woman's subconscious motives may be operating closer to the surface. The boundaries between the real world and the psychic dimensions may be less distinct. By definition, the insane person occupies the edges of social norms. In this way, Amy Denver (the white girl who saves Sethe's life in Toni Morrison's *Beloved*) is insane because her actions do not follow the behavior Sethe has learned to expect from white people. Her unselfish motives in helping Sethe are as strange as her obsession with traveling to Boston to buy red velvet.[2] Sethe's previous experience with a white woman was with Mrs. Garner, who was kind and well-meaning but ineffectual in overcoming the evils of the slavery she condoned. On the other hand, Amy was escaping from the man who had owned her mother and called himself her father. Amy could empathize with Sethe's need to escape the man who had whipped her. The absence of "meanness around her mouth,"[3] the healing force of her hands and the soothing effects that Amy's endless talking had on Sethe's unborn child made Sethe trust her. She named her baby after Amy Denver and arrived at Baby Sugg's house with her daughter wrapped in Amy's underwear.[4] The white girl's own victimization at the hands of Mr. Buddy made it easier for Sethe to trust her. Madness is more threatening to the upper portion of the social hierarchy because the rules that govern behavior in the mainstream of society may not be applicable in the fringes. The behavior of such psychic entities is unpredictable. Furthermore, they arouse fears in others regarding the safety and certainty of mainstream normalcy. Finally, when issues of racism are applied, the person who lives outside society's laws threatens to disclose the inconsistencies and immorality extant in that society.

"Becky" is Toomer's portrait of a poor white woman with two black sons sentenced to exile by a community of southern blacks and whites who publicly ostracized her, praying that God would "cast her out," while they privately fed and sheltered her. Becky wouldn't reveal the father of her children. The 1920s southern society railed against the nameless "damn buck nigger" with "no self-respect" who fathered her children, while they banished the "Catholic poor-white crazy woman" to a life of loneliness.[5] In the beginning of her exile, they thought Becky was harmless; and the cruelty of her sons vindicated their actions against her. People were wary of Becky but did not fear her until they began to think they had been too harsh. Her dogged survival became a symbol of strength and they feared retaliation. For their words that had "filled" the emptiness in her spirit until "she broke," hardened her "mouth . . . in a twist that held her eyes, harsh, vacant, staring."[6] In the eyes of those who had broken Becky's spirit, her complete depersonalization and disassociation from society transformed Becky's mien from a sad crazy woman to a "hant" that might seek vengeance.[7] Becky's tragic life, the mysterious collapse of her cabin and her survival in spite of ill-treatment did little to reaffirm social laws. If anything, her survival raised questions about judgments against her and elevated her status from a wretched, insane woman to that of ghostly transcendence. Society's guilt is projected onto her being and the object of their fear assumes disproportionate powers of witchery.

Lynne, in Walker's *Meridian*, is outcast from white society for marrying a black man. While they live in the South and are happy, Lynne is accepted by the harmless, old black woman she refers to as "Art," and she simply exchanges community ties. Nevertheless, Lynne retains her former enculturation as is evident in her poetic notion of the "noble savage" that occupies her imaginary South. Accustomed to the aesthetic monotony of suburban affluence in the North, Lynne perceives a richness and depth in the South manifest in the old black woman's "tattered yellow dress" and her song so "rich and full of yearning."[8] By labeling their lives as "Art," Lynne ennobles the suffering of the victims of racism. She thus retains her position of lofty superiority despite her efforts to extricate herself from her privileged status. Lynne was not raised in the black community, thus she can never occupy a position in the mainstream of her adopted culture. Furthermore, Lynne is oblivious to the danger she represents to black men who are seen with her in public. Tommy Odds (who is shot) and Truman (Lynne's husband) begin to see Lynne as a symbol of the hate directed against them because of their color. Because Lynne has absorbed this guilt within herself, she is cast out from white as well as black society. Whereas Becky's power ascends in exile, Lynne's power deteriorates. Lynne survives the grief over losing her husband and her child, and she withstands the loneliness of alienation, but not without a cost. Like the woman she so reveres as Art, Lynne is not a threat. Truman survives because he ceases to think of Lynne as a symbol and begins to remember her as a person; however, despite the fact that he loves her, Truman no longer desires Lynne. Only when she is completely beaten does Lynne perceive a similarity between herself and the woman in the tattered dress. The gulf between Truman and Lynne is particularly evident in her question, whether Truman's sexual indifference is attributable to her tangled hair, her odor, her weight or "because [she has] now become Art?"[9] Truman does not understand Lynne's question because he has never experienced the liberal white woman's imaginary South. He is unable to conceive how the South that had persecuted him could be looked upon for renewal. Lynne has hopes that the relationship might be restored if they can just return to the South where they were happy, before the incident with Tommy Odds; she becomes a tragic figure because the "graceful" South she once knew had never been real. Lynne's function as a medial Initiator is mostly evident in the process of change that Truman undergoes. Two significant women in his life, Lynne and Meridian, function to initiate Truman into greater insights about himself and the nature of the inward journey; however, Meridian emerges as an independent entity, whereas Lynne is tragically lost.

Similar to Lynne's experience, Leona's life (*Another Country*) is tragic. Her insanity is never raised to the transcendence of Becky's; nevertheless, Leona's effect on Rufus destroys him. Her function as an Initiator who awakens Rufus to crushing despair, and her pathological need for punishment (which places her at the fringes of society), identify Leona as a medial figure. Leona and Rufus are obsessed with an emotional and sexual ambivalence toward one another. Her ignorant platitudes, "Ain't nothing wrong in being colored," elicit accusations and cruel insinuations from Rufus, "Not if you a hard-up white lady." As Rufus's remarks become more disparaging, "her eyes be[come] more despairing than ever but at the same time filled with some immense sexual secret which torment[s] her."[10] They are physically and verbally abusive towards one another. Rufus's remorse over the times he had raped Leona is inconsolable; however, despite her "unutterably abject" response, he "twist[s] his fingers in her long pale hair" and he "use[s] her in whatever way he [feels will] humiliate her most."[11] Following these violent episodes, Rufus flees to the anonymity of the bars where "no one applaud[s] his triumph or condemn[s] his guilt." Although he realizes his failures before Leona leaves him, "the air through which he [rushes is] his prison and he [can] not even summon the breath to call for help."[12]

Unlike the Trickster figure, whose position of mediation maintains the boundaries and restores the vital balance between human social systems and the divine center, the Witch as the tragically insane woman destroys one's vital connections to the community (which, as in Rufus's situation, may be his only refuge and hope for redemption). The Witch and the Trickster figure occupy medial positions; however, the neutrality of the Witch's power may quickly turn to disruptive expressions of her energy. Part of the Trickster's role is to dissolve false systems of order (which brings about a period of chaos out of which a new order is created[13]). He is always functioning to maintain a critical equilibrium, where the temporal world is distant enough from divinity "so that men are free, yet close enough . . . to guarantee that this [social] structure will not spin down into nothingness."[14] Legba facilitates the process whereby the "divine center" and the "human periphery" are enabled "to find [their] full manifestation in [each] other."[15] This is not necessarily true of the Witches. When the full cycle of the Feminine is allowed its course of nurturance, decay and regeneration, then the medial feminine role might be considered sympathetic to the function of the Trickster (as is true of Pilate and Circe in Morrison's *Song of Solomon*). The characterizations of white women represent only fragments of the archetypal Feminine; therefore, in spite of good intentions, they are incapable of dissolving false systems of order (e.g., racist ideology). The Witch may appear to be benevolent and well-meaning and may even be in love with the black man who, as a result of his love for her, is momentarily (Truman) or irretrievably (Rufus) lost. Lynne's political stance and her self-imposed exile from her own class are acceptable forms of this well-meaning behavior. When she is moved out of pity to allow Tommy Odds to "rape" her, Lynne's benevolence becomes a curse.

Tommy celebrates his victory for organizing his pool-hall friends to vote, by inviting Truman and Lynne to join him at a segregated cafe. Later, Truman, Tommy and another friend are attacked with machine-gun fire as they leave a rally at the church.[16] Deep inside, Truman feels the incident could have been avoided if Lynne had not been with them. Just as blacks are punished for the "crime" of being black, Lynne is guilty because she is white.[17] Lynne has always believed that black people "suffered without hatred." This preconception permits her to feel awe for their particular form of torment and this resulting awe informs her romanticized view of their lives as Art.[18] In Tommy Odds, Lynne realizes the hate behind the suffering. However, Tommy does not use a black wife for a whipping post (like Celie's husband in *The Color Purple*), nor does he stab another black man in the back; he chooses Lynne to be the recipient of the hatred he tries to exorcise from his system. At first, Tommy wants "to force her to have him in ways that [will] disgust and thrill her." He visualizes "hanging her from a tree by her long hair."[19] Lynne resists, then she is passive out of guilt and pity for Tommy, to the extent that she kisses the stump of his arm after he "rapes" her.[20] Lynne surrenders with the most damaging motive, not out of desire or love; she is willing to absorb the responsibility of his victimization into her psyche, as if racism is the original sin only white women can absolve through martyrdom and as if her own victimization issues from some essential character defect. According to Tommy, Lynne's lovemaking with Truman is just an act to atone "for her sins." Through rape, Tommy tries to recover the dignity that Lynne destroys with her pity: "The one thing that gives me some consolation in this stupid world, and she thinks she has to make up for it out of the bountifulness of her pussy."[21] Tommy chooses rape as his opportunity to vent rage and recover his sanity, just as Jesse (*The Primitive*) seeks to restore his sanity through killing Kriss. Initially, it seemed inappropriate to Lynne to scream or actively resist Tommy's attack. Later, she fears the reprisals that are likely to occur if she reports Tommy, but her passivity and acts of kindness only function to strip Tommy of his pride. At the same time, she loses her own sense of self-esteem. Lynne withdraws from her activities at the center and her hair, a symbol of her whiteness and her beauty, becomes tangled and dull. The gradual disintegration of Lynne's soul is mirrored in Tommy Odds, who also looks "terrible. Puny and exhausted and filthy. Dead."[22] Here, the powerful white woman who had joined the cause (like the Trickster, to dissolve social systems that interfere with human potential) in hopes of creating a new order, functions merely as a destructive force regardless of her intentions.

In *Another Country*, Leona's platitudes have a similar effect of stripping Rufus of the dignity in his anger. Yet she is as likable in her directness as she is contemptible in her oversimplification of Rufus's problems. She rationalizes Rufus's violence against her ("He's just lost and he beats me because he can't find nothing else to hit."[23]) in the same way that she finds excuses for the white people in Greenwich Village (they are spiteful because they are lonely[24]), who make their bigoted intolerance of interracial relationships obvious to Rufus. Leona and Rufus interpret what they see from their own perceptions of victimization. Leona's simple platitudes overlay her complex sexual and emotional identity. As ambivalent toward their lovemaking as Rufus, Leona cries out at the same time she "cease[s] struggling."[25]

Initially, Rufus resolves to keep his distance from Leona so he does not have to feel any tenderness toward her. To protect himself from any entrapment, Rufus does not want to know her story; he does not want to hear about her life. Reluctantly, Rufus does feel some tenderness toward Leona and his loneliness and vulnerability cry out in his music, "*Do you love me?*"[26] He can only vent his anger at Leona for as long as he can remain detached from her pain. The love he does feel for her only magnifies Rufus's torment. Only in a violent climax do they find release, "strangling, about to explode or die," Rufus moans, "*I told you . . . I'd give you something to cry about.*" Leona weeps but her "lips [curve] slightly in a shy, triumphant smile," as she tells him, "It was so wonderful."[27]

Leona repeats a pattern that will give her the punishment she thinks she deserves. First, her husband abuses her; then, he uses her family as accomplices to take Leona's child away, on the grounds that she is insane. Leona flees to New York to seek shelter in a new but equally maimed lover. She begs Rufus not to hurt her, yet she is as attracted to his violence as she is to his tenderness. Leona projects a guilt and failure-ridden animus onto lovers seeking a reciprocal measure of pain for their own self-hate.

Vivaldo recognizes the hate–love relationship between Rufus and Leona and cautions Rufus against his tendency toward destruction. The only true empathy between Rufus and Leona is sexual and yet, for Rufus, Leona is the "only chick in the world." Vivaldo accuses Rufus of shattering Leona and Rufus retaliates by challenging him to prove that the possibility exists for something better than self-destructive, empty relationships with women. Attempting to respond to Rufus's dismal picture of love, "fear drain[s] his voice of conviction."[28] Perhaps Vivaldo has not found the "right girl" because he is somehow inadequate, or worse, she might not exist. Vivaldo shies away from the seduction of despair; but there is no outlet for Rufus who "can't forget" something that "hurt so badly, went so deep, and changed the world forever."[29] Vivaldo, the confessor, fears the void that Rufus reveals and he cannot provide the absolution Rufus needs.

Rufus's oppressive image of love is empathic with Vivaldo's experience of the Devouring Goddess: "No matter what she [is] like or what she [is] doing" or what her motives are, what a woman is "*really* doing" is "eating you up."[30] The insane woman and the equally tormented man exchange projections. Although Leona may have benevolent intentions, her naiveté (and inability to fully comprehend the societal forces that threaten Rufus) makes her a less supportive partner than one who might occasionally empathize with Rufus, or at least acknowledge the reality of his fears. Rufus becomes alienated from Leona's simplistic perceptions, yet he loves her. The burdens of the past are only compounded by the tensions surrounding an interracial relationship. The relationship cannot provide the desperately needed sanctuary. What small respite they find in one another only succeeds in amplifying the need for shelter and maintains the framework of madness that borders their lives together. Benevolent in intent, Leona becomes a symbol of destruction in Rufus's life.

Mrs. Dalton in Wright's *Native Son*, another well-intentioned individual, has a comparable effect of destruction on those people she tries to help. From the school of thought maintaining that the poor and minority populations are "culturally deprived," Mrs. Dalton sincerely feels that she is providing a service. This attitude enables the well-intentioned woman to maintain her nonprejudiced image toward those who are needy, while only partially concealing her underlying conviction that they are inferior and somehow responsible for their own indigence. The Daltons give Bigger a job "so that his family [can] eat and his sister and brother [can] go to school."[31] With all their philanthropy and gifts of Ping-Pong tables, the Daltons remain conveniently blind to the fact that it is Mr. Dalton's refusal to rent better housing to blacks that keeps them in the "forest" of the "Black Belt." This is a classic case of blaming the victim for the conditions of his environment. Mrs. Dalton's altruism is shallow and her "philanthropy . . . as tragically blind as [her] sightless eyes."[32]

Mrs. Dalton's blindness extends to her insensitivity toward Bigger. She wants to help by sending him to school and cannot perceive why Bigger does not understand her kindness. She is unable to see the irony of her husband's charities as Max sees it. For all their good intentions, the Daltons still keep a sense of place that excludes Bigger. When he first arrives, the Daltons discuss Bigger's future in a "long, strange" language full of words intended to exceed Bigger's understanding.[33] The day after Mary's death, Bigger is confident that Mrs. Dalton will not ask him too many questions because her shame over Mary's behavior keeps a distance between them; she cannot discuss these matters with a servant.[34] Although the Daltons' world is foreign to Bigger, to a certain degree, he can predict their behavior. What is most unnerving to Bigger is the ghostlike presence of Mrs. Dalton. His first "meeting" with her is startling; her blindness only adds to the illusion of the apparition: "Her face and hair [are] completely white; she seem[s] to him like a ghost."[35] Mrs. Dalton's ghostlike blur and Bigger's fear of being accused of molesting Mary are enough to terrorize him to the point of hysteria when he smothers Mary.[36]

Mrs. Dalton's glowing presence is the opposite of the popularization of the witch clad in black with a black cat, but instead is analogous to the whiteness associated with the Yoruba witches. Horrific, African "ugly masks" (painted white) are symbolic of the forces of the underworld and disease. The terrible and compelling whiteness of Moby Dick is another commonly used metaphor for deadly power. The belly of the whale may be symbolic of the initiate's journey to the underworld or it may be a grave.[37] The Terrible Goddess appears frequently in the archetypal motif of a deadly womb, *vagina dentata*, inhabited by a "meat-eating fish."[38] Mrs. Dalton invokes in Bigger the same fears, helplessness and dissolution that can "be the forerunners of inspiration and vision"[39]; but, in this case, they serve to weaken Bigger, leaving him exposed to "the void." The young Witch (Mary) seduces Bigger, whereas the old Witch (Mrs. Dalton) is a "disintegrating force."[40] The Witch may perform the function of driving the individual toward "positive development and transformation" when he is forced to "fight with the dragon."[41] Only when Bigger confronts the dragon by killing the white woman does he feel like he has truly become human; however, his newfound definition of the humanity he has joined is a product of the same moral expedience that drove Jesse (*The Primitive*) to kill Kriss. The Medial Woman may be associated with the underworld beneath the liminal surface of the water. She may lead the way to spiritual transformation or, like the mermaid or the old hag, she may immerse the hero in a spiritual darkness with no promise of emergence. Mrs. Dalton offers education as possible inspiration to Bigger, yet she has no real intentions of changing the political system that perpetuates his captivity.

During the investigation of Mary's absence just prior to the discovery of her body in the furnace (apropos, as white witches were condemned to die by fire), Mrs. Dalton enters the basement (filling the space behind her "with a flowing white presence") with a suddenness that causes the men to gasp. Her white cat follows her noiseless steps. Even her eyes are white and "stony."[42] Sensing Bigger's discomfort, the cat jumps on his shoulder and, though Bigger "trie[s] to lift the cat down, . . . its claws [clutch] his coat," implicating him as the murderer.[43]

Robert, in Himes's *If He Hollers Let Him Go*, is driven by a comparably unrelenting tension and resentment but, whereas Robert sometimes finds Madge alluring, Bigger's motivation is primarily that of survival. He is momentarily attracted to Mary Dalton, but Mrs. Dalton's presence elicits so much terror from Bigger that his focus instantly shifts to survival. In the moment of crisis both Robert and Bigger's survival reactions are similar; panic overrides rational thinking and both men, assuming the world will believe the worst, frantically try to quiet the women who endanger them.

The well-meaning are dangerous because one can never know when their intentions might revert to unconscious motives controlled by racist preconceptions. Even if there are no underlying motives of racism, naiveté such as that of Lynne or Leona can make them blind to the danger they represent. Truman divorces himself from Lynne sexually, whereas Rufus flees Leona's grasp in death. Bigger's options are comparably limited; "he [can] take the job at the Daltons and be miserable, or he [can] refuse it and starve."[44] The Daltons represent a job and some economic freedom. Mrs. Dalton talks to Bigger about going to night school to finish his education. Mr. Dalton tells him that twenty dollars of his pay can go towards supporting his family so his brother and sister can finish school. Mary Dalton talks about politics and joining the union. The Daltons cannot even conceive of the real benefits that Bigger sees; he will be able to sleep in a bed by himself, maybe even sneak Betsy up to his room sometime, or drink without having to sneak around. These benefits and the thought of having some money in his pocket are more immediately important to Bigger.

The Daltons may be nothing more than stereotypical hypocrites who think of themselves as philanthropists; however, they function as archetypes to the extent of their power to evoke terror in Bigger. The Benevolent Witch typified by Mrs. Dalton is as dangerous as the obvious manifestation of the Terrible Goddess, but for different reasons. The well-intentioned philanthropist puts her recipient in a position where he has no choice but to accept her aid; Bigger has no other option but to put himself in a vulnerable position with the Daltons. Within their home, the Daltons are the only people he can trust, yet he trusts only because he has no other option. Despite a constant foreboding, Bigger has to operate as if he trusted their intentions.

Mrs. Dalton's appearance identifies her as a Witch. In *Another Country*, Jane's appearance functions as an equalizer for Vivaldo (white) and Rufus (black). Whereas Mrs. Dalton deliberately maintains her position along caste lines to preserve her separation from the "Black belt," Jane reduces her socioeconomic status to establish herself on the same level as Rufus. Mrs. Dalton uses long words that exclude Bigger, whereas Jane attempts to engage in a form of verbal combat similar to the *dozens* (an American derivative of African forms of ritual satire and mock insults). Jane is "combative and dirty" and her clothes are "shapeless," "baggy" and often "covered with paint,"[45] which she flaunts to lend authenticity to her claims of being an artist. This negative appeal takes on a positive role in which Jane functions as a bridge between Rufus and Vivaldo. Because of Jane, Rufus feels he can trust Vivaldo. Although white men are "likely to betray" their black friends for women, the type would tend to be a "smoother chick, with the manners of a lady and the soul of a whore." But Jane has neither the soul nor the manners. She is a "monstrous slut" without the soul or sensuality of a whore. Rufus's disdain for her allows him to like Vivaldo, "and she thus, without knowing it, [keeps] Rufus and Vivaldo equal to one another."[46] Rufus's self-hate will not allow him to maintain a friendship with Vivaldo unless, through Jane's mediation, Vivaldo is reduced to his level.

Jane likes to give the impression that she is the liberal Greenwich Village artist with no illusions of class or racial superiority. She will not accept Rufus's judgments because he is not an artist. Rufus sarcastically belittles her statements as "too deep" for them and Jane retaliates by accusing Vivaldo and Rufus of being the real "snobs. . . . I bet you I've reached more people, honest, hard-working, ignorant people, right here in this bar, than either of you ever reach."[47] Jane reveals her ignorance of the nature of their surroundings when she continues the argument long after Rufus and Vivaldo recognize the danger they face.

Leona is similarly out of touch with her environment. A white boy eyes Rufus with enmity and his rancorous "glance flick[s] over Leona as though she [is] a whore," while Leona remains "oblivious of everything and everyone" except for Rufus.[48] Lack of awareness of the codes of behavior in their respective environments places these women in the borders of their communities regardless of professed alliances and status within a social caste. Leona's naiveté enables her to keep her own motivations under the surface. Instead of examining her purposes for maintaining involvement with them, she can continue to wonder why men should be so cruel to her. Leona's passivity helps her feel blameless.

Likewise, the philanthropy of the well-intentioned enables them to uphold a liberal image and remain blameless. Mary Dalton (*Native Son*) and Lynne (*Meridian*) feel compelled to take an active stance in proclaiming their views, yet both women are possessed of misconceptions that tarnish their otherwise altruistic aims. Lynne frames the old black woman as "Art" and Mary wants to eat "colored food." They do not realize that apart from conveying a rich and unique culture, these aspects of African-American existence also evolved in response to poverty. Mary and Lynne choose to romanticize their impressions of black American life, while Bigger suffers embarrassment at having to bring Mary and her boyfriend to his neighborhood and Tommy Odds is shot because he dared to be seen in a public place with a white woman. Mary is insensitive to Bigger's dismay at having to escort her home and up the stairs and Lynne continues to feel that her life with Truman could be redeemed if they could return to the South. The ignorance of the real dangers that exist because of racism makes Lynne and Mary just as dangerous as if they were overtly racist. They attempt to force closure of the gap between social classes and function merely to underline the differences, thereby maintaining social segregation.

Lynne and Mary possess a guilt-ridden sense of responsibility for the social circumstances that separate their affluent upbringing from the lives of the oppressed. The sense of guilt and alienation from their families is the primary motivation for supporting social reforms; their political altruism is secondary. Despite the fact that their attempts are often ineffectual and even may be damaging to the causes they pursue, they hope to find absolution to mitigate some inner sense of emptiness. Lynne and Mary eagerly take on the challenge of political activism. At first, Truman is attracted to Lynne's eagerness and the unrestrained pursuit of her imagination. Later he realizes that Lynne has this sense of freedom because she has never known the limits of social restriction. When Lynne encounters forces she cannot overcome, her life deteriorates and Truman recognizes her true limitations.

Harriet Shippen, in *The Chosen Place, The Timeless People*, is similarly motivated to translate her feelings of uselessness into an act that will give her a sense of empowerment. The need to show her love through controlling her husband's life in some way makes Harriet not only an example of the Terrible Goddess, but also an example of the well-intentioned woman who is nonetheless dangerous because she does not understand the pathological nature of her need for control. "All she . . . see[s] or care[s] about [is] that their life together [is] in jeopardy, and she . . . act[s]" to save her relationship with Saul.[49] Finally, when hope is lost, her gradual decline begins. First, "like many women, she [clings] to the belief that the small rituals of life—the lighting of a lamp, the closing of the curtains at dusk—somehow ha[ve] the power to restore the life of two people when all else fail[s]."[50] Finally, her thoughts creep back through the darkness to similar failures with Andrew and to the "feelings of guilt and horror at herself which she had sought to flee by leaving him" only to "repeat the pattern" with Saul.[51] Throughout her life, Harriet stolidly refuses to admit guilt and her privileged affluence protects her. Her last image of the sea is symbolic of the mushroom cloud that haunted her life and the sounds of the ocean finally engulf her in a "massive detonation."[52]

Women who have been pampered to the point of helplessness experience the atrophy of their resistance to life's adversity. Extreme luxury undermines instinctive modes of living. They are unequipped for survival because they have lost the basic abilities to connect with instinct or yet with a larger social structure. Harriet sees no future beyond her failures but death. She is incapable of change and so she is unable to withstand the dissolution of her false sense of order. Harriet's rigidity is the opposite of the Trickster's infinite order. Harriet's form of order is ultimately unstable because it is so limited and therefore vulnerable to external forces. The

Trickster's order may appear random but it is ultimately infinite and consequently a more stable form of order (unlike Harriet's) capable of transformation. In *Song of Solomon* Miss Butler also prefers to die rather than change her pampered lifestyle. She has silk on her walls that "took some Belgian women six years to make."[53] She can no longer afford to maintain the level of self-indulgence to which she is accustomed. She has to let all the servants go; "without servants and money and what it [can] buy" she cannot exist and "kill[s] herself" in order to avoid doing the work her maid, Circe, has done all her life.[54]

Milkman's Circe, like the Circe of the *Odyssey*, is a keeper of the underworld. Milkman mistakenly assumes that Circe stays behind to maintain the house out of loyalty to her deceased employers when, in fact, she insures its decay so that Miss Butler's prized palace will eventually succumb to the claws of the underworld.[55] In her benign aspect as Milkman's great-grandmother and guide to the underworld, there is the suggestion that this Circe, like Homer's Circe,[56] intercedes to grant immortal life to Milkman in his mystical flight home. She, too, is a Benevolent Witch, one who nevertheless terrifies Milkman. But where the well-intentioned and benevolent white woman, Leona, leads Rufus to a death without redemption, Circe guides Milkman out of the underworld by way of the stile,[57] just as the men of the Odyssey go through the stile to be transformed. Like the falcon-goddess Circe, one of the two birds circling around Pilate's dead body takes the earring that preserves her name, so that Pilate can be escorted to the otherworld.[58]

Despite his childhood images of Witches, Milkman cannot resist Circe's "outstretched hands, her fingers spread wide for him, her mouth gaping open for him, her eyes devouring him."[59] Though her "gummy embrace" makes him dizzy with repugnance natural to a human fear of death and the underworld, he soon recognizes her benevolence and willingness to help him.[60] In contrast, Swille is sexually attracted to the deathly figure of his sister Vivian.[61] Likewise, in contrast to the pampered Miss Butler, Reed takes the pampered prototype to an extreme in the characterization of Ms. Swille. Barracuda, the maid, complains about Ms. Swille's behavior. Ms. Swille claims that exerting effort to feed herself is "anti-suffragette." When she does get out of bed, Barracuda and the other servants have "to rock her in the rocking chair . . . wash her feet and then empty her spoils."[62]

Mr. Swille seems to be attracted only to the dead or near-dead victims of anorexia nervosa. He tries to talk Lincoln into his Camelot vision of "a wife who is jaundiced and pre-maturely buried." Ms. Swille is a "good sufferer but not as good as Vivian." She does not have the tragic beauty of Poe's Death Goddess. "Skin and bones, . . . down to seventy-five pounds,"[63] Ms. Swille is a parody of the fashion model aesthetic; however, regardless of Barracuda's brainwashing attempts to turn her into a docile Southern Belle, Ms. Swille denounces her husband. Then, as is typical of an individual without a core sense of identity, she reverses her opinion. After berating Swille's decadence she relents, melting under his compliments and confessing, "I wasn't boycotting, I wanted you to notice me. You weren't paying attention to me."[64] Here the woman who craves constant attention suffers a pathological gap in self-esteem.

Whereas chapter 1 explored the Tragic Mistress and the Femme Fatale as results of the contemporary disregard of the feminine side of life, the following examples of women with negative self-images explore the pathological results of a lack of positive attention. Regina, in *The Man Who Cried I Am*, is another victim of the I-just-want-to-be-loved syndrome. She chooses mates who are inaccessible (gloomy animus), involving herself with men who do not love her. Her loneliness is extreme at Christmas. The sole survivor of her German-Jewish family, she is always "apologizing to hell and back for being alive with the rest of her family dead."[65] Max's shame over his demeaning relationship with a madwoman, in and out of an asylum, makes him want to punish her. But her despair generates from misplaced love and her frequent trips to the asylum are a substitute for the sanctuary of a lover. Regina exemplifies the negative animus, both Bitch and Goddess, eternally unsatisfied. She is not loved in the way she wants to be loved and the form of love that would make her happy may be a fantasy. She deeply feels a sense of loss and gropes for ways to fill the gaping holes in her need to be loved. Such inconsolable despair is nowhere more poignantly expressed than in the character of Nel in Morrison's *Sula*, who feels the loss of her husband in her empty thighs. This sense of despair, no matter how well cloaked in bitchiness, witchery or insanity, inexplicably fills men with desire and dread and elevates women to the status of Witches and Goddesses. The power of the Femme Fatale lies in man's ambivalent fascination with abysmal despair, and in her affinity with the life-giving Mother and the life-taking Terrible Goddess.

The Femme Fatale's power, like that of Becky in *Cane*, occupies the edge between good and evil. Her alignment is ambiguous. While Becky may be benevolent, she is also taboo. Yet it is partially because she is taboo that the two young men are compelled to move towards the door of her cabin that swings open to them. The "ghost train," a death symbol, finally shakes the foundation of her isolated cabin until it collapses.[66] The young men think they hear "a groan" beneath the mound of bricks that is simultaneously symbolic of her sex and her grave. Out of fear, Barlo throws "his Bible on the pile." Thereafter, the village has its litany for the still undefined spirit of Becky, whose only sin was her carnal relationship with a black man. The Bible thrown upon her "mound" is their precaution against the fear that she and her lover might be more worthy than those who condemned them. In ironic contrast to the awful power they feared lay beneath the wreckage, their talisman seems to be an impotent placebo: "The Bible flaps its leaves with an aimless rustle on her mound."[67]

The weight of Becky's spirit transcends the sacred word of the Bible. A community assumes that the need for social belonging is such a primal human instinct that Becky's exiled soul acquires the proportions of the Goddess. Her essential benevolence or malevolence is immaterial. Becky becomes an object of fear because her power is beyond human control. Similarly, Circe in *Song of Solomon* is a boundless entity. Her hideous appearance is evocative of Witches. Even though Circe's attitude toward Milkman is essentially benevolent, she is nonetheless frightening for the power she emanates. Mrs. Dalton's glowing presence in *Native Son* is unsettling, even terrifying, and her well-intentioned motives emanate from her white affluent background; therefore, she cannot be trusted. Mrs. Dalton, Circe and Becky are the closest approximations to the Witch archetype. They have the potential to turn their power toward positive or negative ends. Like the Gelede witches of the Yoruba, their power demands propitiation; even then they may choose to wield this power capriciously.

Other women may be insane, but they are eventually reduced to harmless figures. Miss Butler in *Song of Solomon*, Regina in *The Man Who Cried I Am* and Ms. Swille in *Flight to Canada*, approximate the archetypal Goddess to the extent that despair is the operative factor in their lives. Their actions may be silly and ineffectual, but they approximate the Tragic Goddess's despair. They do not possess the power to turn that despair into the destructive fury that is the other face of the Tragic Goddess. Their insanity turns inward and is ultimately impotent with respect to their effect on others; instead, they destroy themselves. Ms. Swille is a parody of the tragic woman who seeks a disproportionate amount of attention in order to feel a sense of self-worth. She "boycotts" and refuses to take care of herself when her husband ignores her.[68] Regina invests her emotions with men who will not give her the commitment and sense of sanctuary she needs. Ultimately, she seeks her sanctuary in asylums at Christmas when her loneliness is most pronounced and guilty memories of deceased family are most intense. Unlike Regina, Miss Butler does not suffer from guilt or a low sense of self-esteem; she has no sense of self. Without the empowerment that money can give her, Miss Butler has no independent self-image. In *The Chosen Place, The Timeless People*, Harriet Shippen's sense of self is proportional to the degree of influence she has on her husband's life. When Harriet fails in her relationship with Saul and Miss Butler in *Song of Solomon* loses her money, both women seek escape from emptiness through suicide.

Of the four women, Harriet is the most powerful. She can interfere with Saul's life to the extent of destroying his efforts to bring change to Bournehills. Saul's mistake is that he never realizes the extent of Harriet's power. Saul is also naive. He assumes the motivations of the grant-giving foundations are the same as his own; however, Harriet's foundation is more interested in preserving the status quo than in supporting any real change. Saul's naiveté and Harriet's will to power ultimately undermine the project.

Mary in *Native Son* and Jane in *Another Country* think of themselves as unprejudiced. The danger they represent has more to do with naiveté and insensitivity than with conscious prejudice. Jane is combative and Mary is unthinking. Mary creates a terrifying situation for Bigger, who is already uneasy with white women. He must carry her upstairs and put her to bed, placing himself in an awkward situation. He has no reason to assume that she will defend him later. When Bigger is caught in Mary's room, he desperately tries to quiet her so he will not be discovered by Mrs. Dalton. Although Bigger kills Mary, he does not escape her power to destroy him. Jane manages to place Rufus and Vivaldo in a dangerous situation with her incessant arguing. The men in the bar are quick to defend her and Jane's loyalty to her friends comes too late. Unlike the despairing women who have powerful motives and ineffectual actions, Mary and Jane have superficial feelings with deadly consequences.

Lynne mirrors Truman's inner struggles in *Meridian*, whereas Leona's personality in *Another Country* parallels Rufus's despair. Both women fit into the role of the archetypal anima projection. Their respective breakdowns are not unlike Truman's painful struggle for resolution and Rufus's abysmal despair. Possessed by a gloomy anima, both men tend to search in vain for an ideal woman; in the process they entangle themselves with women who are ultimately beaten by similar forces of hopeless despair. Rufus seeks the warmth and nourishment of a sanctuary figure. He seeks a Mother but paradoxically submits his soul to a patriarchal God, cursing Him as he leaps to his death toward dark water, a symbol of the Feminine. Through the vehicle of Meridian, Truman finds his way back to a place where he can reconstruct his life and begin his lonely process of inner reconciliation. Still terrified, he is no longer influenced by Lynne. Meridian tells him, "in the darkness maybe we will know the truth."[69] He may still be unprepared to face the hardship of his own dark night, but he recognizes the necessity of movement toward the reconciliation of his shadows. Truman's relationship with Lynne led him to a final understanding of Meridian's separateness. In this respect, Lynne was an instrument of transformation who initiated Truman to the dark passage of the underworld. In *Beloved* Amy's intervention has a more direct influence on Sethe's journey to freedom. But Denver's spirit, "charmed . . . from the beginning," was the main force behind Sethe's emotional survival through the journey and, later, in jail. It was Denver's will to live that "pulled a whitegirl out of the hill" to help her mother.[70]

Initiator, Femme Fatale, or Witch, each of these women partakes of facets of the Goddess. Unlike the Terrible Goddess who occupies an extreme pole in the many manifestations of the archetypal Feminine, the archetypes of this chapter pendulate between the poles of good and evil. Lynne initiates Truman into the underworld, whereas Meridian and Amy point the way out. Becky may seek revenge, whereas Circe selectively directs her vengeance at oppression while aiding another victim like herself. The well-intentioned have ambivalent motives that make their effects unpredictable. The Witch occupies a mediating position. She may initiate novices into an abyss they are unable to escape or she can point the way to redemption. Only Circe and Meridian (both black women) function as benevolent Initiators to spiritual metamorphosis. The white women may occupy a mediating position, but their own unresolved conflicts interfere with the process of complete transformation of the psyche. The aberrant Initiator tends to sidetrack those who encounter her on their way toward integration of the psyche.

MOTHER, VIRGIN, WHORE

In her most elementary form the Great Mother possesses the positive, nourishing traits of the Good Mother, as well as the devouring function of the Terrible Goddess. Their symbols may be very similar; the vessel of the positive Mother is the womb (from which release is inevitable), whereas the vessel of the negative Mother is the prison and the grave (from which escape is virtually impossible). "Moreover, the function of the ensnaring implies an aggressive tendency, which . . . belongs to the witch character of the negative mother."[71] Captivity at the hands of the negative Mother may be suffocating. Conversely, release (or rejection) from the Good Mother's nourishment into the unknown territory of life can be terrifying. In *The Primitive*, as oppressive as his captivation by Kriss may be, Jesse is unwilling to risk escape. Even when the circumstances of repression are removed and the restrictions dissolve, the individual "ego" may experience this freedom, "in which an old shell of existence is burst, as rejection by the mother."[72] The negative experience of rejection from the Mother can actually lead to higher levels of mystical participation with the Feminine free from loneliness.[73] Captivity and nurturance, release and rejection, madness and inspiration are some of the axial experiences of the Feminine.

Opposite the pole of inspiration is the madness Jesse experiences in Kriss's apartment. Paradoxically, at the point of utmost dissolution of the ego attributable to " 'negative enchantment' " by the old Witch or young Harlot, "the negative pole ... can shift into the positive."[74] In these extremes, opposite experiences of the archetypal Feminine "coincide or can at least shift into one another."[75] The individual loses his capacity to differentiate between the Good Mother and the Terrible Mother, the positive and negative anima, the young Witch and the old Witch, the Virgin and the Whore. In the struggle to release himself from the captivating Mother, the hero experiences psychic distress that may ultimately lead to transformation and growth. "This phenomenon" (of polar reversal), which is "typical" of the "paradoxical" nature "of the archetype, constitutes the foundation of a great number of mysteries, rites of initiation, and occult doctrines."[76]

The positive anima at the "pole of inspiration" may manifest itself in the form of a Muse or divine Virgin. The Good Mother may be seen in the Egyptian Isis, Babylonian Ishtar and African Yemoja. The Terrible Mother is evident in the Indian Kali, the Haitian Erzulie Ge-Rouge, as well as in the terrible aspects of Yemoja, Ishtar and Isis. The negative anima is found in fatally seductive figures such as Aphrodite, the Lorelei and Lula (*Dutchman*). Whereas, in her seductive aspect, Ishtar may inspire her lovers to spiritual transformation, the negative enchantment of black men by white women is most often a fatal encounter supported by an aberration of the Feminine in White America.

The underworld, as the abysmal realm of the unconscious through which the hero must pass, may be experienced as a nocturnal "sea voyage."[77] This voyage from death back to life is reenacted in the Haitian *retirer d'en bas de l'eau*. Max's underworld voyage takes him through primordial beginnings. Eventually, Maggie ceases to be his Lorelei and she becomes part of Max's spiritual emergence and transformation. Most often, the African-American hero fails to emerge from his underworld ordeal with the white woman. He succumbs to a depression of the will because the object of his inspiration, herself a fragmented entity struggling against the tide of despair, is likewise a victim of a society that upholds empty feminine ideals while ignoring the full round of the feminine archetype.

Whereas the White Goddess prototype of the ancient Celts encompassed the images of Mother, Virgin and Whore, the White Goddess of contemporary African-American literature poses a fragmented mythology. The Virgin and Whore are mutually exclusive, and the Mother image rarely resolves the contradiction of purity and sensuality. It is in these African-American characterizations of white women that we see the extreme degradation of the Great Mother archetype in American society.

The attributes of sensuality, sexuality, purity and grace formerly belonging to the Goddess image are separated into two distinct camps. The tasteless "dead water"[78] type in *Meridian* is relegated to the same class as the Southern Belle in *Flight to Canada* and those "dreadful Catholic Girls"[79] in *Another Country*. Belonging to the other camp are the prostitutes. According to Rufus and Vivaldo, "the greatest lay" can only be enjoyed with a whore.[80] Victims of the Virgin/Whore dichotomy, they must condemn their mothers, or, like the Jewish poets Lula chastises in *Dutchman*, they must forever search for her ultimate image in someone else's "baggy tits."[81]

These broken images appear when an individual lives outside the mythos (it is this outlaw who is the projected image of the negative animus in Madge in *If He Hollers Let Him Go* and Lula in *Dutchman*). Myth forms the matrix against which all further experience can be measured or interpreted. The dispossessed individual retains only the shreds of the entire mythos: the extreme anxiety, emptiness and despair characteristic of a negatively expressed Mother image. There is no longer a sacred canopy in which Rufus can interpret his experiences as reflections of a greater scheme (*Another Country*). He is like a motherless child.

Although an archetype belongs to the collective unconscious and is inherently expressive of common human needs and potentials, it is apprehensible only through the particular motifs and images provided in the specific traditions of a given culture. For a cultural memory to survive within the restrictions of slavery in the New World, the retention of an ancestral mythos must be accomplished in code. This encoded transformation of African myths is achieved, in part, by layering European-American imagery on top of West African forms (e.g., the Haitian adaptation of Catholic rites and nomenclature for *Vodun loa*). The process of coding becomes more obscure and invisible in areas where religious expression is most seriously threatened. In the southern plantations of America, kinship and tribal connections among slaves were deliberately severed in order to weaken any potential resistance to slavery. An underground mythic structure is developed whereby the "crazy nigger" is permitted to sit in the front of the bus despite Jim Crow laws because no one with a full grasp of his facilities would commit such a daring act. This outlawed behavior is allowed as long as it is perceived to be harmless. When the Old World mythos no longer has a broad context in the New World, the individual is forced to adopt and transform New World imagery and live underground (cursing the white man in code) or conform to a system of rationalization for social oppression. If the local circumstances are responsible for providing the mode of expression of archetypal themes, it is easy to see how these local pressures could contribute to a state of pathological imbalance "of neurosis or psychosis" where "dreams and fantasies analogous to fragmented myths will appear."[82] Jesse in *The Primitive* is plagued by such dreams.

The symbols of the Mother can be both positive and negative (e.g., while Michelle provides sanctuary in *The Man Who Cried I Am*, she also beckons death). A negative Mother complex can manifest itself as "homosexuality and Don Juanism, and sometimes also [in] impotence."[83] Don Juanism is revealed in stud behavior (Rufus's approach to Leona in *Another Country*) and also in proving oneself, as in a cause. The cause of the mother country becomes the symbol that white women cease to fulfill when Cecil of *A Short Walk* and Truman of *Meridian* turn to the Pan-African Nationalist Movement.

A negative Mother image may lead to repulsive anima projection experiences. Jane is not just a Whore but a "monstrous slut" without soul in *Another Country*.[84] When white women are not described as bland and odorless, their distinguishing traits are revolting.[85] For Max in *The Man Who Cried I Am*, all of the women with whom he had short affairs after Lillian's death were in some way repulsive. Betsy had to make love "with all her clothes on." Another woman "whined about her career" and had to be drunk first. Frederika "never came, . . . liked jazz" but couldn't keep a beat, had a "few tough hairs on her breasts," and her "crippled labia . . . felt like . . . a piece of warm chitlin."[86]

This "revulsion, . . . rooted perhaps in early experiences with mothers or mother-figures," results in a "tendency [for men] to hold themselves 'virginal' or, . . . to prostitute themselves for their own sex."[87] Though Yves did have ambivalent feelings toward his mother (as Alexander points out) and he had been prostituting himself, his central relationship with Eric is not one of prostitution. Yves finds sanctuary in Eric and this could be interpreted instead as a reconciliation with his Mother image.

The mother's womb is translated into several comparable images of vessels, for example, the bowl, chalice, Grail and cauldron. The cauldron of the witches is the vessel corresponding to the regenerative powers of the Feminine. Later this cauldron survives in popular fairy tales as the

witch's tool for enchantment. The womblike container is similar in function to the Haitian vessel created to contain the reclaimed souls of the
deceased following their emergence from the dark abysmal sea. The
mantic woman, "the lady of the wisdom-bringing waters of the depths" is
"connected with the symbols of cauldron and cave, of night and moon."[88]
This is the inspirational Goddess who is "worshipped in dance, and most
of all in orgiastic dance."[89] This exuberant form of worship is what Reed
names "Jes Grew" in his *Mumbo Jumbo*. Everything that is antagonistic
to femininity, sexuality, ecstasy, joy and celebration is summarized in
Reed's "Wallflower Order."

Male initiates of the feminine mysteries approach the quaternary experience of the Mother-Virgin-Muse-Wise Woman through the anima. "The
vehicle" of transformation, the anima "is the mover, the instigator of
change, whose fascination drives, lures and encourages the male to all the
adventures of the soul."[90] Although the Harlot may inspire negative
feelings, she may also open the passage to transformation. The most
transcendent example of this figure is Silko's Night Swan, who awakens
transcendence in those who honor her while she destroys the men who
refuse her.

In the "Battle Royal" of *Invisible Man*, the Helen figure is an important
symbol in the protagonist's rite of passage from boyhood to manhood. As
clearly as he may see "the price of . . . blindness" as a deformed woman,
he still desires her.[91] The whore is Max's way out of the war in *The Man
Who Cried I Am*, yet he curses her for his need. She wants to know his
name, while Max wants to maintain impersonal distance. The "old and
worn" woman with a sagging "kewpie-doll mouth" looks for something
more human.[92] Similarly, Rufus attempts to keep Leona at a distance.
Later, when Leona is silhouetted against the nameless, soulless myth, her
reality tortures him. Nameless white women are a symbol of admission
into white society for Native American war veterans in *Ceremony*, whereas
the white girl is just an object to "Jiveass Nigger Alias George Washington
Alias Julius Makewell."[93] She wants to tell him her name but he does not
want to know it. Her name and identity are inconsequential because she
is just a symbol for "the white woman." Her defilement is his passage to
manhood.

Miss Pringle, a thrill-seeking whore, is an American tourist in Africa.
She is "an efficient, better-than-average-looking-secretary" who has "been
selling pussy to Nigerians for fifty dollars . . . for only one time."[94] It is as
though, once in Africa, she is freed from the social pressure that would
call for discretion in America (*The Man Who Cried I Am*). The Whore that
is "whitey Aphrodite" is as irresistible as she is repulsive. By opposition

to the form (which requires irresistible beauty) she becomes part of the mythos. She does not have to have a name. The lie, according to Max, is that white men claim that black men should not feel any attraction toward the irresistible and forbidden white women. "Unconsciously throughout his life," the black man is driven "toward whitey Aphrodite, . . . raping [her] when he [can], loving [her] when he [is] allowed to and marrying [her] when he dare[s] to."[95]

The ambivalence apparent in the symbols for the archetypal Mother exists also in the manifestations of the Seductress. Eve is the symbol of Adam's fall into time. His fall from innocence meant banishment from paradise. Likewise it is a harlot who tames the wild instinct of the Assyro-Babylonian Enkidu. He despairs at the loss of his companionship in the wilds and curses her, though she holds no bonds on him. Yet it is only through this rite of passage, this giving up of innocence to the whore, that he meets Gilgamesh. Each represents a mirror image of the other. "One represents an evolution upward from nature to culture; the other represents a devolution downward from divinity to humanity."[96]

The Platonic bonding between Enkidu and Gilgamesh is a "mediation of the opposites of Heaven and earth."[97] This mediation of opposites is itself an archetypal pattern, functioning between upper and lower worlds and within the planes themselves. The *orisha* of Africa and the *loa* of Haiti manifest this "devolution downward from divinity to humanity" by riding or possessing a "horse" or human vehicle. The "evolution upward" is made by the initiates via symbolic transformation through the drums, the *veves* and the *poteau mitan*. Maya Deren describes the drums as the "sacred voice of address to the loa."[98] The *veves*, which are sacred chalk ground drawings that disappear during the ceremonies, are a doorway to the divine world.[99] To "walk the chalk," as Minnie Ransom does in *The Salt Eaters*, is to participate in the world of humanity and in the world of the spirits while holding one's own psychic energies in balance.[100] The *veves* are drawn around the *poteau mitan*, which functions as the "axis of the metaphysical cosmos."[101]

The mediating factor between the opposite faces of the Goddess is contained in the multivalence of her paradoxical nature. She is Virgin and Whore, Sanctuary and Prison, Mother and Lover, forbidden and irresistible. The tension of ambiguity sustains the ambivalence that makes her seduction complete. She represents the multiple facets of the creative unconscious that enables one to establish connections between seemingly disparate forces. Both "prostitute and virgin" are "archaic images of the free woman, as opposed to the domesticated woman."[102] Her penchant for abandonment to the forces of instinct, enables the archetypal Free Woman to direct the energy of chaotic impulses to revitalize static social patterns. Jung has a tendency to relegate this capacity (for tapping into the reservoir of instinctive modes of behavior and creative impulses) to the domain of the pre-technological cultures that he perceives as an analogy for the infant stage of consciousness. Yet this extralogical capacity to find meaning in synchronous events (which the Free Woman shares with the Trickster) is not an inferior or infantile mode of interaction with the world. On the contrary, the ability to move easily between the all-at-onceness of intuition and the sequential ordering of steps is the hallmark of an artist or a healer empowered to envision and to initiate.

Erzulie, the Goddess of the African-Haitian *Vodun* pantheon, is all of these facets of the archetypal Mother-Virgin-Whore. She is often described as a light-skinned black woman, another form of mediation between white and black.[103] The manifestation that most closely resembles the despair of the Femme Fatale that pervades White America (along with the billboards) is the Tragic Mistress. "Erzulie is the loa of impossible perfection which must remain unattainable. . . . The condition of her divinity is his failure" to meet her demands.[104] Similarly, the reification of the white woman in part depends upon the failure-ridden stereotype of the black American male and the guilt-ridden white man. Erzulie Maitresse is but one manifestation of a grieving *loa* who has not been loved enough[105]; the billboard woman has no other attributes to compensate her emptiness. In women who suffer the mirror affliction of a man whose projected anima experience is that of an unattainable dream (as in Gatsby's green light[106]), the despair is like that of Erzulie's. In spite of the many gestures made in devotion to the Goddess, she still feels somehow betrayed, eternally unsatisfied, unloved.

Erzulie Ge-Rouge is the enraged manifestation of a *loa*. When she is not "fed," her murderous instinct is unleashed and, as in Reed's *Mumbo Jumbo*, it takes the soothing manner of Papa LaBas and Black Herman to dissuade her from further expressions of rage. Likewise Ishtar, spurned by Gilgamesh and Enkidu, delivers a curse and the mortal Enkidu dies, leaving Gilgamesh in despair.

Regina is forever seeking love from those who are incapable of providing it. She is a lesser human personification of the Tragic Mistress. Lula, in her inability to find a man who can play her lines correctly, is a victim of her eternal struggle. She is the Flying Dutchman, like Whitman's vision of Poe on a ship of torn sails "apparently enjoying all the terror, the murk, the dislocation of which he was the centre and the victim."[107] She is the Tragic Mistress who has turned to rage for an outlet. Rufus's anima, an effect of a negative Mother complex that expresses itself through rage and despair ("self-castration, madness, and early death"[108]), has made him a suicide. Though death by drowning is a symbol for the return to the Mother, it is the Father, the white God, that Rufus curses: *"All right you motherfucking Godalmighty bastard, I'm coming to you."*[109]

The eternally seeking but unsatisfied Eros finds finality in death. The female manifestation of the Eros may be a Lorelei who drowns the men she loves or, conversely, a Femme Fatale whose role is always tragic. In men, the gloomy anima can be a driving force behind the death wish for the Devouring Mother to engulf them. They may alternately worship the Virgin for her purity or, as Max does in *The Man Who Cried I Am*, despise her for her inaccessibility while cursing the Whore for their need. The Witch may enable or impede personal revelation. Matriarchal systems extant in prehistoric periods were ultimately suppressed by the later, patriarchal societies and the balance shifted toward materialism and technological advancement. The lament of an African-American blues lyric, "Motherless children have a hard time when their mother is dead," expresses the despair over the loss of the vital regenerative, nourishing and transformative capacities of the complete cycle of the Feminine.[110]

CHAPTER 3

Social Stereotypes

POLARITY: THE STEREOTYPE AND THE ARCHETYPE—BREAKING BOUNDARIES

The stereotype is distinguished from the archetype by its inherent limits. Whereas the archetype belongs to the universal unconscious, the stereotype resides within the bounds of linear, polarized world views. According to Webster's Collegiate definition, a stereotype is "a standardized mental picture that is held in common by members of a group and that represents an oversimplified opinion, affective attitude, or uncritical judgment."[1] A stereotype operates in a particular time and place and is conceived as an immutable type with no other attributes. "When someone calls a woman 'a man eater' they are generally stereotyping her, putting her in an immovable position without recognizing the archetypal form of the man-eating mother that is asleep, or astir, in all women" (and, via the anima, in all men).[2] The primordial woman is the original archaic image out of which all subsequent feminine representations are developed. Kali devours her newborn child, yet this "man eater" is equated with life. Thus, the archetypal Mother is both the symbol of regeneration and death. The same image of fecundity is inseparably connected to the process of decay. Kali represents the power of time as Eve represents man's initiation (or fall) into the existence of time. Although "carnage and cannibalism are characteristic traits of the archaic goddess," it is likewise from Kali in her terrible affect that "mercy can be implored."[3] Life emerges out of death, and decayed matter nourishes new shoots. Life moves inevitably to death and the cycle is repeated. The stereotype, unlike the archetype, is never cyclical nor does it partake of a multiplicity of traits that balance one another. The stereotype represents an imbalance. The woman who is a stereotypical "man eater" is a polarized entity without individuality. Her attributes exist only in relationship to her ultimate destructive function. Therefore, the stereotype has a fixed, normative identity bound by time and space. Archetypes exist outside of time and space and are operative as recurring images unhindered by the social and political structures in which they are manifest.

Categorizing the world of experience into discrete types is a means to create order out of multiplicity and to render the transcendent intelligible. However, the system for intelligibility should not be mistaken as the equivalent of the reality it attempts to comprehend. A dialectical process is used to differentiate levels of experience. Modern thought leans toward convenience and neatness; that which is apprehensible and verifiable is "real" in the rational sense. The ontology of the psyche is vague and uncertain. René Descartes's *cogito* asserts the existence of the thinker but not the thinking process or psyche. According to Jung, matter has replaced spirit as the Western symbol for what is ultimately real, yet spiritual materialism has no more certainty than the psyche's domain. Western rationality depends upon dualism as a system to interpret experiences. What a phenomenon is, is often defined by what it is not. On the side of what is verifiably real are facts, time, space, body, natural laws, action and visibility. That which is invisible, spiritual, uncertain, ambiguous and conceptual is relegated to speculation. Out of the tendency to polarize experience into real and unreal, science and faith, thought and feeling, chastity and lust, sobriety and joy, emerge the two worlds of stereotype and archetype.

Stereotypes are definable entities with predictable actions within a predictable world. The domain of opposition and linear logic codifies the expectations of modern man. Operative modes of being are determined by "should" and "ought" and the multiple facets of the archetype are divided into that which is acceptable and that which is suppressed. The singular difference between Western dualism and African religious hierarchies is that the African world view contains a mediating force between the physical and spiritual dimensions. Neither plane is fixed. The invisibles partake of the visible plane through possession of devotees. The physical world intersects the invisible to the extent that spiritual events become readable through physical signs. Distinctions between zones begin to break down and the study of a network of interrelated events as signs takes ascendancy over the impulse to separate, categorize and analyze. Through the sacrifice of clarity, a greater gestalt is achieved, whereby the seeker does not aim to dissect but to experience the vision in its entirety.

Modern alienation and fragmentation are the result of perceiving ourselves and our experiences as separate and unique without connection to
the infinite. Reed distinguishes the linear Protestant (Atonist) system of
rationalism from a mythical system (Jes Grew) that knows no class, no
race and no time (*Mumbo Jumbo*). Representative of the world of the
archetype, Jes Grew is the "manic in the artist who would rather do
glossolalia than be 'neat clean or lucid.' "[4] The Atonist's urge to categorize
and define the content of the psyche can result in a series of unreconcilable
dichotomies (e.g., reverence is opposed to laughter; the Goddess cannot
be one and many at the same time). Nowhere in Christianity does one find
"an account or portrait of Christ laughing. Like the Marxists who secular-
ized his doctrine, he is always stern, serious and as gloomy as a prison
guard."[5] Whereas the African-Haitian *orisha* of order (Damballah) is
simultaneously the *loa* of chaos, Reed's Atonists attempt to purge the
world of laughter, celebration and "hysteria" in order to create the rigid
control consistent with their needs for rulership. Osiris (of Reed's poem,
"why i often allude to osiris") prefers to dance, whereas his temporary
usurper (the Atonist, Iknaton) wanted to rule.[6] The Atonist Christ is never
seen "laughing until tears appear in his eyes like the roly-poly squint-eyed
Buddha . . . or certain African loas, Orishas."[7] Whereas the Atonist "tech-
nique for 'curing' [a host's] hysteria" was "electrifying it lobotomizing it
or removing its clitoris,"[8] the *Vodun* attendants (e.g., Reed's Black Herman) feed, celebrate and drum the *loa* until it leaves the host.

The West lost its knowledge of the names and rites of the invisibles
"when the Atonists wiped out the Greek mysteries" in search of clarity.[9]
The cult of Dionysus was undermined by the illumination of the more
austere solar deity, Apollo. By reducing the importance of passion, intuition and sensuality in the spiritual life, the need for a dominant feminine
figure in the mysteries was similarly reduced (or transformed into a
virginal Mother). According to Reed, both Christian and Islamic doctrine
"agree on the ultimate wickedness of woman, even using feminine genders
to describe disasters that beset mankind."[10] The Atonist perceives the
world as divided into fixed, unrelated types, whereas a philosophy of
correspondence assumes a collective psyche out of which the archetypes
generate and interrelate. By suppressing the generosity, lust, joy, humor
and sensuality of the Rada side of *Vodun*, Christian fanatics in Haiti
invoked the aggressive rage of the Petro side. "Suppression always destroys first what is gentle and benevolent; it inspires rage and reaction,
encourages malevolence," thereby "creat[ing] the very thing which, the-
oretically, it would destroy."[11] Similarly, the archetypal White Goddess is

released in all her fury when her beneficent powers are denied in a patriarchal system. The Atonist milieu might be defined as the world of the stereotype, whereas Jes Grew and its antecedents are archetypal.

The judicial, governmental and religious strata in American society are quite distinct, but the regulating forces of secret societies within Africa and Haiti are closely aligned with spiritual forces. African religion (and its descendants in Haiti and the Americas) retains the principle of unity with the earth as the primordial Mother. The Yoruba Ogboni society "is a society of titled elderly men who worship earth as a source of moral law." They can preside over "primary matters of law" because they are beyond the "distractions of petty ambition and hierarchic insecurities."[12] Abiding in the phenomenal world, the Ogboni demonstrate their symbolic allegiance to the supernatural, metaphysical earth by turning their clothing (and the inner self) inside out. Thus revealed, their symbolic nakedness prompts the revelation of the source of imbalance within the community. "The mystic number of this . . . society is three." The symbolic sculpture is the *edan*; two figures, male and female, are linked by a chain representing the fusion of "contradictory concepts to suggest a third [entity], the presence of the earth."[13] Operating within the context of a mediating force, the Ogboni elders have discovered and absorbed the secrets of the crossroads figure, Eshu-Elegba.

"Boundaries—physical, social, religious, and even metaphysical—dissolve and reform in [Legba's] presence." Legba "lives where separate worlds meet and can move back and forth between them." He is not a creator but a shaper of human interaction. Signifying Legba's great powers of transformation, his libidinous energy "forces responses that reveal possibilities [that otherwise would be] hidden" and discloses "that the limits of this world can become horizons."[14] Through his outrageous behavior (which might include gluttony, mendacity and seemingly destructive pranks) the Trickster "seek[s] to dissolve boundaries in such a way that a meeting brings harmony, not conflict."[15]

In a world that requires mediation between opposing poles to maintain a vital balance, "delight is the substance . . . [that] brings us near to the divine state."[16] Sexual union (and not fecundity per se) is the image of divine mediation for Shiva and Dionysus, ancient Indo-European mediation figures. At the heart of the Dionysian mysteries is the "revelation of sexuality as transcendency."[17] Unlike the asexual transcendency of Christ and Mary, the *loa* retain their vital sexuality. "The confrontation of boundless sex with wholly bounded sex brings forth neither chaos nor a new absolute." On the contrary, this confrontation of opposites "joins center and periphery, centripetality and centrifugality." Legba reveals the nature of the threshold "into the larger world of human community."[18] The contrast between the savior of contemporary Christendom and the Tricksters (Shiva, Dionysus, Osiris and Legba) centers around the absence (Christ) or presence (Trickster) of sexuality and mirth.

In Legba, the "deeply ironic vision, which yokes together what is and what may be" is central to the Fon way of life. Furthermore, the African "vision" of the ordering processes in the cosmos has "remained celebratory, neither freezing into stoicism nor dissolving into hedonism."[19] The existence of destructive stereotypes demonstrates the problems inherent in static social structures. In his efforts to preserve some place in his identity that was pure and unsullied by moral corruption, the southern white slaveowner created an image of sacred white womanhood that ultimately became the tool of depredation. Social structures that promote negative stereotypes reveal the danger of rigidity. Legba's function is "to stir up as well as to allay, to rechannel far more than to neutralize, the various forces present in . . . dangerous social situations."[20]

The purpose of any "social structure" is "to create a network of symbolic harmonies, enabling people [and societies] to pass through the process of dissolution and reintegration . . . not only without harm but with continued growth." Misdirected, these structures "can calcify and block real passage," (as in the case of the sexualization of racism).[21]

A Trickster figure or enlightened author provides the needed interference to break through the strictures that inhibit human growth. He can expose the errors of judgment common to a group of people that stereotypes white women while promoting harmony with the universal attributes of the Feminine "asleep or astir" in all individuals. Whereas the former belongs to a limited set of experiences within a narrowly defined universe, the latter belongs to the infinite.

SEPARATING THE ARCHETYPE AND THE STEREOTYPE

Although this study of the image of white women is primarily an investigation of archetypes, the stereotypes peculiar to black-white relations provide the structural context through which archetypal forms may be perceived. Furthermore, any attempts to mediate the chaos of the psyche in the modern world must focus on exposing the specific results of racism while addressing the psychological dimensions of spiritual transformation in general. That a universal spiritual revolution is needed (such as that embodied in Jes Grew of *Mumbo Jumbo* or Betonie's medicine in *Ceremony*) does not imply absorption into the middle-class mainstream. On the contrary, in order for any spiritual healing to occur, issues of racial oppression must be identified, exposed and resolved.

More insidious than prejudice, institutionalized racism allows even the educated (who believe themselves to be unprejudiced and well-meaning) to continue conventional practices that give unfair advantages to whites. The stereotyped behavior of the well-intentioned Mrs. Dalton (an inadvertent supporter of institutionalized racism) parallels her archetypal function as a Destructive Goddess (*Native Son*). Her tendency to treat Bigger as a child is a paradigm of the false superiority inherent in the oppressor's condescension toward the oppressed. The "tendency of racism" is to objectify the dominated population into commodities for "pleasure or profit; . . . the stereotypes . . . of the white population then depict them as animals or children, the better to justify such less than human patterns of relatedness." The racially oppressed become "convenient targets for the psychic projection of those character tendencies and desires that Western man has suppressed in himself."[22] Unable to establish an internal integration of polarized forces, those who block measures to ensure greater equality legitimize the dehumanization of racial minorities by assigning to them the negative spectrum of behavior.

Spiritual revolution involves the realization that all opposing forces are interpenetrating parts of a growth process that may be represented as an evolving spiral (a Neolithic symbol for the Feminine), contrary to the Protestant image of linear organization: good versus evil, animal versus human, nature versus culture. If we define negative stereotypes as projections of suppressed facets of the psyche, then the movement toward integration necessitates an ability to tolerate unpleasant forces within the self. In other words, negative stereotypes cease to function as a means to preserve institutionalized racism once a society recognizes its participation in a full spectrum of human behavior.

Archetypal forms of the Mother, Daughter, Terrible Goddess, Virgin, Harlot, Initiator, Destructive Bitch, Femme Fatale and Mistress exist consciously or unconsciously in all women. Through the anima, men also participate in the archetypal forms of the Feminine. Archetypes may be defined as regular, recurring patterns of human experience unbounded by time and geography. Specific representations of archetypes may be found in the mythic structure that supports the beliefs and values of a given culture. Archetypes exist a priori and contain the collective memory of the human species as well as the potential for transformation. The archetype in itself is formless and difficult to define, whereas manifestations are easily recognizable within the context of a specific culture. Because the manifestations of an archetype can be very specifically described, they are often hard to distinguish from stereotypes. The archetype is boundless while the stereotype is restricted to local attitudes. "A stereotype is a stricture . . . literally a printer's mold cast in metal."[23] Usually, the stereotype has no other reference outside the corresponding social pattern (e.g., racism) that creates fixed roles and images, whereas the manifestation of the archetype always refers to an archaic remnant of memory that supersedes the limits of time and circumstance. When the fixations of a social structure encounter the mediation of archetypal forces, the opportunity for growth emerges. The images of the present are confronted by the infinite and limits dissolve. According to Nor Hall, the true nature of the Feminine cannot be encountered until the primordial patterns that lie beneath the stereotype are rediscovered. Therefore, "wherever the archetypal nature of words and images has been intentionally recharged by referring to roots of meaning there is a correspondingly greater freedom to explore the parameters of feminine identity."[24]

Fictional characterizations may be examined by referring to both the stereotypes and the archetypes they represent. Examination of a character in reference to an archetype leads to a broader understanding of the workings of myth and the collective unconscious. Studies of stereotypes lead to conclusions about the historical evolution of social attitudes. When part of the intent of a novel is the exposition of social problems specific to a cultural context, the investigation into archetypes and stereotypes is applied toward distinct, though related theories for change. If we apply Jung's model for individual psychoanalysis to society, then healing is best accomplished by providing an analogy to fragmentation and alienation through myth. When a local context is seen in relationship to the broader context of the collective unconscious, individuals may recognize their participation in the archetypal Feminine and find their way to expanded fulfillment. Whereas the social scientist may examine stereotypes to find solutions for more immediate change in the social, political or economic structure of society, the necromancer seeks a form of change that will permeate all levels of consciousness.

To the extent that social stereotypes may be analyzed by reference to deeper structures, there may be considerable overlapping of the socially constricted definition of a character's stereotype and her archetypal function. The stereotypes of this chapter may be categorized as follows. The woman who perceives herself as *deformed* attempts to define black men as evil in order to elevate her own stature. "*White Trash*" or sloppy, lower-class women invoke disgust either through their gross naiveté of social problems or through their inability to fulfill the dream of the beautiful White Goddess. The *Thrill Seeker* is an upper- or middle-class woman who fulfills her fantasies by "slumming" with black men. The *affected* woman emulates a statured social position in order to elevate her own sense of worth, whereas the *political Do-Gooder* seeks absolution through her efforts to create social change. Hernton's *"White-Negro"* woman takes on the cultural attitudes of blacks and denies her background as a white woman, and *exiled* white women who marry black men are banished from their families. *Empty*, barren women are perceived either as innocuous figures or dangerous entities. Finally, the white women perceived as *objects* for social mobility are despised for their ultimate powerlessness. Any of these types may participate in archetypal qualities of the Feminine; however, the distinguishing element between these types and the Terrible Goddess, Witch, Initiator, Harlot, Mother, Virgin and Confidant Sage is in their definition as socially constricted types bound by the conditions of racist attitudes.

A stereotype exists within a time and space framework, whereas the archetype is atemporal. Taken out of the context of American social structure, these white women can be seen as fragmented projections of another character's inner world. These negative aspects can be attributed to a destructive anima or the shadow self of the black characters. However, just as the victim of racism is not the cause of his own victimization (neither through "innate wickedness or genetic defect,"[25] nor because of his "cultural deprivation"[26]), he is not the prime mover behind the negative stereotyping of white women. Regardless of the attitudes black male and female characters may possess toward the white woman, they have not created the image. The white woman may be the recipient of the rage and frustration incurred through the history of racism, but this transferral does not originate in the African-American consciousness. Rather, the invective directed at white women begins with the birth of a nation founded on colonialism. Ironically, although the officials who maintain a corrupt system are predominantly white upper-class men interested in protecting their financial positions, the blame for the inequities is often stated in the white woman's name: "The old liberal whores from the social sciences are . . . turning new tricks every day under the baton of the madam in the White House, conducting from the score of his new oratoria, *Benign Neglect and Malignant Intervention*."[27]

It is common for an individual to despise traits in another person that are evident (though not accepted and therefore censored) in one's own personality. The black man's self-hate is fostered by the indoctrination of whites and blacks alike that he is inherently inferior. Instead of searching for the cause of pathological violence in the family life of the murderer or rapist, one must acknowledge the more powerful forces of institutionalized oppression that undermined his growth toward healthy adaptation from the very beginning. By focusing on the "alleged defects" of the black American child and his family, well-intentioned social reformers nevertheless undermine any significant change because they have conveniently "diverted . . . attention" away from "racism, discrimination, segregation, and the powerlessness of the ghetto" experience.[28] The focus on "Blaming the Victim" not only perpetuates the powerlessness of subjugated minorities, but also reinforces both the self-hate that prompts a compensating objectification of the white woman as the embodiment of luxury and freedom and the subsequent desecration of the myth of sacred white womanhood.

Although stereotypical modes of perceiving white women are generally expressed through the tormented psyches of black men, black women also suffer in comparison to their reified image. Thus negative projection may come from both camps. In *Who Is Angelina?* Sammi is seen through Angelina's eyes as a "slumming" white woman. Angelina is attempting to purge herself of empty and self-destructive habits and Sammi, as the shadow self, is the mirror of those traits Angelina has rejected within herself. Michael-Mary Graham in *Song of Solomon* is an upper-class snob seen through the eyes of her maid Corinthians. The affected mannerisms of Michael-Mary are but mirrors of the same affectation Corinthians displays toward her lover. Once she knows that her suitor Henry Porter has "occasional yard work in [the] part of town" where she works, Corinthians is relieved that "she had never . . . mentioned . . . the man to anyone."[29]

There is a tendency in Calvin Hernton's *Sex and Racism in America* and in Eldridge Cleaver's "Primeval Mitosis" (*Soul on Ice*) for both authors to analyze white women only in relation to black men. According to Hernton, the major attraction to white women is the forbidden quality in the relationship. The more taboo the white woman becomes, the more expansive the myths about her. The more she is mythologized, the more she is desired. Cleaver attempts to deduce the universal "primeval mitosis" as the original cause of conflict, whereas Hernton confines his analysis to stereotypes within the arena of a local sociopolitical context.

Seen in isolation, the image of the white woman in these novels is, for the most part, negative. She is, as Hernton maintains, the symbol of bondage and freedom. Apart from their effects on other people, these women are often characterized as fools and it can be argued that characterizations of white women in African-American literature are analogous to the early image of blacks on television. From this point of view, white women are also the victims of oppression. Minority writers are often accused of reversing oppression in their characterizations of white women. Perhaps they are simply being accurate in revealing the victimization of white women. If oppression is an externally imposed restriction on the individual's capacity to become self-realized, then these women are oppressed by the system that created them. One should not go too far in pardoning criminal behavior because the perpetrator was a victim. White women may be victims but, if they accept the indoctrination (according to Reed's Ian Ball) while "drooling over the burnt flesh" of black men and bringing their children along to attend lynchings, then they share the moral responsibility for the actions they condone.[30] *Reckless Eyeballing* exploits all the stereotypes including anti-Semitic southerners, black men who are "wife beaters and child molesters"[31] and white men who are "fucking little children . . . pineapples and dead people."[32] None of these behaviors is excused. Nevertheless, the pathologies point to a need for healing.

White women and black men hold a similar position in the hierarchy of power, according to Cleaver's "Primeval Mitosis." The split of the "Unitary Sphere" into male and female, mind and body dichotomies is further divided by class distinctions. "The Class Society projects a fragmented sexual image." The white elite male takes on the "Administrative Function" of the mind while black men are relegated to the position of the "Brute Power Function."[33] To counterbalance the "physical weakness" of the white man, his white mate has to be "Ultrafeminine" in order that he may appear "masculine" in "contrast."[34] Fearing "impotence," the white man harbors a "secret aversion" to the white woman's frailty.[35] Instead, he is drawn to the physical strength and domesticity of the black woman. The white woman "is physically inadequate while mentally voracious"; therefore, her sexual complement is the black man.[36] The accuracy of this world view is not the issue here. What is evident in Cleaver's picture of the American social structure is that no one (not even the "Omnipotent" white man) escapes degradation in a lord and bondsman framework.

In the initial stages of the Civil Rights movement, powerlessness is a position of affinity between black men and white women. When the women's movement coincides with the Civil Rights movement, both Truman (*Meridian*) and Cecil (*A Short Walk*) find allies in white women. When the movement becomes divided and several separatist groups emerge, white women are no longer welcome, and black men who become involved in an interracial relationship are ostracized. Unlike Velma (*The Salt Eaters*), who must find a "colored" bathroom, as a white Lynne (*Meridian*) can still enjoy some comfort in her Civil Rights efforts. A renewed respect for the beauty of black women corresponds with the nationalist preaching of Garvey's disciples. Black women are the embodiment of race consciousness for their overprotective men. Truman returns to Meridian, wanting her to have his "beautiful black babies."[37] Cecil chastises Cora's friendships with white people in general and criticizes her lack of "race pride"—yet he keeps his white feminist lovers in the background (*A Short Walk*). Cora has had to work all of her life; white women are fighting "for the right to work." Cora "had that right all [her] life" but does not have the right to work in the kinds of places where white women can work. Angry at this hypocrisy, Cora tells Cecil she plans "to walk into a nationalist meetin" and "preach on the '*White* woman question.' "[38]

The black woman is expected to uphold a Pan-African image commensurate to the black nationalist's romantic notions of Africa, whereas the white woman counterbalances the earthiness of the black feminine image with a commercial image devoid of emotional depth. "Anne—the American white woman—ha[s] the leading role, her smiling face on the products, the covers of magazines."[39] Black women, Asian and Jewish women are "undergoing torture in order to look like her."[40] According to Reed's Johnnie Kranshaw, white women are "the most privileged women on earth, but all they do is complain."[41] At the same time Cleaver's Lazarus describes the white woman as a "cancer . . . devouring [his] brain," he sees her as a religious object. His "dreams" and "nightmares" are filled with images of her long hair "like a mane on a Palomino stallion."[42] In *Reckless Eyeballing*, Reed's Ian Ball describes Anne as an interfering gossip,[43] a "conniving spidery creature" who attempts "to control those around her by dangling the golden apple of artistic success" before them.[44] The old European fairy godmothers were benevolent gossips present at childbirth and the formidable Muse brought divine inspiration. Reed's white gossip and Muse are reduced to pitiful, sexless women. "Over seventy percent . . . are opposed to penetration. They want to be cuddled." Johnnie Kranshaw continues, "They ain't nothin' but a bunch of brat women."[45]

Black women become figureheads of race pride, earth and Africa—the antithesis of brittle, sacred white womanhood. When her dedication to Civil Rights turns to pity, Lynne becomes just another oppressor (*Meridian*). Yet black women are not without their respective negative roles in these novels. Opposite the strong image of independence gained by Velma and Meridian (black women who survived the disappointment of the movement), is the image of Lillian (*The Man Who Cried I Am*). Lillian survives by conforming to middle-class mediocrity. A member of Hernton's "orthodox" middle class, her values are modeled after the "white, Protestant world."[46] She models her "ideas about dress, social etiquette, charity work, political matters, private manners, and public morals" after the white woman, her "alter [ego]." Contrary to Cleaver's black domestic woman, the black woman of the orthodox middle class "is far more rigid, repressed, and neurotic than any other female in America."[47] Whereas Lynne's loyalty to the movement is suspicious because she is white (*Meridian*), Lillian never attempts to support a movement toward change. Similar to Clay (*Dutchman*), Lillian takes on the identity of white middle-class existence and offers no resistance to conformity. Lillian will mask whatever injuries she has experienced as a result of racism; otherwise, any confrontation with oppression might reveal that her social position is really tenuous. Compared to the white women with whom Max becomes involved, Lillian is the Femme Fatale who stands in the way of his career. She cannot tolerate any of his radical writing because it might jeopardize their place in society. Lillian wants Max to have a normal life. Jesse's wife Becky (*The Primitive*) is similar in character type to Lillian. Both men would have to sacrifice their integrity as writers in order to support the middle-class existence desired by their wives. Lillian and Becky would have to give up all notions of stability to encourage their husbands' resistance to middle-class repression. By remaining fixed in their notions of security, Lillian and Becky stagnate. Max and Jesse suffer remorse for marooning the women they love. Margrit acknowledges Max's need to write and Kriss pushes Jesse to his confessions, where he finds his "simple street." It is the white woman who is the Muse in *The Primitive* and *The Man Who Cried I Am*.

When the stereotype of the white woman provides a positive role (such as that provided by Margrit), black women are frequently perceived in negative roles. As soon as the positive image of white women is demeaned, black women regain importance. Truman's selection of a white woman to replace his black girlfriend is even more crushing to Meridian, whose image of the white woman makes Truman's preference incomprehensible. She was raised with the stereotype of white women as "sexless, contemptible and ridiculous" creatures, desired only by "their empty-headed, effeminate counterparts—white boys." Unlike the stereotyped white men who smell like "boiled corn and . . . glue," white women are odorless like "dead water" because they do "not sweat." Meridian was taught that white women are even incapable of managing a household; "without servants all of them would live in pigsties." The "homely ones" go to college, while the others "s[i]nk into a permanent oblivion" after high school. But not all white women are portrayed as "frivolous, helpless creatures"[48]; neither are they the only victims of derision in these novels.

There are just as many weak and broken characters who are not white women. In *Flight to Canada*, Mr. Swille is the exaggerated stereotype of the southern white man; Mammy Barracuda delights in beating

Mrs. Swille and Cato, the black overseer, is a clumsy, "infernal idiot."[49] In *Song of Solomon*, Ruth is a pitiful woman and her daughters, Lena and Corinthians, spend most of their adult years scarred by their parents' unhappy marriage. In *Who Is Angelina?*, the black female protagonist has similar problems to those her white friend, Margo, is experiencing. Toby Crawford is a pompous black fool and Larry's new girlfriend is a hypocritical, pseudoradical black nationalist. Although Booker sends his white ex-wife 'guilt money,' "he's all black now," preferring the "simpleminded chocolate mama starlet type" to white women.[50] Morrison's Jadine (*Tar Baby*) and Young's Angelina undergo struggles in their quest for identity similar to the soul-searching of Cass (*Another Country*) and Margrit (*The Man Who Cried I Am*). In *The Salt Eaters*, the so-called leaders of the Civil Rights movement entertain themselves in hotel rooms while Velma and the other marchers have no shoes and no food. Obie lives with Velma for two years before he knows how"to identify" her orgasm.[51] While Velma absorbs the symptoms of the psychic struggle of African-American existence, Obie is ineffectual, disconnected; "his whole johnson [is] getting raggedy—his home, his work." Although he sits "on a bench in a basement talking to a locker," Velma is the heroine and the vehicle through which the transformation of old medicine within the New World can effect a healing. Obie is too removed from the process to know how to help: "The fissures at home had yawned wide and something fine had dropped through."[52]

From looking at these characters it is evident that white women are not the only examples of image projection (Jung's analysis) and maimed personalities (Himes's analysis). As a sociological stereotype, the white woman in these novels is the shadow of White America just as much as she is the black man's anima. She is the epitome of emptiness and yearning that all women have felt. She is both entrance and barrier to freedom and the retrieval of undefined loss.

According to the tenets of Western dualism, two entities that are defined as opposites are polarized and unreconcilable. If individuals accept this system as their own without recognizing their ability to transcend its limits, then they are unable to reconcile internal conflicts. A black man's survival within a rationalist system depends upon his rejection of the opposition (i.e., white woman/anima) within. In order to escape self-hate he projects the hate outwards; he must kill her in order to survive because it is impossible to acknowledge his internal struggle. The aberration resulting in this logic is the conviction that the outside world has taken on the essence of the inner demons. Working from this logic, he has no choice but to kill the woman, the self he cannot absorb and reconcile. Until he kills Mary, Bigger has no identity in the white world. There is no sacred canopy or "Jes Grew" to create a safe atmosphere within which the individual can afford to take risks of self-exposure. Bigger tells his lawyer, "After I killed that white girl, I wasn't scared no more. . . . I was my own man then, I was free."[53] In reality, he is not his own man; in the act of killing Mary, he becomes the stereotype white society has expected all along. Although he becomes a haunted man, at least Bigger's existence as a man is acknowledged in the white world.

Analogous to Bigger's projection of inner demons, the political hierarchy of the Western world projects unacceptable contradictions of its self-image as the benevolent master onto the lower stratum of the social hierarchy. Survival of a positive self-image and the rationale behind social oppression depends upon the deeply rooted need to put oneself forward at another's expense. However, the traits of selfishness, deceit and cruelty are incompatible with cherished notions of a charitable image. Unacceptable traits are projected in the form of demonic urges onto blacks to preserve the Protestant notions of purity in the Western world and to absolve white society of its guilt. Considerable defenses are raised in order to deny participation in the dark side of consciousness; therefore, it becomes even more essential for the dominant group to project hate and evil externally.

Ultimately, the Atonists of Reed's *Mumbo Jumbo* project the responsibility for their own hatred outward onto Jes Grew. Calling it evil, the Atonists defeat themselves by undermining the benevolent force and vital energy of delight embodied in Jes Grew. Patriarchal systems evident since "the period of Aryan (Indo-European) conquest and colonization"[54] ignored the importance of the Goddess. Without the female counterpart of creative energy embodied in Shiva, and without the "spark which flies between them: attraction (*râga*), delight (*ânanda*), pleasure (*kâma*), love," the links that bind human experience are severed.[55]

BETWEEN THE ARCHETYPE AND THE STEREOTYPE: MEDIATION AND THE TRANSCENDENT SYZYGY

Whereas the judicial process in American society is often administered with stereotyped prejudice, the Ogboni society of Nigeria is, in theory, comprised of elders who have transcended temporal boundaries and conceive of justice as bringing to balance the forces of opposition. The Nigerian Ogboni members have moved beyond the anima/animus conflict. The shadow self and anima/animus have been integrated in the psyche and the transcendent psyche appears in the image of an old man or woman. As transcendent figures, the elders are spiritually capable of making judgments to resolve issues of community conflict. A reconciliation of diverse energies is experienced in a state that simulates infancy when the secrets of Legba are understood and the individual returns to the primordial, uroboric unity of the Earth Mother, Onile.

Members of the Ogboni society are able to reconcile conflicts of violence because they have reached an age when sexual differentiation and political affiliation are no longer important. Kinship ties are not as strong and destinies in the dual worlds are complete. Like Eshu-Elegba, they are beyond time and the limitations imposed by time, and therefore they participate in seemingly contradictory phenomena. The crossroads figure, Eshu-Elegba, stands between the physical and metaphysical worlds. He stands at the gates of time mediating opposition. He is neither good nor evil but can be the bearer of both. Likewise, the White Goddess is neither good nor evil. Her power is neutral. *Ase* is androgynous, and can be light or dark; it has the potential of destructive action as well as compassionate force.

In a Pan-African system, it is the negative aspect, *aje*, perceived most often in the white woman. There are no formal rituals to appease her power. Her will is capricious and her *aje* cannot be challenged. Like the Yoruba Mothers, she must be praised and obeyed. This is clear in the stereotypical southern white woman who controls the black man by threatening to cry rape if he does not comply with her wishes. Her generosity is less reliable than that of the Gelede who, if they are properly honored, will turn their forces toward the good of the community. Depraved characterizations of white women are an anti-aesthetic to the Yemoja archetype. In her totality, Graves's White Goddess is analogous to the African Yemoja; whereas the white women characterized in these novels are fragmented, incomplete, unresolved women. The imbalance of power given to the white woman compensates for hidden weaknesses in her identity and fragments of her personality become exaggerated and magnified.

The archetypal *ase* has all the power necessary to provoke fear. The invisible *ase*, born of a pre-dualistic world, is superseded by the white woman's means of exercising power. Her color is her status and her vehicle for exacting punishment. The dominant society's overconcern with absolute control produces not a balance of forces but a pseudoequilibrium of enforced inequities. The "powerful dualism" of Western man is a prototypical model for the specific form of tensions acted out between people from opposite ends of a social hierarchy. The actual opposition is between the atemporal, pre-dualistic, archetypal world and the dualistic, spatiotemporal world of the "Protestant world view, which sees good-evil, life-death, child-adult, animal-human, heaven-hell, . . . as polar opposites rather than as interpenetrating realities."[56] It is the position of Legba to maintain the disequilibrium, the tension between worlds so that, through struggle, we can attain the transcendent anima/animus experience. Opposition is not inherent in the *ase* but exists in the mask in which the *ase* appears. The writer-artist works with the force of the *ase* to create the mask. The characters act out the healing pattern mediated by the necromancer, thereby exposing the fissures that need mending.

Derision is the form taken in Efe/Gelede ceremonies to compel conformity, assist individuals in their return to spiritual health, and restore harmony to the community. This derision is also a means to debase one's enemies and reinforce social values. At the beginning of the Gelede masquerade a male dancer (Oro Efe) appears in a costume combining the leg and arm bracelets Legba wore to appease the Mothers in the early days of creation, with layers of material amplified with wood breasts and bustles to suggest the opulence of the Mothers. The Oro Efe thus joins symbolically with Legba and the Mothers to open the ceremony with criticisms for those members of the community whose behavior is considered to be detrimental to the whole social structure. At the same time, he sings praise songs to the Mothers.

Often, the sheer outrageousness of the satirist, like the "shucking, knee-slapping, wet-eyed laughter" of the black people in *Sula*, masks the authentic "pain that rest[s] somewhere under the eyelids." Celebrative affirmation of life on one hand, and mockery on the other, are a defense against one's adversaries, "otherwise the pain [will] escape him even though the laughter [is] part of the pain."[57] Another disguise for the collective injuries resulting from white oppression is the "crazy nigger" (e.g., Shadrack in *Sula*), who gives the appearance of living outside the struggle. His identity as a "crazy nigger" does not imply that Shadrack has no "sense or, even more important, that he ha[s] no power."[58] His laughter enables him to live outside the law. His craziness gives him the right other black men do not have to violate the white man's order. Shadrack leads the people of Bottom to destroy the dreams created by white men and to begin to rebuild their own purposes. Shadrack stands between the two worlds as a mediator. A stereotype of the comic buffoon, he manages to escape violence from white men while inflicting exile upon himself. Here Shadrack may operate (as do Legba and Ghede) to mediate opposition within his world; however, unlike the *loa*, he is ultimately a sacrificial victim relegated to the lonely world of the outcast.

The Ghede of African-American fiction is Ishmael Reed. Like the Oro-Efe, he ridicules the ills of society in verse; no one is immune to his scrutiny. Like the griot of West Africa, he extols the value of knowing one's history; like the calypso singer, he challenges us to learn what we do not understand. The modern griot must be a repository of world history and myth. Reed's LaBas learns that the Work of the Old World must expand to address the global consciousness of the modern world (*Mumbo Jumbo*). Through derision, Reed reduces the power of the Atonists with mockery. Similarly, the Goddess in *Flight to Canada* is so outrageous as to be absurd. She is reduced through laughter to a silly woman. Her *aje* is no more than a bunch of ploys to get her husband to notice her. Even in the mockery there is seriousness, for to appease the destructive power of the Mothers, they must not be ignored. Their importance must be recognized and, with songs of praise, their powers channeled for the good of the community.

A character's individuality is defined by her unique role in time. She also finds her existence and definition according to the degree to which she accepts or rejects her counterpart in the unconscious world. If the real woman rejects any aspect of the archetypal Goddess within, chances are that she will project this self-hatred outwardly, making the internal conflict a physical fact. The inner battle is between repression and integration. If opposing facets within the psyche are accepted and integrated into the whole of the individual's life, then she will have no need to project a negative affect onto another person. However, if the individual is trapped in a dichotomy that forces a rift in the psyche, she is forced to externalize the irreconcilable differences of the inner self and battle to the death. The marginal characters survive the battle because they are borderline figures who allow for inner contradictions to exist. Jesse and Kriss in *The Primitive*, Lula and Clay in *Dutchman*, and Madge in *If He Hollers Let Him Go* cannot reconcile their internal battles. Velma in *The Salt Eaters*, Meridian and Truman in *Meridian* and Pilate and Milkman in *Song of Solomon* transcend the limits of time to learn the secret of Eshu-Elegba to escape the boundaries of polarity. They find their answers in the transcendent self, the integrated syzygy.

WHITE TRASH: DEPRAVITY AND DEFORMITY

The social stereotype is a mask, often functioning as the anti-aesthetic of the White Goddess. Whereas the stereotype in *Invisible Man* is a superficial white nymphette with little characterization, the internal world of Leona in *Another Country* is more developed. Her socioeconomic profile is that of an ignorant, lower-class, white woman from the South. This, along with her bad grammar, places Leona in the category of "poor white trash." From Rufus's perspective, Leona provokes violence. Leona is both terrified by and attracted to the morbid violence of the relationship. Although violent sexual dominance fantasies may have various interpretations, the analysis that seems to fit Leona explains that she is seeking punishment for her own self-hate and guilt. Her need for punishment emerges consciously in her sexually ambivalent desires for tenderness and cruelty. She is not psychologically prepared for real meanness and cannot fathom its source. She acknowledges that her ex-husband "was rough" but she "didn't think he was *mean*." She drinks heavily so she can "stand living with him."[59] She prefers the identity of a victim over the type of debasement (e.g., losing her child) that challenges her self-worth. Similarly, Leona rationalizes Rufus's anger but has ambivalent feelings about punishment and meanness.

In their relationship, Leona and Rufus find a form of opposition that mirrors their internal conflicts. Leona's final action fits her apparent passivity. She always appears to be the victim, unjustly accused, just as Rufus feels he is unfairly judged by the white world. Rufus is painfully aware of his environment, whereas (ironically) Leona's survival depends upon maintaining the ignorance of her participation in the southern way of life that perpetuates violence. Ultimately, Rufus resents her whiteness and her unintentional complicity with the forces of racism. Yet he would like to have hope. His rage is directed at the cruelty of the hope she represents. Rufus's socialization has made him overly anxious about the opinions of others, whereas Leona's indoctrination has made her oblivious to the point of insensitivity.

Vivaldo and Rufus have similar fragmented experiences of love and women. They cannot reconcile sexuality with the ideal of purity ostensibly existing in real love. They cannot accept the dual aspects of the Virgin and the Whore of the Goddess. They are locked into a dichotomy in which one form annihilates the other; and so, they are doomed to pine after the unattainably pure or to settle for a whore whom they despise for revealing their own depravity. Leona's veil of innocence frightens Rufus; it is easier to condemn her as a whore than to confront his motives for punishing her. The conjured image of his actions and guilt threaten insanity. Like the American society Baldwin discusses in *Blues for Mister Charlie*, Rufus "closes his eyes . . . in order to protect himself; . . . compulsively repeats his crimes and enters a spiritual darkness which no one can describe."[60]

Similarly operating in a spiritual void, Freddie (a black bus driver) and Margie (his white wife) face profound disappointment over unfulfilled expectations (*The Salt Eaters*). Margie's unhappiness is apparent in her lethargic sloppiness and Freddie's disappointment is expressed in anger.

She is blamed indirectly "for his chafed neck and his jounced nuts, his loss, his threatened pension." Freddie arrives home from work and tells Margie he "ran over a coon, . . . not to be confused with the coons your daddy used to lynch." Instead of crying for him or commiserating with him, Margie cries "for herself and some dead animal."[61]

Margie is condemned by a social mold that forms her character. Fulfilling society's expectations of the stereotype, white women in Margie's class are either excused for their behavior or despised. Freddie berates Margie's failure to provide for the small luxuries at the end of the day. She absorbs the blame for his "loss" because of her association with inaccessible dreams. She cannot compare with the commercial image of the white woman. Her depravity becomes a betrayal and her "blubbering" over a dead animal is inexcusable because she has never been perceived as an individual human being beyond the role she plays. The theory of environmental conditioning would rationalize her flaws as products of her surroundings, whereas the American ideal of individualism would condemn Margie for her inability to overcome the limitations that society has imposed. Mistakenly perceived as the cause of despair and disillusionment, the Margies are only an effect, victims of a local mythos that does not empower them to bestow the dreams with which they are identified. The truth actually lies somewhere in the middle. The white woman is responsible for her own fate; however, environment plays a critical role in the formation of values and attitudes that will influence her choices and her faith (or lack thereof) in her essential self-worth.

Margie's most contemptible flaw is her inability to perceive Fred's needs. His dream of a woman is simple and he is angry with Margie because she violates his dream. Apathy is not an emotion generally acquired in a stable, content household. Her lassitude implies a certain resignation to unconquerable problems. Margie's lethargy is manifest in the "dirty movie-trailer house smelling like spoiled chops burning in an unclean oven." There's "no tub run," no iced tea, "no decent meal" and no "intelligent conversation" waiting for Fred at the end of the day. The outlet for her disappointment contained in an apathetic attitude is a flood of tears for a "dead coon on the highway."[62] The irritation Margie inspires is not from anything she does; it is what is missing in her character that is contemptible. She is supposed to be a symbol of the luxury that is withheld from Fred. Instead, she represents a prison of filth.

Reed's parody of the southern plantation owner (Mr. Swille) insults Lincoln's "frowzy, dough-faced" wife who "looks like a Houston and Bowery streetwalker who eats hero sandwiches and chews bubble gum." Because Ms. Lincoln does not fit the billboard stereotype she, like the "laundromat attendant" she resembles, is equally deserving of contempt.[63] Unfortunately, the satire is not that far off when one analyzes the more common situation between Margie and Fred. Margie's failures in themselves are not hateful; however, her inability to meet the demands expected of the white woman further reveals the harsh realities of Fred's existence.

Margie is motivated by disappointment whereas Leona is motivated by a need for punishment commensurate to her guilt. Madge in *If He Hollers Let Him Go* follows yet another pattern of southern white womanhood. A sense of deformity encompasses her sexuality and overshadows her tentative self-image. Madge's lack of self-esteem is apparent in her attraction to black men, who, according to her Texan upbringing, are little better than sinful animals. Her sense of esteem is regained when she sees herself in relation to a black man. And this sense of superiority is further induced when she discovers that she is sexually repulsed by him. Madge's vulnerability is exposed when her sexuality is challenged by Robert, who makes it clear that she is unappealing. Her rape fantasy operates as a defense against the threat to her esteem that occurs when a black man, her "inferior," finds her unattractive. If she can cry rape, she can also regain her position of control, and thereby discredit his appraisal. This pattern is typical of the southern white woman for whom the black man became the personification of her "unconscious sense of sexual poverty," and of "everything that was wrong with her life and her society." The white man must portray the black man "as a savage rapist to soothe his guilt," whereas the white woman is compelled to "accept this image" in order to convince "herself that she [is] *sexually* attractive, if not to white men, at least to black 'savages.' "[64]

Madge's ambivalence toward Robert is related to an inner sense of deformity. The white woman's deformity does not always have to be attributed to physical ugliness. Her deformity is attributed to some lack of character and in her mind she is "fit to relate only to men whom [she] also conceive[s] as deformed—black men."[65] This psychological process operates in Kriss (*The Primitive*) and in Leona (*Another Country*). Leona's sense of failure as a mother and a lover is a typical example of Hernton's description of a woman who seeks atonement through punishment in her relationship with a black man. She knows her relationship will alienate her; "white men will sneer at her, and society in general will look down on her."[66] This is the punishment she seeks for the "nameless guilt that eats at her self-esteem." If alienation from white society is not enough to fulfill the need for atonement, then she may seek "a more direct, carnal form of punishment from the very hands of her black lover."[67] Rufus is the "sexually sick" black man who uses Leona as an "object for symbolic mutilation" and a vehicle for "escape from" self-hate.[68]

Likewise, Richard in *Blues For Mister Charlie* fits the stereotype of a "would-be-great" musician for whom white women symbolize the depravity of a New York lifestyle. After taking "as much shit as [he can] stand from the managers" and the audience, Richard leaves a gig to look for "some pasty white-faced bitch . . . to make some down scene" if he can manage "not to strangle her" or beat "her to death" first.[69] The white woman becomes a symbol of depravity and, in destroying her image, the black man feels cleansed. At the same time, he gains a false sense of power. "Any oppressed group, when obtaining power, tends to acquire the females of the group which has been the oppressor."[70] She is simultaneously the symbol of freedom and oppression, and the sexual image of the black man is based on the same mythology that makes her elusive. Her inaccessibility creates a high-risk situation that is attractive in the Freudian sense of taboo and ambivalence.

Southern black men have learned to fear even looking at the White Goddess because of her sacred position in society. Even if the attraction exists, the risk is far too great for any form of demonstration. Black men like Bigger (*Native Son*) learn to avoid white women. Because of the existence of this fear in black men, white women must be the aggressors. Even they are trapped by the sacred image they bear. The chastity myth has made the Southern Belle the white man's discarded and empty mannequin. Feeling sexually inept, she turns to the myth of the black man's savage sexual prowess. And, in order to perpetuate her clean image, she blames the affair on his bewitching irresistibility and cries rape. To admit complicity with the black man would be to forfeit her sacred position in society.

Contradictions implicit in the white woman's outward revulsion and inward attraction to black men create a dangerous situation for her victims. "It is as hazardous to 'go along' as it is to refuse" because there is always the threat of being caught "or of the woman getting angry; in either case she can, to save face or take vengeance, yell 'rape.' "[71] This type of American white woman "intrudes upon [the black man's] space, glares at him with lust in her eyes, and when he pays no attention accuses him of reckless eyeballing, causing her husband and his friends to lynch" him.[72] The protagonist of *Reckless Eyeballing* attempts to market a play that posthumously vindicates a man for the "crime" of "eye-raping" a white woman. Ian Ball is Reed's parody of a young black writer who compromises his own sense of truth in order to win approval from feminists who advocate censorship of any material with negative stereotypes of women. Cursed in utero to lead a double life, he is a victim of censorship; yet, he avenges himself by secretly "shaving off the hair of feminists whom, he felt, were smearing the reputations of black men."[73] Cora Mae is Ball's stereotype of the "radical feminist lesbian, part owner of a bookstore" who, "in the sixties, with heavy makeup, miniskirt, eyeshadow, rouge, blond hair with black roots [was] a sleaze and a tease."[74] To appease his feminist producer, Ian prostitutes his art and changes his storyline to claim that Ham Hill (accused of eyeballing Cora Mae) was just as guilty for "eye-raping" as the white men were for lynching him.[75] Cora and Ham Hill are both victims; Ian has remained politically neutral to gain acceptance into the feminist circle he secretly victimizes. His hopeless ambivalence is emphasized by the chrysanthemum he leaves with each victim.

Without societal taboos, it would not have been necessary for Bigger to become frightened when Mrs. Dalton came to Mary's bedroom (*Native Son*). At worst, he would have found himself in an embarrassing situation. The innocent act of putting the drunken Mary to bed would not have been an occasion of terror despite his momentary attraction to her. And yet, it was the taboo in part that aroused Bigger before he was aware of Mrs. Dalton's presence. At the same time that whiteness is proclaimed as godly and clean, blackness is the devil and dirty. That a white woman might be attracted to his blackness is even more inviting to a man who has been convinced that he is to be despised. A symbol for purity, the white woman becomes the positive anima image for the depraved sense of humanity experienced by the black man.

Both Leona (*Another Country*) and Jo (*Blues For Mister Charlie*) possess the ignorant naiveté that is attractive to a man seeking power. Beneath the innocence they can submerge all awareness of injustice and convince themselves that racial problems do not exist. The result is that white men like Lyle can continue to hide their guilt under her oblivious acceptance, and the black man appears to be increasingly paranoid. Jo never asks Lyle about the shooting. When she discusses Lyle's motives with Parnell, Jo is willing to believe that Lyle shot Old Bill out of passion for Willa Mae. She is more willing to attribute the killing to his passionate love for another woman than to believe that the man she married killed for no justifiable reason. Jo is sexually aware enough to guess that Lyle's feelings toward her and her own feelings toward Lyle never reached the extent of Parnell's passion for Pearl. Jo's thoughts during the church social and her reasons for wanting to marry Lyle (he wanted her) betray her lack of southernly virtue. Jo is not sexless; she is simply repressed.

The black men involved with Leona, Margie and Madge respond to the stereotypes they perceive. Although these women have more depth of characterization than the true stereotype (i.e., an oversimplified, standardized image that lacks individuality), their respective partners are unable to perceive an individual beyond the image. In this respect, Jo is distinct from the aforementioned women. Although Lyle is not particularly perceptive, he does not respond to Jo as a type; he simply lacks the sensitivity to comprehend motives beyond his own. Rufus, Freddie and Robert are conditioned by environment to respond to white women as types. Any natural sensitivity they might possess is further impeded by the expectations set up by stereotypes.

THRILL SEEKERS, "SLUMMERS" AND SOCIAL AFFECTATIONS

The stereotype of a Thrill Seeker coexists with the stereotype of the black man as a "superior sexual animal."[76] "Segregation, the myth of sacred white womanhood" (and the sexual deprivation that the myth implies), in addition to all of the other attitudes that contribute to the sexualization of racist patterns, "have distorted and vulgarized her perception of black men as sexual beings."[77] The Thrill Seeker may perceive the black man as representing a new experience, exotic and exciting or, if she is fully entrenched in the image of herself as chaste and pure, then he might become irresistible, savage and magically compelling. Depending upon the level of social restraints, the white woman might act out the thrill seeking in a clandestine way or she might openly "slum" with black men.

In *Who Is Angelina?*, Sammi rejects her middle-class background by "slumming" with black men. That her lifestyle is as shallow and destructive as that which she rejects is of no concern to Sammi. "Like, I'm as guilty as the next person when it comes to that bullshit." From Bloomfield Hills, Sammi is "one of those spoiled rich girls" Angelina remembers from "college who was spending her life practicing up to be a sleaze."[78] Whereas the Thrill Seeker wishes to maintain her advantageous position in society while secretly acting out her fantasies, the Slummer consciously rejects her social position. Sammi has "all the attributes: bleached hair, too much makeup, studied bad manners, and a foul mouth" along with open disdain for her upbringing, "where everybody's ripping off the corporation or the government, fucking and sucking off everybody else and then getting indignant . . . when somebody gets caught."[79] Her casual morals fit her new image. Sammi is Alex's lover. Alex is Renee's ex-husband; Steve is Renee's newest pursuit. While the foursome is crowded in the bathroom snorting cocaine, Angelina walks in just as Sammi is "licking Steve's upper lip and nostrils."[80] The truly unliberated liberated woman (Sammi) tries to imply that Angelina is repressed, as if cocaine use or urinating in front of a group of self-consciously uninhibited people was the vehicle to self-discovery.[81]

Like Sammi, Jane (*Another Country*) is a middle-class dropout who has descended into the bowels of the city to "find herself." She believes herself to be the quintessential artist who can understand and communicate the pitiful world of her limited bar crowd: unemployed, downtrodden, degenerate white men. Jane considers herself to have more "soul" than Rufus will ever have because of this "artistic empathy." Rufus's most cruel insult is his attack on Jane's credibility as an artist. Jane is particularly vulnerable to Rufus's sarcasm because the authenticity of her image is questionable. At any time (like the "dog-faced hippie"[82] of *Who Is Angelina?*) she can "take a bath" and drop back into the society she rejects.[83] Whereas Leona (*Another Country*) or Margie (*The Salt Eaters*) may represent "poor white trash," Jane and Sammi have pretensions of belonging to their romanticized image of the oppressed world. Slumming white women simulate the "foul language" and the "bad manners" and (like the "dog-faced hippie" who berates Angelina for reporting a thief to the police) "talk all that ignorant horseshit and get a whole lotta black people's . . . heads split open in the name of revolution."[84] They lack the "true convictions or even the maturity to know what they really want."[85]

Renee's more subtle, civilized version of thrill seeking (*Who Is Angelina?*) contrasts with Sammi's gaudiness. Renee is upper middle-class, a second-rate artist, one who might fit into Hernton's description of the white women who are "phonies, psychological disorients. . . . They do not understand that the energy driving them" toward "misfits emanates not out of any personal commitment, or intellectual grasp of the 'system,' . . . [or devotion to] art" nor out of a great "capacity to love the black man" but (like the deformed "white trash") out of a "diseased concept . . . of themselves."[86] Renee is "into" everything—a pseudosophisticate who finds intimacy with a ridiculous black man. She married Alex, got divorced and is now "into" Steve. She paints and is "into a different phase now—browns and blacks and whites and grays. . . . 'Lately I've been doing a lot of portraits,' " she tells Angelina.[87] And of her latest lover, Renee reports, "Steve I can get lost in. He's that vast."[88]

Renee projects a pseudoartist image similar to the pseudopoetess, Michael-Mary Graham (*Song of Solomon*). Michael-Mary Graham is an affected socialite. Unlike Hernton's pseudoartist, Michael-Mary does not take on the affectations of the minorities; instead, she uses them for inspiration. Corinthians gives "her house the foreign air she like[s] to affect." The name "Corinthians Dead" appeals to Michael-Mary's "poetic sensibility."[89] What is "vast" to Renee is "quaint" to Michael-Mary, analogous to the white romanticized notion of a "noble savage." Michael-Mary keeps her distance with her affectations. Renee's approach is more subtle, though no less manipulative than Michael-Mary or Kriss. Kriss (*The Primitive*) wants her escort to be civilized in public but in her bed, it is his "savage" blackness she wants. Out of her own confused emotional orientation, Kriss manipulates Jesse's behavior until there is good reason to fear him. Madge (*If He Hollers Let Him Go*) also falls within this category of women who "*enjoy* 'fearing' Negroes because this adds to the 'thrill' of being 'overpowered' by them."[90]

The white women in Himes's *Pinktoes* are conspicuous in their thrill seeking. Still, they depend upon Mamie to orchestrate alibis and discretionary precautions. They are unconcerned about Mamie's opinion; they have only their standing within white society to protect. Mamie's power throughout the parties is notable in the games she plays, alternately exposing the faults of some while covering the lies of others. Her solution to the "Negro Problem" is to capitalize on the intricate relationship between sex and racism. What is "white and black poetry" at Mamie's is what Hernton refers to as the "sexualization of racism." "He" says "Jim Crow" and "She" responds, "Oh, you suffering Negro." "He: Denied my rights. She: Oh, take my delights." The male and female narrators are depersonalized stereotypes of the black man and the white woman.[91]

The clearest example of the Thrill Seeker is the nameless wife in *Invisible Man*. She is "the kind of woman who glows as though consciously acting a symbolic role of life and feminine fertility."[92] Under the pretense of interest in the "powerful primitive" and "throbbing vitality of the movement," she performs her seduction.[93] As she proclaims the freedom the Brotherhood has given her, her victim is thinking, "And if I were really free . . . I'd get the hell out of here."[94] He is caught in the trap that many of Hernton's informants speak of—that of the rich and powerful woman who seduces unwilling men to her room. As he watches the self-consciously provocative woman answer the phone, the "brother" remembers "forgotten stories" of rich "wives" who "summoned . . . male servants, . . . chauffeurs . . . [and] Pullman Porters" to their rooms during their husbands' absence.[95]

Sybil, another white executive's wife, desires a "domesticated rapist."[96] Sybil begs the protagonist of *Invisible Man* to rape her, then falls into a drunken sleep, awakens and asks, "wasn't I a good nymphomaniac?"[97] Although Sybil is "just the type of misunderstood married woman" he "would have avoided like the plague, . . . her unhappiness and the fact that she was one of the big shots' wives made her a perfect choice" for his plans.[98] Interested mainly in obtaining information from her, the Invisible Man entertains her fantasies of "Brother Taboo-with-whom-all-things-are-possible" until she asks him to rape her.[99] When he tries to change the subject, suggesting a walk in the park, Sybil pleads, "But I need it." She coaxes, "You can do it, it'll be easy for *you*, beautiful."[100] He mentally appraises her and, like Hernton, concludes that Sybil's fantasies have been part of her training throughout her life. The black man's sexuality is "made into a great power and [white women are] taught to worship all types of power." Despite all the taboos, "some are bound to want to try it out for themselves. The conquerors conquered. Maybe a great number secretly want it; maybe that's why they scream when it's farthest from possibility."[101] A contradiction among many, "she lay aggressively receptive" waiting for him. Impatient with his stalling, Sybil cries, "Come on, beat me, daddy—you—you big black bruiser. . . . Hurry up, knock me down! Don't you want me?"[102] Briefly, the "brother" does want "to slap her" but ultimately Sybil falls asleep and, when she awakes, he appeases her by convincing her that she was actually "raped." Later, Sybil wants to follow him into Harlem when the riots start, but he puts her in a taxi to go home. In the middle of the chaos, he sees "a body [hanging], white, naked, and horribly feminine from the lamp post." This horribly feminine apparition is only a mannequin, yet he is uneasy, "What if this one, even *one* is real—is . . . Sybil?"[103]

Under pretenses of possessing social conscience, these women nevertheless (like Mrs. Dalton in *Native Son*) perpetuate social distance. Sybil and the nameless wife use their status and superficial interest in the Brotherhood to seduce a black man. The social distance and the taboo underlies the thrill they seek, but they use the issues of equality to provide the opportunity for their seduction. Although not all women who become involved in pursuits for social equality are "insincere, or are merely out to 'slum' among Negroes,"[104] . . . "it is not too rare to find young white women 'using' their liberal ideas as an *excuse* to 'slum' among" blacks.[105] These women are moved either to prove themselves as individuals who live their altruistic ideals or they are motivated to defy "parental control, usually of a domineering, successful father."[106] Jane in *Another Country*, Renee and Sammi in *Who Is Angelina?*, Lynne in *Meridian* and Mary Dalton in *Native Son*, all fit the category of "college students or young adults from good middle-class homes in the North and the Midwest,"[107] often from liberal backgrounds who are motivated by defiance or by high-sounding principles to be sexually consistent with their lifestyle of liberalism. Upper-class women (e.g., the women from *Pinktoes* or Sybil and the nameless wife of *Invisible Man*) seem to be motivated by ambivalence. Like the southern white women, they may be motivated by guilt, sexual privation or an inner sense of deformity. They use their social status to maneuver black men into positions in which they cannot refuse (i.e., reject) the white women who seduce them. All of these women affect a social image consistent with their own needs for self-esteem. Any confrontation about their behavior poses a threat to that esteem. They can no more admit the pretense of their actions than take the risk of being rejected.

In *A Short Walk*, social pretense is obvious to the child, Cora, who observes the behavior of white and black upper and lower classes during the "Rabbit Ears" show. Affecting detached superiority, the upper-class whites are there "to be amused by the audience as well as the show." Each "assume[s] the same studied, half-amused, tolerant expressions." Conforming to social custom, "black people buy ice cream after the poor whites have first go at it, rich white people don't eat food sold in public."[108] White prostitutes "tip the candy butchers to pass their notes"[109] in order not to be confused with "the laughing black fancies" who drop their notes in the aisles. The black and white notes are easy to distinguish: "Honey Dripper . . . 22 Adams Junction (Enter John's Alley)" or "Miss Smith . . . Privacy and good taste . . . Over tearoom."[110]

Through other forms of condescension, the more asexual upper-class women in *Song of Solomon* promote the chasm between themselves and their "inferiors." Grace Long suggests that Susan serve tea and butter cookies to Milkman, causing Susan to leave the room when she knows that it is Susan that Milkman has come to see.[111] For someone who seems to be aware of the social graces, she has no tact and refuses to acknowledge that her presence is not wanted.[112] While Renee (*Who Is Angelina?*) is a less offensive character than either Michael-Mary Graham or Grace Long, she is also affected. She throws "good California liberal" parties in her boyfriend's apartment, including her ex-husband and his girlfriend in her invitations.[113]

Lynne (*Meridian*) and Mary Dalton (*Native Son*) do not affect their interest in social equality. They genuinely believe in the rightness of their pursuits. Furthermore, they feel partner to the racial guilt of White America. "The source of guilt may come from any number of experiences . . . which at the time may have nothing to do with race or sex." This sense of guilt may "stem from a sense of 'failure' for not having lived up to the expectations of one's parents."[114] Mary immerses herself in the Communist movement, whereas Lynne becomes involved in the Civil Rights movement. Both women forsake their respective backgrounds and are somewhat ashamed of their upbringing. Privileged with a wealthy, northern, liberal upbringing, these characters are "full of theories and high-sounding principles."[115] More often than not, the efforts of women like Lynne and Mary are resented as much as the philanthropy of Mrs. Dalton. Although Lynne gives up her privileged life and lives in the same poverty and alienation as her black friends, she always has the choice of returning to the affluence of her upbringing. Nevertheless, her ethics interfere with taking that choice. Although these women are naive, they are sincere. Lacking significant power, the difference they make is minimal.

THE EXILED AND THE "WHITE-NEGRO" WOMAN

A white woman who marries a black man is generally exiled from her family regardless of her social class. Lynne in *Meridian*, Charlotte in *The Man Who Cried I Am* and May in *A Short Walk* are all ostracized by their families, who likewise reject the children born of the interracial marriage. Those women turn to the black community for a sense of belonging and begin to take on the actions and attitudes of their adopted culture. Lynne plays basketball with the men and sits on the porches with the old black women; May's home is filled with the cultural heritage of a sailor and Charlotte's friends are Harry's friends. Whereas May has faith in Apolinario's love regardless of the cost, Charlotte sulks: "When things [are] rough, she ma[kes] a point of reminding Harry how much she ha[s] given up to marry him." Instead of leaving, "she stay[s] and sulk[s]."[116] Charlotte knows Harry is having affairs and she retaliates by seducing his best friend. Finding some solace from loneliness in sexual sanctuary with Max, Charlotte complains: "But I love him and that's what hurts so" and she beseeches Max to hold her."[117] As if to convince Max that she is sincere in her love for Harry, she tells him that she is pregnant with Harry's child, although later they name the baby Max.

Hernton maintains "that the attraction or motivation of white women . . . to associate intimately with Negroes is predominantly sexual."[118] If sex is not the primary motivation, then altruistic love can help "an authentic relationship between a man and a woman withstand the pressures of the world."[119] Furthermore, "altruistic love is most frequently evident" when "there are powerful forces working *against* that situation" (i.e., interracial marriage).[120] May's marriage to a Filipino (*A Short Walk*) is characterized by an unselfish love that increases in spite of (or maybe, because of) her mother's disdain. May's priest supports her mother's belief that "there must be some reason why God made us all different and wants to keep us each to our own."[121] May's mother writes, "A white woman

that lays on her back for the pleasure of a oriental is a hore at heart. . . .
You wallow in filth like a pig."[122] Lynne (*Meridian*) is also rejected by
her parents. Moreover, they are unsympathetic when she calls them after
her daughter Camara was murdered. Although she remembers her father
as a "gentle . . . fair" man, his response to the news that her daughter is
dead is: "So's our daughter."[123] Lynne had ceased to exist for her parents
when, years before, Lynne's mother followed "her to Truman's house."
When it became evident that "she had tracked her only daughter . . . to a
black neighborhood . . . they heard her screaming from three blocks
away."[124] The sound "would never leave her" even in death. "Even when
she [was] most happy," Lynne could not forget her mother's screaming.[125]
Similarly, in *A Short Walk*, even when May is "in Apolinario's arms" her
mother's harsh "words write themselves across [her] closed eyelids."[126]

Aware of the taboo entailed in marrying Charlotte, Harry feels "like
Sisyphus rolling that goddamn stone" and wonders if there will ever be a
time "when a black man will not marry a white woman he loves *simply*
because she's white."[127] Charlotte's father never accepts her marriage to
Harry and she cannot visit her mother with the baby when he is around.
When her father dies, Charlotte misses her mother, or at least feels as
though she should be with her, but cannot bring herself to go. Homesick-
ness and Harry's estrangement contribute to Charlotte's deepening despair. Her sulking is analogous to the effect of a negative animus. Yet she
does love Harry, "what he is, where he came from, how he survived." Like
Desdemona, she "defie[s] custom . . . thriving, loving, finally on Othello's
talks of his deeds."[128]

Max is the best man at Charlotte and Harry's wedding. Before he meets
his future wife, Maggie (a white woman), Max dates his white secretary,
Mary. His appraisal of Mary and Charlotte correlates with Hernton's
analysis of white women who become intimate with black men. Mary
"never object[s] to anything. That [is] what [is] wrong with her."[129]
Although Mary is neither attractive nor homely, she is "beaten." Unmar-
ried, in her "middle thirties," Mary will "always [be] a secretary, always
alone, friendless." Nevertheless, Mary fulfills the expected sexual image
that, because she is forbidden, she is also "capable of every conceivable
act in bed."[130] The taboo enhances anticipation that in turn creates a
self-fulfilling prophecy of mythologized sexuality.

Max meets Margrit at a "seemingly innocuous place where you proved
you were a hippy."[131] The atmosphere becomes a stereotypical European
"mixed" party; therefore, his first impression of Margrit is based on his
expectation that she will be like all the white women who like jazz and go
to these parties to satisfy their curiosity by seducing a black man. In reality,

Margrit came to the party with a girlfriend and, although she has stereo-typed expectations of her own, she is not completely aware of the image she represents. She does not really like jazz and she is equally disillusioned with the clichés and a series of empty relationships.[132] Max realizes later that Margrit reminds him of his black wife more than the white women with whom he has associated since Lillian's death.[133] Contemplating her relationship with Max, Margrit reflects on the white girls who marry black men: They "always seemed to be doing penance." Although Margrit is not completely assured of her life, she feels distinct from the women who are completely passive beside their black husbands, who seem like "mere extensions of them, as if they ha[ve] . . . lost all perspective of them-selves."[134] But Margrit does not fit the stereotype of American white women. She is Dutch and does not have the same cultural inhibitions. She has more affinity with the Confidants discussed in chapter 4 of this volume than with Charlotte or May. As a result, Max and Margrit's relationship moves deeper than the stereotype. As a couple, they encounter their greatest challenge in America. Max feels the ominous threat of his sur-roundings more deeply than Margrit, who is mystified by his behavior. Margrit tries to reach him in a dark but superconscious "labyrinth, . . . lost, but from where she had to commence her search for him."[135] Unable to decode her internal dialogue, she runs toward a "blinding light so she [can] see him and lead him out," but everywhere she encounters the metaphor-ical creatures of Max's internal horror. Struggling to reach him, Margrit hears Max calling to her innermost core, "keep going left, baby, the heartside."[136] The spiritual sickness of a maligned society is unavoidably actualized in the labyrinth that prevents them from reaching one another. The white women involved with black men defy custom and bring alienation upon themselves. Even in a loving, well-adjusted relationship, the price is high and the loneliness inevitable.

Of all of Hernton's types, the "White-Negro" woman is the most difficult to find in pure form. In all respects, the White-Negro woman has assimilated into her adopted race consciousness. She is treated as though she is black. She is one of the most complex types and the only type, according to Hernton, who receives acceptance. There are a few, like Sammi in *Who Is Angelina?*, who try to assume a black identity and fail. There are others (e.g., Lynne and Charlotte) who, by marriage, become accepted within the community but are never completely transformed into the White-Negro woman. There is always a flaw that unconsciously works on the white woman's motivations or, assuming she is free from social restraints (i.e., Margrit), the world nevertheless invades. In Lynne's case, the internal flaw deepens the anima/animus cycle of the Femme Fatale.

Abandoned by white and black society, her daughter dead, Lynne is unable to recapture a strong sense of self (*Meridian*). As the Femme Fatale, Lynne's hopelessness places her within the category of the insane and harmless women mentioned in chapter 2. By themselves, Lynne and Leona (*Another Country*) are harmless. If white men see them in the company of black men, these women become a more potent symbol of danger.

Margo, the trustworthy friend in *Who Is Angelina?*, is the closest fictional equivalent to Hernton's image of the White-Negro woman. According to Hernton, the White-Negro woman distinguishes herself (from other liberal white women who become intimate with black men) by her "*soul*."[137] Angelina is grateful for a friend like Margo "who, in many unofficial ways, [is] blacker in expressing herself than Angelina." Margo has "soul, and soul, like blood, [goes] way beyond pop ideas of sisterhood or brotherhood."[138] Rather than being defensive about her money, Margo easily acknowledges that she can afford to take the theft of Angelina's apartment lightly. She offers money to help Angelina, encouraging her friend to go on a trip "to get [her]self back together."[139] Margo is not without her problems. Her numerous relationships with men have soured, including her most recent one with Leonard, who Margo finds upstairs at a party "layin back grinnin in the dark while some bitch is going down on" him.[140] Margo drinks heavily and, like Angelina, is disillusioned with Berkeley. The White-Negro woman and the exiled white wives of black men adopt black culture and find in it some of the acceptance and empathy missing at home. They seek out outcasts like themselves and, whether the motives are altruism, love, sex, guilt or deformity, these women see in their black friends the same frustrations and hardships with which they are so well acquainted.

THE EMPTY WOMAN AND THE OBJECT

Stereotypes of empty-headed white women are abundant in American society. Physical, emotional and spiritual shallowness are all relegated to the death aspect of the White Goddess. In view of this image, it is clear why black women would be offended by their lovers' attraction to white women. When she becomes aware of Truman's growing intimacy with a white woman, Meridian aborts her baby. Thereafter, she is never able to reconcile Truman's betrayal despite his inevitable return to her. After her experiences with Truman and the Civil Rights movement, Meridian's sexual identity and self-concept take a cathartic journey, similar to Velma's in *The Salt Eaters*. Without this personal catharsis, Velma and Meridian would be lost, tragic figures. Velma and Meridian transcend the results of their victimization within the movement and are capable of forgiveness and generosity in their judgments of men. Leona in *Another Country*, Becky in *Cane* and Lynne in *Meridian* do not return from the borders. In general, the white woman in African-American fiction who risks the venture inward rarely returns from the pilgrimage with her self and soul intact. Lynne attempts the internal catharsis without a supportive environment. She emerges beaten and empty.

Another form of the Empty Woman is the superficial personality who models herself after the pretty doll who does not think too much. This empty woman prefers belonging to a shallow image (that gives her an identity within a community) over the solitude of the inward journey. In its extreme, this vacancy of spirit could be read as a zombie-figure (Vivian in *Flight to Canada*) but, in the human reality, she is the "Dumb Blonde." The denial of her sexuality and depth and the eerie tragedy that surrounds her image, assign her to the realm of the dead. The negative association is her irresistibility. Of all of the stereotypes, the most beguiling myth is her pedestal. According to Hernton, the myth of sacred white womanhood "was not created by the southern white woman," nor was it promoted "by the black woman [or] the black man." The "southern white man" created the image to assuage his "guilt," which "stemmed primarily from his persistent, clandestine activities with" black women.[141] Furthermore, it follows that if he found black women irresistible, his wife might be vulnerable to the same "animal" attraction towards black men. Despite her desexualization "under the fierce indoctrination of puritanical asceticism" the southern white man plotted to "ensure the 'chastity' of his woman." The South was compelled to "create a symbol" commensurate to the need for absolution for the evils of slavery. This symbol would justify "the *entire* 'southern way of life.' . . . Sacred white womanhood emerged in the South as an immaculate mythology to glorify an otherwise indecent society."[142] The southern man created the " 'rape complex' " to "maintain and protect" his "way of life." Either the white woman remains oblivious of the "sexual immorality of the South" or, "out of a sense of guilt through complicity," she pretends to be unaware.[143] Assuming the role of sacred white womanhood, she is cast into an empty life. "Despite whatever progress has been made, the southern white woman remains a victimized product of her culture, with nobody on whom to avenge her sexual rage except" the black man.[144]

Although the "rape complex" creates the necessity for the white man to protect the southern white woman against the black man's "eyeballing" and sexual "savagery," her symbolic role as the repository of the myth of the pure South is similarly in need of protection against the critical scrutiny of a black woman who sees the southern white woman as a useless creature.

Sofia in *The Color Purple* is the epitome of the "uppity" black woman, whereas Miss Millie exemplifies the helpless southern white woman whose self-worth is predicated upon her position of authority. Miss Millie's need to continually reassert her power is implicit in her insensitive, patronizing gestures (patting Sofia's children on the head and apportioning unsolicited praise of their "strong, white" teeth as if they were animals). Sofia's response ("Hell no") to Miss Millie's invitation ("All your children [are] so clean, . . . would you like to work for me, be my maid?") is incomprehensible to the woman who bases her existence on remaining blind to the injustices she condones.[145] The mayor smiles benignly in approval of his wife's kindness and slaps Sofia for her insolence. Sofia is brutally beaten for hitting back and her final punishment is to be forced into becoming Miss Millie's maid.[146] The mayor and his wife are comfortable in their assertions that Sofia assaulted the mayor for no apparent reason. Miss Millie is able to preserve her identity of benevolence as long as it is Sofia who is the criminal. Only through upholding the lie of her own moral superiority can Miss Millie remain blameless for not allowing Sofia to see her children for five years. The need to cling to a sense of superiority is necessary to fill the spiritual void that issues from her complicity with the immorality of racism. Moral and spiritual emptiness translate into Miss Millie's underlying inadequacies such as an inability to manage her own home or to learn how to drive a car. When, after five years, she drops Sofia off to see her children, Miss Millie is unable to put the car in reverse. In frustration, she destroys the engine and is once more dependent upon Sofia to get her home. Sofia was unable to spend any real time with her children because Miss Millie "couldn't ride in a pick-up with a strange colored man" nor did she feel comfortable driving home with Odessa.[147] She thus ensures, whether or not she initially intended to withhold visitations, that Sofia's imprisonment is complete.

Although Millie's daughter, Eleanor Jane, has kinder instincts toward Sofia, she still possesses a level of self-importance tantamount to tactlessness. Eleanor Jane allows her child to make a mess of Sofia's ironing while seeking affirmation that Reynolds Stanley Earl is "just a sweet, smart, cute, *innocent* little baby boy." Furthermore, in spite of Sofia's apparent disinterest, Eleanor Jane wants to know, "Don't you just love him?"[148] She feels that her kindness should entitle her to some transferral of affection to her son. Yet Sofia never wanted to be in Miss Millie's household to begin with and she has no special affection for Eleanor Jane's family. Furthermore, the child is likely to grow up indoctrinated to continue oppressing Sofia. Eleanor Jane has never felt loved by either of her parents and her husband is too absorbed in his job and his poker games to be concerned with her. Sofia's approval of her only achievement (having a child) becomes all important because Sofia is the only person from her household to ever show Eleanor Jane affection. She completely disregards Sofia's suggestion to leave her husband because her role as his wife is her only identity.[149]

According to Ned (the pontificating friend of Cecil Brown's Mr. Jiveass Nigger), the "mind" of the southern white woman and "her soul ha[ve] been washed out with . . . store bought beauty"; and the women who end up "imitating that dead, dry bitch . . . ain't no better . . . [than] Miss Ann."[150] Ned uses his irritation at a particular white woman as an opportunity to berate all white women, claiming that if anybody "will listen to black people, it's the white woman." Ned attributes the lynchings in the South to the image of the southern white woman. "A white cat gets married and his old lady doesn't fuck, she 'makes love' and so . . . he goes out and strings up some niggers, thinking the niggers are getting it, . . . but the truth . . . is . . . the bitch ain't got nothing to give."[151]

The association of barrenness and chastity with the Death Goddess and/or Witches is not peculiar to the South. In many cultures, including the Yoruba, barren women are treated with care lest they turn their powers against society. Barrenness in contemporary society is not necessarily associated with childlessness, but is a description appropriate to all women who have been relegated to the dull, unresponsive, empty life of sacred white womanhood. Vivian (*Flight to Canada*) is the most extreme example of the Death Goddess discussed in chapter 1. The terrible whiteness of Vivian is comparable to the horrific whiteness of the mannequins swinging from the lampposts in *Invisible Man*. Both apparitions of whiteness are analogous to the horrible whiteness of the whale to which Cleaver alludes in his poem, "To a White Girl."[152] Like Melville's Moby Dick, the white woman is described by Cleaver as the black man's nemesis, a "symbol of the rope and hanging tree." He is driven to pursue her even if it kills him. This allusion to the horrific whiteness of the whale and the bloated, white bellies of fish (a common insult referring to the skin of aging white women as well as the stereotype of the white women's passionless, passive lovemaking) is also made in *The Primitive*.[153]

The stereotypical southern white woman becomes a symbol for the lynching rope. "While she [does] not actually lynch and castrate" black men "herself, she permit[s] her men to do so in her name." Furthermore,

Hernton claims that she experiences the same "perverse sexual ecstasy" that the white man enjoys when she hears "about lynching and castration."[154] She fills the void created by the privation of her sexual identity with bizarre fantasies of inflicting punishment on and receiving punishment at the hands of black men.

Although the essential spiritual energy (*ase*) is neutral, a barren woman is a threat because her *ase* is extremely vulnerable to witchery. Whereas Velma's rage (*The Salt Eaters*) and personal loss create a void that is ultimately filled with a spiritual identity, the emptiness of the sacred white woman is filled with animosity. With the aid of a healer, Velma's *ase* is directed toward the regeneration of the world. The unfulfilled woman lacks a central direction for her energies. Without a channel, her natural drive for growth is frustrated, resulting in a form of alienation akin to the "mothers' " negative *aje* in the context of traditional Yoruba myth.

Jo's southern indoctrination in *Blues For Mister Charlie* prevents her from exploring human sexuality too deeply. On one side is Lyle's refusal to credit her thoughts with any importance (she is too delicate); on the other side is her fear of learning that her husband is a murderer. She would rather believe that his reasons for the shootings were justified.

Unlike Joe, whose motivations arise out of a southern upbringing, Renee's sentiments are more liberal (*Who Is Angelina?*). A social outcast, Renee's investment in art and the intellectual avant-garde lacks substance. She changes her life cosmetically but her personal melodramas are never entirely convincing to her friend, Angelina. In the midst of some crisis Renee's face will "take on an expression, . . . an intense contraction of facial muscles" that forewarned "the end of some world whose realness she'd never been convinced of anyway."[155] Lacking a central orientation to her psyche, Renee's emotional responses are frequently disproportionate to the situation. One time she reacts to the fear of failing a final exam by comparing the importance of her minor trauma with the end of the world. Her responses are fashioned for effect to elevate her self-importance. After college, Renee seeks to promote an air of unflappable nonchalance by inviting her ex-husband and his girlfriend to her New Year's Eve party at Steve's apartment. Renee affects detachment as she and Sammi are being "fondled by both men's hands."[156]

There is an equally superficial stereotype of black men that corresponds with Hernton's stereotype of the pseudointellectual white woman. Renee's new "discovery," a "Soul Train" black man, wears a "beach-ball Afro and technicolor clothes replete with stacked-heel shoes." While Angelina regards Steve as "quaint" but effusive with his "theatrical" gestures,[157] Renee thinks that she has discovered his "vastness." What the white woman "discovers" is a man without a core sense of self. Renee's discovery has no more soul than the other type to whom white female outcasts are drawn: unkempt, " 'broke,' talkative . . . but terribly illiterate . . . humming [and nodding] his head to . . . jazz music, mumbling ceaselessly about *his* 'oppression.' "[158] The black man who has been convinced of his "depravity" finds "ontological affirmation of [his] being"[159] through association with the "immaculate" white woman who regards him as an "exotic beauty."[160] "In the mind and the life of a black man" the white woman simultaneously embodies "his freedom and his bondage." She becomes a symbol "of temptation and repulsion, love and hate." His sexual identity "in the South is predicated upon the existence of the white woman who is inaccessible." And because she is beyond his reach, "he hates what he cannot love; he wants what he cannot have . . . [and] degrades and mutilates" the object of his "humiliat[ion] and derange[ment]."[161]

Emptiness is a many-faceted phenomenon in the image of the white woman. One version is the nameless sexual object; another is the passionless, sexless woman. In *Ceremony*, the nameless white women make the equally unknown Laguna men feel like Americans, but only in uniform, "and then by God . . . [they are] . . . U.S. marine[s] and [the white women come] crowding around."[162] That white women are portrayed as an illusory panacea in minority literature in general is also evident in John Okada's *No-No Boy*. Like Tayo (*Ceremony*), Ichiro experiences postwar disillusionment. He finds himself caught in the middle of opposing world views, neither of which fits his experience. He is neither Japanese nor American. The only time a Japanese-American man of Ichiro's generation feels like an American is in uniform (e.g., Bull finds his American soldier's identity in the company of a white girl). Kenji believes that the abolition of separatist communities is the only solution to the problems particular to Japanese Americans. "They screamed because the government said they were Japs and, when they finally got out, they couldn't wait to rush together and prove that they were."[163] He advises Ichiro to find a place "where there isn't another Jap within a thousand miles." Kenji tells Ichiro to "marry a white girl or a Negro or an Italian or even a Chinese. Anything but Japanese."[164] Not only the white woman, but any woman racially or culturally removed from the Japanese, is Kenji's tool of liberation from the problems of separation and isolation. Simultaneously the symbol of liberation and oppression, these women are no panacea. Nevertheless, they are coveted as objects.

Although they may be portrayed primarily as objects, at least there is a sexual identity. The more profound and pitiable insignificance of Mrs. Pribby (*Cane*) provokes disgust. Her weak eyes betray a shallowness and a sense of futility in her soul. Mrs. Pribby is the opposite of the "Art" perceived by Lynne in the old black woman of the South (*Meridian*). Whereas the eyes of old black women are soulful and yearning, the eyes of old white spinsters "are bluish and watery from reading newspapers."[165] The 'noble' old black women are romanticized, whereas the old white women are simply empty. The patchwork quilts, bungalows and tattered dresses (which form Lynne's collage of black womanhood in *Meridian*) are a powerful contrast to the lifeless, mechanized clicks and bolts (of the "endless rows of metal houses"[166]) that belong to white women with soulless eyes and sweatless bodies who sink into the "permanent oblivion" of mediocrity.[167] Marshall establishes this contrast between the cold eyes of a white woman (with "the tone and texture of a winter sky as the first snow gathers") and the warm fey eyes of black women (*The Chosen Place, The Timeless People*).[168] The "inner sunlight" of Merle's eyes "amid that nameless and irrevocable loss . . . make[s] a person feel she can read his life with a look."[169] The eyes of black women always connect back to life while the eyes of white women are metallic and inanimate. When these women are not relegated to mediocrity, the void experienced in their lives is "filled" through wielding power, as is the case with Harriet Shippen (*The Chosen Place, The Timeless People*) and Miss Claybrooks (*The Life and Loves of Mr. Jiveass Nigger*). Like Harriet, Miss Claybrooks's "light blue" eyes appear "to have something of cold steel in them" and their only "softness" derives from her "peculiar style of blinking."[170] She uses her position to manipulate George, who appraises her as a "cold bitch . . . [with] thin, cruel, dry lips . . . a red-neck cracker!"[171]

The Barren Woman and the Object, like many of the stereotypes here mentioned, may be elevated to the status of a Goddess to the extent that she poses a threat to the psyche or to one's existence in general. Her own emptiness can betray her companion's hidden fear of meaninglessness. The difference between her emergence as stereotype and archetype in African-American fiction has to do with whether or not the nature of her power is perceived to transcend the local consciousness of race. When the danger assumed in the figure of a white woman takes on mythic proportions then she is empowered to undermine the stability of a society. A society can react by appealing to her for assistance or by undermining her sense of worth. A white woman who loses faith in her own vitality is not a threat.

CHAPTER 4

The Confidant-Sage

The white woman of African-American fiction who functions as a trusted friend becomes a manifestation of the Wise Woman when she is able to assist other people in their transformation to a higher level of consciousness. Whereas the archetypal Sage is at once complete in her self-awareness and in harmony with the cosmos, her imperfect human manifestation is always in the process of reaching toward self-actualization. The Confidant's capacity to assist others along the way to fulfillment issues from insights gained in the process of confronting her own shadow and animus projections.

The archetype of the Wise Woman completes the cycle of ascending symbols of the Feminine. Beginning with the formative character of the Great Mother, whose function centers around nurturing the child (or infant stage of consciousness), the early Mother image can either release the psyche to further growth or bind the individual to fearful neediness. The Terrible Goddess ensnares her victims. To the extent that the victim is able to escape the grasp of the Destructive Mother, she can function as a medial figure who inspires the psyche to further growth. The second group of archetypes, the Medial Woman, functions (in a transformative capacity) to lead the psyche to the trials of the underworld. The earthly woman who fulfills this function may only facilitate a partial emergence from the underworld or she may become an unwilling captive in the abyss with her companion. Finally, the Wise Woman encompasses all of the higher capacities of the Goddess and of human insight with "a wisdom . . . infinitely superior to the wisdom of man's waking consciousness." If we equate the waking consciousness with masculine facilities and the powers of the Feminine with the unconscious mind, then the infinite Wise Woman exists within every human psyche. When awakened, the Sage, "as a source of vision and symbol, of ritual and law, poetry and vision, intervenes, summoned or unsummoned, to save man and give direction to his life."[1]

This is a Mother on a higher level interested in the whole, mature individual "who governs the transformation from the elementary to the spiritual level." The archetypal Wise Mother is not an abstract, disinterested deity, "inaccessible to man in numinous remoteness and alienated seclusion."[2] She is a vital participant in the lives of humanity. Her wisdom is still earth-related, central to the heart, as opposed to "the 'upper' wisdom of the head."[3] She is the repository of the collective unconscious and the history of consciousness. The manifestations of the Great Goddess "in all times and all cultures . . . appear also in the living reality of the modern woman, in her dreams and visions, compulsions and fantasies, projections and relationships, fixations and transformations."[4]

The individual who has integrated rather than denied her shadow side and negative animus is fully armed to make intelligent choices in the context of conflict. No longer moved by uncontrollable forces, the mature individual can assess the cost of succumbing to destructive urges, and can make decisions based on true knowledge of her potential. This is not a person who has buried her crimes but she has faced them. She is not free from the experience of pain, but she is no longer driven to desperate acts as a result of pain. The human woman who sometimes operates in the role of the Wise Mother/Confidant has reached a stage in which the mutually compensatory functions of the conscious and unconscious are mediated by a third level of awareness, which allows for opposites to be reconciled. She has reached a plateau of adaptation and integration; however, this process is never complete (as in a "once-and-for-all 'cure' "[5]) nor is the individual free from future problematic situations. To the extent that she is aware of the powerful forces that operate within her, the integrated woman can circumvent highly debilitating conflicts. "Knowledge of the regulating influences of the unconscious . . . does render much bad experience unnecessary."[6] Furthermore, greater insight into one's motivations and idiosyncratic behavior can have a "vitalizing influence."[7] This individual can function as a Wise Mother for others to the extent that she can assist others in crisis without surrendering to overprotectiveness and control. The human Confidant performs the transcendent function by allowing the individual to rely on his own resources, retain his independence and achieve "liberation by [his] own efforts."[8]

The Confidant-Sage is someone who can provide comfort and the kind of advice that shows she has suffered too, and so her words have deeper impact than the platitudes of women who cannot or, like Leona of *Another Country*, will not understand. These women have kept themselves open to empathy. The Confidant is, by definition, loyal and compassionate. To the person who is unready for such introspection, the Confidant's insight is threatening. When Rufus (*Another Country*) surfaces just before his suicide, Cass's empathic depth frightens him. Although the realization that another person has shared similar torments can provide a brief reprieve in commiseration, this short respite is not enough to sustain Rufus. Instead, "the sympathy on her face" increases his hopelessness and gives clarity to his pain, so that the pain is exposed in bright relief against a darkness he cannot bear. Although Rufus turns to Vivaldo automatically, he is unprepared for Cass's perceptive insight; "he wonder[s] why she should look like that, what her memories of experience could be." Rufus "never imagined a girl like Cass could know" the darkness he feels.[9] Cass does know despair. Hers is a different set of experiences than the despair Rufus encounters; nevertheless, she has known the inescapability from the inner torments of her psyche.

At first, Cass finds her sanctuary in a role with Richard in which she is in control. She creates a nest and roles for each of them to play. Richard is probably all that he can be, but he falls short of the image Cass ordained for him. Cass loses respect for Richard even when she realizes that she has made him what he is. Had he resisted her molding, Cass might have maintained respect. She judges him as "second rate" with no "real passion" nor "any real thoughts of his own." Yet, at one time, she had been happy to mold him. Cass changes and outgrows Richard's mediocrity. Although she succeeded in creating Richard according to her patterns, her "triumph" becomes "intolerable."[10] Finally, his malleability irritates her.

Reed's play, *Mother Hubbard*, parodies women who want their men to be tender but despise the pliancy of the end result, labeling their "liberated men" who cook and clean as "weak." Olympia, a female boxer, explains to her trainer, "At first it was a novelty—a man cooking, cleaning . . . [but now,] he's boring."[11] Olympia dismisses her husband and Rudolph complains, "I can't figure women out. They [complained that] we were macho brutes, . . . insensitive, . . . that we didn't know how to cry, . . . that we neglected them. So, we became more tender, did the housework and made dinner, . . . studied foreplay, . . . let them finish sentences, . . . and now after all of that we're boring, we're not exciting enough, we don't have ambition, we're lethargic."[12] These are precisely the problems Cass begins to encounter with Richard (*Another Country*). "Liberated men" like Rudolph and Richard lose their appeal in much the same way as the stereotypical housewives whose middle-aged husbands left them to find more intellectual, exciting lovers. Cass only accepts Richard as the image she creates and, when the image becomes stale, she realizes the shortsightedness of her manipulations. It is her failure that enables Cass to understand Rufus. She survives her failures and confronts her guilt. She is not "cured," nor is she a complete manifestation of the archetype; nevertheless, she functions as a vehicle to transformation.

In a society that has become increasingly complex, the functions and roles of the Trickster and the Goddess become hidden or repressed. The vehicles for their emergence are no longer clearly outlined as they are in a tribal context. The human beings who function in and out of the generative, nourishing, medial and transformative roles often do so unconsciously and without the supportive canopy of a wider mythos to assist their rituals. Cass's role as a Confidant may arise out of an adaptation to her environment that appears incomplete in the form of resignation; however, she exists within a fragmented society in which even partial spiritual transformation often occurs in the fringes instead of within the mainstream. The vital spirit of a world mythos is needed in order to create an environment that will support the growth of the psyche.

Through Cass, Baldwin gives us the answer to the vicious cycle of repeating crimes to conceal guilt. "The thing is not to lie about them—to try to understand what you have done, why you have done it."[13] This is the only way Rufus could have forgiven himself; this is the only way the oppressor type represented in Lyle (*Blues For Mister Charlie*) can change. Otherwise, if he cannot forgive himself, he will "never be able to forgive anybody else" and he will "go on committing these same crimes forever."[14]

Cass is able to forgive herself enough to be honest with Richard instead of continuing to protect him by lying about Eric. Cass's role with Richard comes out of a need to be needed. Similarly, she feels that she can help Eric. The need is mutual, each helps the other through a painful transition. Careful not to repeat the same crimes she committed with Richard, Cass consciously avoids invading Eric's nest.[15] She has no illusions about the relationship; she knows it is temporary and that her role is "to help him endure the weight of the boy who had such a power over him."[16] Eric, in turn, awakens in Cass a world of "ambiguities whose power she had never glimpsed before."[17] He has opened for her the grey area between loving and not loving Richard. He has awakened in her another level of awareness and sensitivity. Yet her own vulnerability does not inhibit her almost motherly tenderness toward Eric: "She moved slowly out from beneath his weight, kissed his brow and covered him."[18] Theirs is a brief relationship that provides mutual sanctuary. What sanctuary Cass provided Richard in the early years of their marriage was always conditional, dependent upon whether or not he fulfilled her expectations. If he failed, she protected him from her disappointment. If he succeeded, his actions confirmed Cass's conviction that she was doing the right thing. Cass imposed her will in the guise of being a good wife. Later, she realizes that "she could break him" for in order to fight her will "he would be compelled to descend to stratagems far beneath him."[19] A sanctuary relationship is one of shared support; however, a sometimes subtle but definite distinction exists between healthy support and devouring protectiveness.

There is an element of the gloomy Femme Fatale in Cass. For her, there is no hope; we are what we are and the best we can do is be honest with ourselves. It is this fatalism that makes her mysterious and limits her role as the Wise Mother. She does not fit the mold of the Mrs. Pribbys (*Cane*) and Margies (*The Salt Eaters*) that Rufus might be able to understand and despise. Her appearance is "frail and fair" and she often alludes mysteriously to an ancestor who "had been burned as a witch." Cass is part of that "plain old American stock," a self-descriptive phrase she uses that would appear to demystify her image. Rufus can "never quite place her" in his image of "the white world to which she seem[s] to belong."[20]

The Devouring Goddess becomes apparent in Cass's analysis of a woman's understanding of men. A woman uses a man's need of her "to undermine him. . . . Women don't see men the way men want to be seen." They perceive the vulnerability in men, "all the tender places . . . where blood [can] flow."[21] This is the arena of the Terrible Goddess, the unconscious destructive force to which we are all vulnerable.

The world of Eldridge Cleaver's "omnipotent observer" is visible, tangible, verifiable, not allowing for such "fantasy." In a comparable role, Baldwin's Richard discredits Cass's insights as invalid. Yet what she "dream[s] up" is just as real as the rational world;[22] only the actions and effects of intuition are less visible. The beneficial qualities of the unconscious (feminine) are frequently overlooked when logic is the preferred vehicle for apprehending the real world. "In the patriarchal development of the Judaeo-Christian West, with its masculine, monotheistic trend toward abstraction, the goddess, as a feminine figure of wisdom, was disenthroned and repressed."[23] Men like Richard make the mistake of underestimating the power behind Cass's perceptivity (Eros/anima) and see only the mask of innocence. It is Eric, her comrade, who perceives these realizations in Cass. It is to Eric that Cass confesses: "You begin to see that you yourself, innocent, upright you, have contributed and do contribute to the misery of the world." Furthermore, this process "will never end because we're what we are."[24] As Cass's frank appraisal of her faults unfolds, Eric watches the girlhood depart from her eyes. Yet she does "not seem precisely faded" or old. There is a transcendent quality to her expression, a "scoured" look. The same phenomenon of mystery that Rufus saw is the "invincibly impersonal" aspect of Cass's insight that Eric perceives.[25] This description of Cass most closely approximates the unromanticized wisdom of the mature, positive anima, the "completion of the self" to which Jung refers. However, Cass must still function and adapt within the limits of her society. To do this she, like any other human being, must possess "an emotional equilibrium" that enables her to be "malleable, to adjust [her]self to others without fear of loss of identity with change." This emotional equilibrium "requires a basic trust in others, and . . . confidence in the integrity of the self."[26] Cultivating trust in society is difficult in an age of fragmentation and alienation. The "normal" experience of the Goddess and the Trickster may involve denial, repression, splitting, reification or projection. "The condition of alienation, of being asleep, of being unconscious, of being out of one's mind is the condition of the normal man" in contemporary American experience.[27]

At first the process of integrating one's shadows and past crimes into the psyche is terrifying. The instinctive response may be to deny or repress the threat to one's self-esteem. Within a supportive environment (which Cass finds in Eric) the individual may amass the courage to face the crimes she has committed. Part of the process involves releasing claims of being above the common man (i.e., she must forfeit megalomaniacal delusions). Cass has consciously fabricated a positive image to compensate for unconscious guilt. She resigns her lofty position and risks facing her mistakes. Although she may lose her innocent self-image, Cass gains genuine knowledge of herself. Consequently she is better equipped to handle future crises. Cass sacrifices blind assurances of her innocence for transformation in the psyche. She achieves some release from fear and her insights are empowering. Her future may be dismal, but given the conditions of her experience, she is functioning at a higher level than she had been in her previous life with Richard.

May of *A Short Walk* is another Confidant whose empathic ability arises from her own struggles with the unresolved conflicts in her life. An Irish woman who married a Filipino-Chinese man against her mother's will, May is Cora's "close[st] friend-girl . . . [who] knows how to look at matters and trace meanings and feelings down to the core."[28] Yet, like most of us, she cannot apply the same wisdom to solving her own problems. Despite the cruel letters her mother writes, protesting May's marriage to "that full-a-pee-pee," May is attached to her mother and misses her people.[29]

"Sometimes I miss Irish things. Everyone has *people*, Cora, not just you and Apolinario."[30] May is naive too. She believes that Cora's love for Cecil is the reason she follows him and that Cora is a self-sacrificing wife—"women do everything for true love."[31]

Although she is naive, May is perceptive. She perceives Cora's unhappiness about being pregnant. Not understanding the complexity of the relationship, nor the distance that Cora feels from Cecil, May assumes that Cora is unhappy because Cecil does not love her.[32] Although May is reluctant to condone abortion, she will not let her religion stand in the way of helping Cora when she is desperate. To Cora's bleak description of love and marriage May answers, "Then you haven't loved yet. It can be beautiful, it should make you feel good even when life is going wrong."[33]

May is not too accommodating to be human. Her optimism is shakable in spite of her devotion to Apolinario. Apolinario is a "blackshirt" and May is anxious "because someone told her [blackshirts] are Fascists. . . [and Cecil] says they're a bunch of racist bastards. . . . May has a very gentle nature, so these things hit her hard."[34] May faces not only alienation from her mother and from her people but also from the church. Her own problems make May receptive and nonjudgmental toward her friends. May is "heartsick" over Apolinario's thefts but she "can't go to confession anymore. Apolinario says" she "must not confess it to the priest" and, if she cannot confess, then she cannot take communion.[35] Although she is despondent over the complications in her life, May is not the type of character to lose herself in despair. Her love for Apolinario is unconditional and she is prepared to sacrifice everything. Unlike Cass, May does not seek to interfere with her husband's life and her protection is authentic. May's denial of family and religion would seem to be extreme and potentially destructive if she was really forsaking a life that was central to her self-concept. A self-effacing approach to a relationship would be as destructive as Cass's manipulations or Richard's pliancy. Yet with May we have the sense that her emotions are clear, her sense of self intact, despite the obstacles imposed upon her love-conquers-all philosophy of life.

In *Who Is Angelina?*, Margo is a loyal friend and confidant who also has her problems. Her lifestyle is very similar to Angelina's, with one difference—she is receiving alimony and does not have to worry about money. She is able to take theft lightly. Described as a "White-Negro" woman in chapter 3 of this volume, Margo is a marginal character typical of the Berkeley stereotype. Young tempers her too-good-to-be-true friendliness with segments of character development that show how Margo can afford generosity and a carefree lifestyle. With all her "enviable alimony pouring in" and "theft insurance," Margo can afford to "laugh it off" when she is robbed.[36]

However, Margo did not arrive at her more optimistic attitudes without a cost. Her relationships with men continue to be unstable and she is a "problem drinker."[37] Nevertheless, she is still capable of sensing her friend's desperate need for change. As she leaves Angelina at the departure gate, she describes her ethics: "You know me. I'm basic. I got scruples all right but I'm a good American too. I wear my scruples light."[38] Margo and Renee are of a class that can afford the luxury of analysis. And, like so many people who have "had their head shrunk," they will reveal "anything about themselves, no matter how private or inconsequential, and whether you wanted to hear it or not."[39] Angelina is willing to tolerate Margo because, beneath the chaos of Margo's life, there is an essential warmth and kindness that is lacking in Renee.

Both Margo and Angelina are struggling inside. The Berkeley atmosphere no longer fulfills their needs. Margo comes to Angelina depressed about Leonard, about Berkeley and her life. Hoping to rid herself of a heritage of collective guilt, Margo moved to the West with the idea that she would "set the record straight" and "prove that not everybody from the South was the devil." She describes herself as a "typical Southron" girl, a sheltered "middle class . . . virgin until [she] was twenty."[40]

In spite of Margo's problems and all of her changes, Angelina is relieved to have a friend like Margo who is "blacker in expressing herself than Angelina was or would ever become."[41] Unlike Reed's Ms. Swille and other southern stereotypes, Margo is trying to prove that not all southerners are bad. Sammi is superficially "out to get" the establishment. She practices to be a sleaze, while Michael-Mary Graham, Grace Long and Miss Butler (*Song of Solomon*) cherish the affectations of the rich. Ms. Lincoln (*Flight to Canada*) is portrayed as eccentric and Margie (*The Salt Eaters*) as a whimpering slob. Baldwin's Leona (*Another Country*) and Jo (*Blues for Mister Charlie*) are ignorant fools. Of all the southern-born white women in these novels, Margo is the only one who appears to redeem the negative stereotype.

So far, each of the Confidant characters has been of a certain type. Cass is part of the New England stock who does not fit "in the white world to which she seem[s] to belong"[42]; May is a part of the white ethnic minority from which she is alienated because of her mixed marriage; Margo is a southerner trying to set the record straight in Berkeley; and Margrit (*The Man Who Cried I Am*) is a white European woman unconcerned about proving herself against a record Margo is trying to set straight.

After a long separation, Max and Margrit recognize each other's vulnerability. They continue to provide a sanctuary for one another, yet their estrangement is reinforced by the one thing that Max cannot share: his illness and his death. In America, it is his race that makes Max feel vulnerable in Margrit's presence. In Europe, it is his illness that creates the barrier. Though the "soft look had deceived her," Max's "amber-colored pupils" reveal his sickness.[43] Yet he cannot allow her to pity him, and he cannot allow himself to surrender to her mothering. Despite her apparent protectiveness toward Max, Margrit is also vulnerable and Max cannot face telling her about his cancer. Her sympathy might weaken his resolve to carry out a mission tied in with his self-searching quest for meaning. Most likely, she is strong enough to bear the knowledge of his imminent death, but Max is compelled by his image of her as "fragile" and "vulnerable" (and his image of himself as independently strong) to keep quiet.[44]

Max and Margrit are always confronting images. During their first meeting each is impressed by those qualities distinguishing the other from the same tiresome mold. Avoiding pretense, Max asks her straightforwardly to be his girl during his stay. Unlike the stereotype Margrit anticipates, Max ends their first evening together by kissing her on the forehead. After four days together, Margrit is left with the realization that she is attached to Max. His imminent departure reveals the emptiness in her life. A marriage at the age of nineteen lasted only one year. Margrit found that she could not be happy with the complacent life that other girls were content to accept. Her subsequent experiences with pickups were "just as narrow" as her life with her husband. Now that she is "almost thirty" she fears the labels "old maid," "lesbian" or "whore," and "managing an art gallery ha[s]n't helped" her image.[45] She fears life alone without Max more than she fears the problems of an interracial relationship.

But Margrit does not have the experience or the foresight to see that in America his "vulnerability" beside her will "be publicized, [and] his manhood . . . challenged."[46] She cannot see what Max sees in the faces of white men. She thinks, "How lovely we are together," while Max sees the "realities."[47] "His manhood [is] put on the line as never before."[48] In Margrit's eyes, Max is overreacting; he is "paranoid."[49] Max responds with "accusing" eyes; he is "incredulous that she had not seen or heard or understood."[50] Oblivious to the threat of sailors swarming around them, or the hostile stares of other whites, Margrit is hurt that Max will not kiss her publicly.[51] Max buys guns to defend them from white animosity. Margrit's denial of the oppression Max experiences creates tension between them; she has adopted the "American" way of blaming the victim for being paranoid.[52]

She realizes too late that Max's awareness is closer to the truth than her rationalizations. In the end her insights are almost too lucid and her daydreaming of well-being too desperate, as if she knows he is already gone. Sitting in the café where they used to drink Pernod, Margrit decides to tell him he was right. In her scenario Max will "get back to his writing" and "anytime he felt they should go to the country to take target practice, she would go, gladly." They will share dinner "at their window" and then "they w[ill] go home."[53]

In Max's nightmares of the cobalt machine, it is Maggie who inflicts pain.[54] Maggie is his tormentor and yet it is Maggie whom he cries out for in the end. Margrit becomes a princess in a tower waiting for Max to come home. In the end, she is portrayed as an innocent; the drama in her mind assures her that Max will come home, that they will sit as they used to, talk out their problems and go home. But Max is dead. He called out her name when he died—a woman whom, because of "images," he could not kiss on the street.

Although the confidants are imperfect models of the archetypal Wise Mother, they present a more positive image than most of the other individuals characterized in African-American fiction. Even the archetype of the Good Mother is not unequivocally positive in every respect. To the extent that any manifestation of the great Goddess functions to seriously impede spiritual growth, she is negative. Conversely, to the extent that any real woman functions as a manifestation of the empowering capacities of the Goddess, she can be a positive force in the lives of others. After many painful realizations Cass is ultimately capable of more positive influence in the lives of others than she had been with Richard. Despite the perennial conflicts with which they engage as human beings, May, Margo and Maggie function as positive enablers.

CHAPTER 5

Cover Your Mirrors at Night to Keep the Nightmare Away

Mother, Mother, child who brings peace to the world
Repair the world for us

Gelede song from Ibaiyun

Why should they be afraid of her? She is just a woman.

Walker, *Meridian*

Lynne was not "just a woman"; she was an object of "billboards, . . . car and soap commercials." Black men saw her as "a thing of movies and television . . . [not] as a human being." She represented a "route to Death, . . . their mothers had feared her even before they were born." Her long straight hair epitomized beauty, "not because it was especially pretty," but for the power and fear associated with her image. Fascinated by Lynne's hair, the children in *Meridian* "loved the tails of horses," another symbol of the White Goddess.[1]

The white woman—or, more specifically, the image of white women and black men portrayed in these books—and the pattern of negative associations attached to sex and racism in American society are symptomatic of more insidious habits of behavior set in motion by slavery. Combatting images associated with negative stereotypes of the black American male, the historically necessary defensive behavior of fictional black men (e.g., Max and Rufus) around white women has been labeled paranoid. White women react to the negative stereotype of the slumming-tease-looking-for-a-rape-fantasy-to-be-fulfilled with similar defenses, which obscures any real feelings they might have. The white woman is also a victim. Rarely do we see this victimization with clarity through her eyes. Posturing may take the form of Margo's attempt to "personally set the record straight" (*Who Is Angelina?*),[2] Madge struggling with her sexually ambivalent feelings toward a black man (*If He Hollers Let Him Go*) or Margie sinking into apathetic lethargy as she "blubber[s] over a 'dead coon'" (*The

Salt Eaters).[3] Whatever form the defensive reaction takes, it is the response of a victim whose internal balance is seriously threatened. She has no yardstick with which to measure her motives against the picture of an ideal self nourished by an integrated society.

Within an integrated mythic structure, the individual can find guidance for making appropriate choices that will benefit the community while fostering self-realization. The Yoruba concept of the inner self (*ori inun*) encompasses the "character, personality, and potential of an individual."[4] This spiritual head is the seat of a woman's *ase*, which is essentially neutral but can be directed for the benefit or the detriment of the whole. Experiences of depersonalization and alienation from the community support systems have the effect of diminishing *ase* as well as interfering with one's capacity to direct *ase* toward positive ends. Shreds of an impoverished mythos are internalized and acted out and become manifest in the everyday life of the victims. In this way, images of white women become part of the psychosis and disintegration that pervades contemporary life in the New World.

Continuity within a mythic configuration depends upon communal reinforcement of the values inherent in that structure. A community provides support to the individual's process of growth within the mythos by alternately praising behaviors that are consistent with social mores or condemning antisocial patterns that threaten the well-being of the society. Yoruba Gelede ceremonies combine songs to honor the ancestors, deities and the Mothers with instruction and reinforcement of collective values. Throughout the night ceremonies for the Gelede, the Oro Efe singer performs his function as a cultural repository, and a spokesperson on political, earthly and spiritual matters. The Oro Efe is a manifestation of the wise necromancer who is empowered and sanctioned by the spirits to speak the truth. Ritual insults and satire challenge errant individuals to modify their actions and atone for transgressions. Thus exposed before the community and the spirits, one is forced to look inward to acknowledge the offense and work back to a state of balance. All efforts of the arts, the state, religion and esoteric sects are directed toward harmony. Acts of propitiation call forth the "benevolent intervention [of the Mothers] in the affairs of the community," while derisive songs enforce behavioral codes "by ridiculing, condemning, and cursing all who contravene the wishes of these owners of powerful ase."[5] One outcast can offend the spirits, upset the fragile cosmological balance and therefore harm the community.[6] "The community, well aware of the dire consequences of wrongful actions by any of its members, adds its combined force in verbal concurrence."[7]

Some Oro Efe costumes include mirrors, possibly referring to the Oro

Efe's ability to reveal fissures in the social fabric as he "holds up a mirror to society."[8] Mirrors also allude to the liminality and whiteness associated with feminine manifestations of *ase*. Mirrored reflections of light approximate the same dramatic effect of the white masks against the darkness of the night ceremony. Generally the Goddesses are associated with the color white because of its allusion to water and coolness. The white deities are those who function covertly, whereas the red deities (e.g., Shango and Ogun) signify overtly aggressive action. In the African diaspora to the New World, the syncretic layering of gods retained this essential symbolism. Erzulie and Damballah are white *loa*, yet the aggressive manifestation of Erzulie is red. The surface of water is a mirror that interfaces the corporeal plane above the water with the world of the invisibles below. The liminality of the Mothers refers to their alleged ability to "move freely between realms, unlike ordinary mortals" or to transform into flying creatures and nocturnal animals.[9]

Duality is expressed in the "concentration of vital force . . . that can manifest itself in both positive and negative ways."[10] The exceptional concentration of *ase* in women is attributed to their more secretive inclinations to be self-contained, persevering and composed.[11] Balancing the hot, overt forces of masculine *ase* is the "cool, covert, patient approach of the mothers."[12] Balance is central to the entire aesthetic and way of life for the Yoruba. Beauty is contained in the balance of attributes exemplified in coolness. Ideal modes of behavior are embodied in the concept of the personal character (*iwa*) that manifests coolness. If "we live generously and discreetly, exhibiting grace under pressure" we approximate the notion of divine coolness. Here, "fully realizing the spark of creative goodness God has endowed us with . . . we find the confidence to cope with all kinds of situations." In this way, *ase*, "mystic coolness," and character become one and the same.[13] One's *ase* can be diminished through improper modes of living. In order to fully realize one's own divine spark, "one must cultivate" the ability to interpret "significant communications," to recognize truth "or else the lessons of the crossroads—the point where doors open or close, where persons have to make decisions that may forever after affect their lives—will be lost."[14]

Personal destiny, like *ase*, must be earned. Correct decisions are just as critical to the attainment of internal potentiality, *ori inun*, as they are to the balance of *ase*. In the time before birth, the primordial union with life and with the Earth Mother, Onile, is experienced. Entrance into the arena of humanity is an entrance into an existence of opposing forces. At birth the "primeval mitosis" of the uroboric experience occurs, and the struggle for wholeness begins. From birth until death, dual forces are at work, and the soul must struggle against the forces of death, disease and decay. The inheritance of lineage, political ties, religious affiliation and sexual identity affects personal choices. At critical points of passage, the individual relies on Ifa divination for guidance. Whereas Ifa's position is one of revealing the continuity of social order, Eshu-Elegba is responsible for the growth and transformation of the social structure to encompass new experiences. The essential structure of Yoruba cosmology and the West African diaspora in the New World is one of fluidity that allows for a layering of multiple, oftentimes competing forces. As a form of "true sociotherapy," Ifa divination reveals "the meanings hidden in the sacred language of social order from the beginning, yet always needing to be rediscovered in the present."[15] Through Ifa, the intentions of Olorun are made known. Through the Oro-Efe songs of the Gelede, the ancestral invocations of the Egungun, and the judicial mediations of the Ogboni, the concerns of the Mothers are communicated. Between Olorun as Sky and Onile as Earth lies the marketplace of human existence wherein the purposes of the eternal ancestral self are played out through the transient activities of everyday life. Between the creative and destructive forces, and the oppositions of sexuality, aggression, life and death, is the guardian of the doors, the gateway figure, mediator of all opposites.

Eshu-Elegba stands thus between the wisdom of age and the beauty of youth, the beneficial and destructive aspects of the Mothers, between men and their gods, the *orisha*, between fire and calm, between the competing forces of heredity and destiny. He is the intersection, the fulcrum.[16] All of human life is a struggle to maintain character and balance despite the burdens and obstacles of destructive forces. The good is encouraged through praise. Those who fall under the weight of fire and lose composure are challenged through ritual insult. A society that is not whole cannot provide the base from which support can be given to heal the ills that pervade it. Ritual challenge meets a long-term system of defenses and, where there is no longer a universal code whereby a formula for healing can be understood, the words fall upon ears that cannot hear. A mind that is divided against itself suppresses guilt and fear and the pain festers. It needs exposure to heal, exposure in a spiritually safe situation. Similarly, sociotherapy requires a candid reassessment of the social structure that, though it appears to produce greater instability and disintegration at first, ultimately leads to a more stable reintegration of a higher order.

Whereas the sociologist would be ridiculed for suggesting a need for spiritual and creative healing, the novelist need not be concerned about the tangibility of his implied suggestions for sociotherapy in terms of verifiable steps for legislation. Nevertheless, because of their more natural alignment with myth, the characters in a novel who propose creative healing can often point the way toward actual change.

Keeping this in mind, we can look at how these novels address the problem of spiritual disintegration, racism and oppression. The white woman as a symbolic form has already been addressed. However, the image of the white woman in these novels and her role in preventing change, continuing the tide of oppression or, in rare cases, her role as Initiator or nurturing Mother as a means to positively effect the healing process needed for social change are issues I have attempted to approach throughout this book.

In the works of Ellison (*The Invisible Man*), Wright (*Native Son*) and Himes (*The Primitive* and *If He Hollers Let Him Go*), the tone is one of anger. These authors do not give us a neat, simple way to change the world, but they do provide us with the first step by exposing oppression. Without truthful exposure of the effect of racism on the human spirit and on the fabric of our society, we have no way to address the problem. Ellison, Wright and Himes air these issues in such a way that they cannot be denied, covered up or ignored, which is a very real step toward change.

On the other hand, Baraka (*The Slave*) and Walker (*Meridian*) portray the effects of prolonged and unmitigated oppression through the actions of violent and non-violent revolutionaries. Baraka addresses issues that precipitate the violent eruption of revolution and Walker reveals the steady process of disillusionment as it unfolds in the lives of Civil Rights workers. Each individual must undergo a personal transformation before any real healing occurs.

Furthermore, Reed, Morrison and Bambara allude to the eruption of the spirits, long repressed, that intervene to assist a spiritual revolution. It is these last three authors that really develop the idea of the artist-necromancer-shaman who initiates the repair of the psychic, spiritual, corporeal and earthly fabric of contemporary life. The necromancer uses the past to assist the present; the necromancer recreates the world not in the image of times past but through an integration of the past and present mythos. Thus, Papa LaBas prevents disaster from taking its foothold in New York (*Mumbo Jumbo*). Moreover, Velma's metamorphosis sets off the cataclysmic events that promise a new era of hope and spiritual regeneration in *The Salt Eaters*. And finally, Toni Morrison's Shadrack, Pilate and Circe show us that the spirits are active in the world in the form of human beings who, despite their private experience of hell that makes personal survival impossible, intervene for others and effect a far-reaching change (*Sula* and *Song of Solomon*).

It may be true that the works of Himes, Ellison, Wright and Baraka are angry. They may not offer the same sense of hope that emanates from Reed, Bambara and Morrison; however, if readers can take the risk to feel uncomfortable, angry, guilty and fearful, then they can see the healing behind the anger. Anger is a necessary, almost instinctive defense system that alerts us to something terribly wrong in our world. Without the ground breaking of these writers, it is doubtful that it would have been possible for the necromancers of the 1980s to reveal themselves. The earlier generation of African-American writers lead the way to the generation of writers that have given us not only heroic characters that have survived despite the brutalities of the society in which they live (the personal heroism of Celie in *The Color Purple*, Meridian in *Meridian* or Papa LaBas in *Mumbo Jumbo*); they have spun the fibers to heal the psyche. It is the voices of African-American fiction that speak of true hope and confirm that the forces behind ceremonial healing do exist. Reed labels this collective force "Neo-HooDoo."

"Neo-HooDoo believes that every man is an artist and every artist a priest."[17] The priests of the ancient, esoteric cults of Africa do not relinquish the hold of oppositions, sexuality, family and worldly images, like ascetics practicing self-denial. Instead, they move beyond the point where these ties have a limiting effect on balance and judgment. Their wisdom transcends even the junction where the guardian of intersections is needed as a mediator. Progression toward spiritual growth takes them past the nurturing Mother, the seductive Initiator, the crossroads figure, the shadow and the animus to the Transcendent Mother. The elders of the Ogboni society express their complete inner exposure to the Mother by wearing their clothing inside out, a sign of interior integration that implies the suspension of worldly ties in order that they may preside in judgment without partiality to anyone but the Earth Mother, Onile. Thus, the fully integrated psyche becomes a necromancer at the intersection of forces, with the wrong side of the cloth, the inside, touching the ground. They can wear the mask of deformity, of the anti-aesthetic, because they have surpassed the stage in which character and primeval wholeness can be ruffled by aggression. They have survived the test of fire.

Ultimately, the individual's journey parallels that of the priest with similar struggles and tests of fire. The initial phases of Jungian movement toward individuation or "self-consciousness" proceed in a direction that is analogous to Baldwin's admonishment that we have to be conscious of what we have done, and are doing, out of guilt, in order to forgive ourselves and break the circle of repeated crimes (*Blues for Mister Charlie*). The interior revolution begins with the reconciliation of the shadow. Neither silencing the object of guilt nor annihilating the oppressive part of the psyche will result in healing. Real revolution is not simply an exchange of oppressors as in Walker's notion of taking "our turn" (*The Slave*)[18]; it is a revolution that seeks to find its balance, the dance of the new *loa*, the mediating force, taking its turn.[19]

If indeed the original split within the world psyche further subdivides sexually and racially (as Cleaver suggests in *Soul on Ice*), then a spiritual revolution should result in the reconciliation of opposing forces through mutual recognition. The recognition occurs through projection. The white oppressor sees his own crimes against the oppressed repeated in the mirror of the slave revolt. At first, the discomfort arising from this exposure will appear destructive of even the seemingly beneficial aspects of the prevailing social structure. In fact, what occurs is a disruption of a false sense of equilibrium in order that negative cycles of behavior can be broken.

The neurosis of Western society lies in the dependency upon logical positivism that seeks verifiable truths to the exclusion of mystical encounter, and on the clarity of the differentiation process of definition as a means to accumulate knowledge instead of the intuition of correspondence as an approach to acquire wisdom. Classification schema devoid of essential meaning yield a metronomic existence, and a time comes when the absolutism of a "two plus two equals four" notion of sanity must be questioned as in Reed's query, "Can a metronome know the thunder or summon a God?"[20] Plato warns us in *Phaedrus* that when notions of truth and beauty are lost, then the efforts of rhetoric are meaningless. In the process toward rationalization, the focus should be on the true nature of things, "avoiding the attempt to shatter the unity of any part, as a clumsy butcher might do."[21] Socrates tells Phaedrus that only when we are aware of the essential similarities among things can we make the appropriate classifications. The classifications provide the basis for definitions and premises for deductive and inductive reasoning. These linear approaches to investigating reality tend to focus on cause and effect relationships, whereas synchronistic cosmological systems find meaningful relationships where there are no causal connections. Similarities, analogy, and intersection or synergy belong to the old pagan existence. Coincidence and correspondence between objects and events were at the heart of the old homeopathic magic, unverifiable and therefore insignificant in the current abuses of rationalism, science and logical positivism.

The "synchronistic principle . . . suggests that there is an inter-connection or unity of causally unrelated events, and thus postulates a unitary aspect of being," wherein the unique growth process of one individual becomes a model for social renewal and the social transformation is a mirror of the processes at work in the cosmos. The concept of causality "breaks everything down into individual processes" and, while a cause and effect theory may be "necessary if we are to gain reliable knowledge of the world" such a theory, by itself, "has the disadvantage of breaking up, or obscuring, the universal interrelationship of events."[22]

In *The Salt Eaters*, the separate lives of people in Velma's world collide at the same time that other important signals appear, signifying the dissolution of the old order and the emergence of a new beginning. Thunder "crack[s] . . . as if the very world were splitting apart,"[23] and Campbell has sudden insights about the effect of Damballah's presence on the restructuring of the world. Jan responds to a spiritual signal to open up to change and surrender her grasp "on notions that might" hold her back.[24] Each individual establishes new alignments with their own messenger: Nilda with "the Deer of the Sun,"[25] and Velma with the drums saying, "barrier dropping."[26]

Physical and psychic signs foretell the new beginning: "a crab . . . attacked a fisherman; . . . a fig unripe . . . dropped from a tree and burst open,"[27] and Minnie gets a message from her "back molars."[28] Freddie thought he saw his friend Porter alive again.[29] At the same time Velma "started back toward life."[30] These moments coincide meaningfully, not by "mere chance."[31] Each individual is his or her own network of cosmological connections that weaves together the social fabric. It is the role of divination to illuminate the interrelationship of events, past and present.

The tools of divination, whereby traditional cultures receive guidance through times of passage and crisis, are "at once a part and an epiphany of the unique constellation of forces and events making up any given moment."[32] Through instruction that recounts the actions of the ancestors in similar moments of critical passage, clients of the diviner can apply the sacred verses to their own lives. In this way, the lessons of the past are brought into dynamic communion with the present. Furthermore, the conviction that all events (no matter how apparently trivial they may seem) are meaningful and significant increases the individual's sense of connection to community.

Instead of a linear succession of events and progression from nature to culture to the absolute, as an evolutionary dialectic would assume, mythic synchronicity entails a suspension of time and a principle of simultaneity that permits contradictions to exist. At the same time the Trickster is in the center of the divine cosmos, he is also a vital presence in the human fringes.[33] "Harnessing dissolution to rebirth," he creates new order out of chaos.[34] To promote growth and engender greater fulfillment, the Trickster upsets safe, womblike complacency, inertia and rigidity. The spiritual unfoldment of the psyche (and, as above so below, the subsequent mani-

festations of change within the everyday events of a society) beyond
uroboric unity with the Mother to infinite relatedness of apparent oppositions "is truly recapitulative—not linear and evolutionary, but spiral and
epigenetic." The principle "of the simultaneity and correspondence of all
planes of being and consciousness" encompasses, via the Trickster, "the
passage out of an incompletely realized center, into the wild, and back into
a center enlarged by both departure and return."[35] This enlargement of the
social order occurs each time the individual is initiated to a higher level
of being.

Whereas Georg Wilhelm Friedrich Hegel's philosophy tends to assume
an absolute dialectic with the ascendency of ideas and Karl Marx's
dialectic is primarily material, the Trickster operates simultaneously in the
divine center and the human extremity dissolving and maintaining boundaries to enable the process of human transformation. Both Hegel's theory
of lordship and bondage and Jung's process of individuation point to the
necessity of recognizing affinity in apparent opposition. Neither process
occurs without painful struggle. Similarly, "the trickster brings out in the
open conflict, lust, and dread that they might become agencies of communion, not disunion."[36]

According to Hegel, the split between lord and bondsman occurs first,
whereby one appears to benefit at the expense of the other.[37] The ascendency of reason on the one hand and empiricism on the other over the
powers of intuition as a means to expand one's understanding of the
cosmos is a lordship and bondage relationship that elevates the masculine
proclivities above the Feminine. Similarly, the relationship between an
oppressive class and subjugated minorities is analogous to the relationship
between oppositions inherent in the psyche. Hegel's *Phenomenology of
the Mind* is a microcosm that can be applied to the history of suppression
in human society (e.g., black/white relations, matriarchal/patriarchal systems) and in the history of psyche. Through the process of revolt and
change the individual selves become aware of their ultimate affinity rather
than their inequality. Only through this life-and-death struggle can true
freedom be obtained. The purpose of the whole process is for the self to
become independently conscious of itself. Just as the master evolves to
the position of self-assertion, he realizes it is not independence but
dependence that has been achieved at the expense of the slave, and what
has been achieved is detrimental to his spiritual health. This is the despair
and guilt of Western society. According to Hegel, through bondage the
slave becomes aware of his negative existence and begins to act on
cancelling that which caused him to fear (the master); however, nihilation
of the master without complete transformation is just as injurious to the

slave's individuation as the master's oppression. The cycle never attains completion and healing as long as revolution motivates only the exchange of prison guards and their captives.

The soul encounters its first awareness within a uroboric unity in which everything is perceived in the infantile consciousness as an extension of itself. The experience of well-being within the nourishment of the womblike paradise is followed by the psyche's fall into time. Here the divided consciousness becomes aware of its distinctness and the initial awareness is marked by fear and adversity. Subsequent struggles to balance with opposition may take the form of (a) *annihilation*, in which the individual seeks complete negation of the other; (b) *repression*, in which the lord (interpreted as the individual waking consciousness and/or the subjugating class in society) seeks to control the slave (unconscious self or oppressed group) through denunciation or reduction of the other by undermining the means by which the other can survive, grow and find self-expression; or (c) *fusion*, in which the master changes the identity of the slave to fit him/herself or the slave exchanges roles with the master. The fourth and final stage of integration involves recognition of one's projected anima/animus in the other and affirmation of the essential unity that supersedes apparent differences. Here the individual retrieves his or her identity, embracing and cherishing, without fear of threat to his or her psyche, the differences in others because he or she fully realizes the unitary aspect of life.

Servitude is not only a fact in human history; the self divided into dominant and subordinate selves is likewise a phenomenon of the development of the psyche until a level of integration is reached in which the central self moves from recognition, to tolerance, to acceptance, to affirmation and utilization of its many polarized facets in healthy adaptation to the environment. "The reconciling affirmation, the 'yes,' with which [conscious and unconscious facets of the psyche, lord and slave] . . . desist from their existence in opposition, is the existence of the . . . expanded" self. The enlightened soul retains its identity while allowing for the existence and affirmation of the other, all the while "possess[ing] the certainty of itself in its complete relinquishment and its opposite: it is God appearing in the midst of those who know themselves in the form of pure knowledge."[38]

The master of the Western world is the conscious mind sublimating the bondsman, or unconscious mind. The conscious mind as master becomes aware of the poverty of reason as a symbol of false independence. The master becomes aware of its dependence upon the slave (i.e., intuition, creativity, imagination) and attempts to discredit this pagan of the past.

The slave, primarily concerned with the need to exercise all the imagined fantasies of freedom, comes into awareness of what it is by virtue of what it does not have and, unrestrained, the id takes over. The bondsman cancels out the oppressive and self-destructive mind and a new order emerges. In either case, the healthy self has a mechanism by which one of the two can circumvent the self-destructive activities of the other and assume control.

The process of self-preservation persists in a similar way as in the mind of an angry child. Holding his or her breath out of spite, the first signal the child receives from the unconscious is pain and discomfort. If the child persists in holding his or her breath, he or she will pass out. The unconscious has taken over and the child will breathe again.[39] As all necromancers and griots inform us, we are on the verge of this change. The "our turn" of Reed's new *loa* is not simply an exchange of masters. It is the unconscious self, the creativity and the correspondence, of the Old World that will intervene and have us breathe again.

This analogy of the critical balance between opposing parts of the psyche enables us to understand the role of the childlike qualities in the Trickster. "In play" the child "leaves the world and creates a counterworld so that he [or she] might return to ordinary existence" with an increased capacity to perceive "in it the harmonies and meanings he [or she] has discovered in himself [or herself]." The rebelliousness of children "is inextricably bound to their creativity." This helps to explain the paradoxically arbitrary, willful and destructive behavior of the Trickster as seen in Legba, and the Indo-European Shiva. Similarly, the Dogon of Mali mythologize the playfulness of children in the figure of Ogu-Yorugu, "aware that play takes the child outside the restrictions of everyday space, time, causality, social reality, and bodily needs so that he [or she] might come to know these restrictions more as horizons than as absolute limits."[40] The Trickster reveals through playfulness the potential expansiveness of boundaries.

Conversely, the Trickster's outrageous behavior mitigates against stultifying rigidity. This explains how Satan came to be associated with Legba in the New World, not by his inherent evil, but for his apparent antisocial behavior that is ultimately used for the benefit of the social structure "to challenge goodness creatively." The ground drawings for Eshu-Elegba "associated with the crossroads, sudden changes of fortune, and 'devilish,' that is, unpredictable, behavior," include "Satan's pitchfork, a pinwheel sign of sudden change and motion, a crossroadslike sign, and additional mystic points . . . recombined."[41] Another way in which Eshu-Elegba mitigates restrictive ways of conceiving the world in terms of dichotomies is to recombine vital, overt, sometimes even outrageous sexuality with the divine center, which tends to be removed from sexuality in the missionary notions of mystical encounter. "Because of his provocative nature, Eshu has been characterized by missionaries and Western-minded Yoruba alike as 'the Devil.' "[42]

Instead of relegating childlike rebelliousness, on the one hand, and outrageous sexuality to the domain of the devil, on the other hand, healthy adaptation involves acceptance and integration of the many selves into the whole psyche. The process of individuation is one of "open conflict and open collaboration at once," between the conscious and the unconscious mind, between master and slave. "Conscious and unconscious do not make a whole when one of them is suppressed and injured by the other,"[43] but only when the true quaternity of the self is resolved with the anima/animus syzygy and the shadow.

The syzygy to which Jung refers is portrayed in *The Salt Eaters* in the relationship between Velma's mud mothers as the shadow, the weak animus male images of Freddie and Obie, the oppressive animus as political power structure, the transcendent Wise Mother Sophie and the androgynous Abraxas figure of Damballah (the Haitian manifestation of the Fon Da and Aida Wedo, who restores health). The completion of Velma as a fully individuated self occurs when she has absorbed all of these experiences in her process of transformation and participation on the eve of society's rebirth.

In Africa, the creative force is represented by an androgynous pair of twin deities that the Fon of Dahomey call Mawu-Lisa; a union of sky and earth, who gave birth to Da, Aida Wedo, identified by a serpent or a rainbow as a bridge between the created worlds and Mawu-Lisa. It is Da who maintains the order and balance, and the Christ/Antichrist figure of Legba mediates opposition. According to Fon myth, Mawu (the maternal element in Mawu-Lisa) wishes to keep her youngest and most indulged son, Legba, with her and tells him "that she will not give his brothers authority over him. . . . Instead she . . . appoints him to visit his brothers' kingdoms and to report back to her."[44] Legba's position as intermediary (between the other deities [*Vodun*] and Mawu-Lisa, and between the *Vodun* and humanity) is assured by his ability to speak the languages of his brothers and Mawu-Lisa. No one else knows the language of Mawu-Lisa. "He alone knows and links the speech of primordial intimacy and the many tongues of less numinous realms."[45] And, considering that the spoken word is believed to be the vehicle for *ase* to express itself, Legba becomes the key to all efficacious communication. Legba guards the gate. The syzygy is expressed in the individual who, like Legba, bridges opposition, maintains a calm expression while balancing fire, keeps the aesthetic of cool while displaying and harnessing the anti-aesthetic, absorbing instead of casting out deformity and realigning the psyche to make it whole.

In *Song of Solomon*, Pilate is the transcendent figure, as is Circe. Hagar has the clinging, immature love of childhood that seeks to devour and be devoured, whereas Milkman's brief sanctuary with a woman who bathes him in a gesture of comradely love washes his spirit clean. His shadow, Guitar, cannot hold him down. He takes flight to the metaphysical Africa where he is no longer the motherless child.

The external "projection can only be dissolved" when a man realizes the existence of all facets of the feminine aspect of his psyche. "She is the vital compensation for the risks, struggles, sacrifices which all end in disappointment." At the same time she is the "solace for all the bitterness of life" and she is the "seductress who draws him into life . . . into its reasonable and useful aspects" as well as "its frightful paradoxes and ambivalences where good and evil, success and ruin, hope and despair counterbalance one another."[46] The loving and terrible Goddess is manifested historically in the "Virgin Mary, who is not only the Lord's mother, but also, according to medieval allegories, his cross." In India, " 'the loving and terrible mother' is the paradoxical Kali."[47] Yemoja and Onile occupy this position among the Yoruba.

The struggle for "self-consciousness" and independence is universal. Individuals project their shadows and anima/animus onto tormentors with whom a confrontation is possible. This, too, is universal. And the final battle within—when there are no immediate tormentors to blame—that is also universal. However, the identification of a sociopolitical problem with the cosmological forces of creation and destruction is not to be used as a justification for continued oppression. By denying the inherent abilities of a creative imaginative force within society to initiate change, rationalization can foster resignation to the inevitability of defeat, providing us with an opportunity to relinquish responsibility for healing. Just as there is often a tendency to explain away the destructive effects of the Goddess type by categorizing her in social-political packages, Himes cautions against the tendency to use the universal to rationalize (and in this way, avoid thorough examination of) the particular, individual pain. The writer must resist the tendency to say, "I must free myself of all race consciousness before I can understand the true nature of human experiences, for it is not the Negro problem at all, but the human problem."[48] The anima image projection, though universal in concept, is unique and individual in experience. This book does not attempt to rationalize this image of white women and how it came about, but to relate a particular frame of opposition (oppression, of lordship and bondage) to a deeper source, that of extreme rationality and dualism, an all-or-nothing philosophy that has no balance, no Legba, as mediator.

When applying a Jungian approach to the analysis of the sexualization of racism, the first step is to identify the shadow. In Jungian terms, the shadow is recognized usually in a person of the same sex. So with writers such as Wright, Baldwin, Baraka and Himes, the shadow comes out in the more brutal tendencies of Bigger, Rufus, Walker and Robert, respectively. Once the shadow (unconscious) has been recognized and integrated, the anima or animus can be approached and balanced. The negative animus is expressed as the omnipotent observer/oppressor, whereas the negative anima is expressed as the Terrible Goddess. The balance is not achieved by an oppressed group simply taking its turn, suppressing the opposition. This is the solution that Walker takes, continuing the Hegelian cycle. The real revolution is Baldwin's sense of coming to terms with our crimes. In "introducing a new loa," Reed adopts the healing force that, like Osiris, would "rather dance than rule."[49] The celebratory emphasis of a spiritual force as embodied in Osiris, Dionysus and Jes Grew is contrasted against the decadence of the power-hungry Iknaton or the cultural persecutions played out by the adherents to the "Wallflower Order." Once the anima/animus is recognized, the transcendent self, the new *loa*, can enter.

Like Socrates, Himes underlines the necessity to seek truth before rhetoric. Hiding from truth will result in the "black Baudelaire[s]" of American society who rationalize their position with rhetoric, obscuring truth and delaying the crisis of change.[50] Clay in *Dutchman* and Lillian in *The Man Who Cried I Am* are examples of the black middle class "seek[ing] to hide . . . [their] battered soul[s]," and "scars of oppression." Desiring only "to be permitted to 'play the game' as any other American," he will hide his injuries and be "opposed to anything he thinks will aid in his exclusion."[51]

To play the game and believe it is to hide the shadow. For a short time, the Jesses and the Clays reap the rewards of playing the game. At the end of the contest with a white woman, Jesse faces punishment and Clay dies an undignified death. Clay's mouth "work[s] stupidly" at the hand of his slayer Lula,[52] whereas the white professor, who controls the drama being played out (in the triangle between his wife, her black ex-husband and himself), manages a last retort in spite of Walker's attempts to repress him: "Ritual Drama. Like I said, ritual drama."[53] The price for playing the wrong game is exposed in the twisted fates of Jesse and Clay.

The "dwarfed, beaten personalities" of black characters (e.g., Rufus, Bigger, Jesse) are revealed in the process of exposing the truth of oppression.[54] If this process exposes "a pathetic sense of inferiority . . . hate and fear and self-hate, this then is the effect of oppression on the human personality." Also included in the "daily horrors," "realities" and "experiences" of the African-American are"homicidal mania, lust for white women, . . . paradoxical anti-Semitism, arrogance, [and] uncle tomism."[55] Rather than ignoring these aberrations, true healing requires uncensored exposure. The black American author "perform[s] his service as an artist" through "round[ing] out his knowledge of the truth" when he "discover[s] that nothing ever becomes permanent but change."[56]

In his critical essay Himes concludes that in spite of injury and hatred, the "indomitable quality" of growth persists within the African diaspora, as it does in the spirit of all individuals. Although "it is a long way, a hard way from the hatred of the faces to the hatred of evil, . . . the Negro will discover" that there are also "white people whom he will encounter along the way" and that all "will be growing."[57] Furthermore, the growth of a society depends upon the participation of all of its members in the transformation to new levels of awareness. Rather than pursue a separatist direction acknowledging only an African heritage, Himes notes that the writer "will find that he [or she] cannot accomplish this departure because he [or she] is an American."[58] Along similar lines, Silko's Tayo (*Ceremony*) realizes that white people are only the tools of witchery and that healing cannot be accomplished through separatism or reversed oppression, but only by including white people within the context of a ceremony that assumes a global consciousness.

Throughout my initial exploration of African-American portrayals of white women, I confronted the question: Is this a case where the oppressed reverse the action, and take their turn, beginning with discrediting the oppressor's women? Is the image accurate or fair? The voice in contemporary African-American literature is certainly an authentic one that persists in relating recurrent experiences of white women. The experience, however, is a fragment, a portion of the old myths that surface as symptoms of a pathology. Although it is true that this image of women is limited, it must also be noted that she is not the only character who is in some way maimed. There are only a few characters in these novels—Velma, Meridian, Pilate, Milkman—who survive, transcend, attain strength, self-hood and realization of spirit, proving the "indomitable quality" of growth that, despite alienation, survives.

When the "counteraction" of the unconscious (upon the will of the conscious mind) "is suppressed it loses its regulating function."[59] Jung relates an example from the book of Daniel when Daniel's insights are suppressed as a regulating influence for Nebuchadnezzar. "At the height of his power [the Babylonian king] had a dream which foretold disaster if he did not humble himself." Nebuchadnezzar refused to hear Daniel's interpretation. Subsequently he "fell victim to a psychosis that contained the very counteraction he had sought to escape: he, the lord of the earth, was degraded to an animal."[60] Nebuchadnezzar's wonders did not guarantee him immunity. Like the Tower of Babel that was once a monument, not to the insolence of mankind, but for the worship of the gods, Nebuchadnezzar was ultimately associated with the error of hubris because he did not humble himself.

Regardless of whether one or twenty Babylons fall, there always will be a replacement for counteracting the unconscious until we evolve beyond the need to assert power over others in order to experience a reduced realization of ourselves. Until then, it is only through the mirror of the projected shadow, the anima/animus, the other, that we may see ourselves. It is when we see ourselves at the expense of the other that we engender more corruption and guilt and continue the Hegelian cycle.

Russell Banks presents us with characters possessing different views on governmental corruption and evil in *The Book of Jamaica*. The Rastafarian Terron sees each example "of their corruption and incompetence as another welcome sign of fire to come," whereas the white American sees it as "another depressing episode in the history of the New World." And whereas "evil confirmed and deepened Terron's belief in good," it only "confirm[ed] and deepen[ed the American's] pessimism."[61]

These two viewpoints are summarized on a broader scale in Bank's epigram by Octavio Paz: "The role that causality plays in our culture has its counterpart in the role played by analogy among the Meso-Americans. Causality" is linear, "successive" and "infinite: a cause produces an effect, which in turn engenders another."[62] This linear thinking is the foundation for the viewpoint of conflict that traps the victims of the White Goddess in these novels. Seen as an irreconcilable contradiction, the negative anima of the Western man is cast out and murdered (or made a powerless fool) in order to preserve the status quo. The struggle itself is based on paradox that is not reconciled through rationalization. The victims of the White Goddess are the victims of the "sane" world they elect. The insane world referred to by Clay (*Dutchman*) as the world of Bessie Smith and Charlie Parker is a world based not on causality, but on the paradoxical union of synchronic and diachronic systems. The homeopathic world of the ancient worshippers of the horned Cernunnos or the hermetic world of the Gnostics, and the African-Americans who retained their inheritance of synchronicity also operated on correspondence and on cyclical relationships, much as the Rastas of Bank's novel. Like Betonie's view of white witchery

in Silko's *Ceremony*, like the necromancer Himes, the Rastas perceive a
Babylon that must inevitably succumb to the rhythm of change. The
perception of evil at its height only strengthens the belief in the coming
good.

> Analogy or correspondence, by contrast, is close and cyclical: the phenomena evolve
> and are repeated as in a play of mirrors. Each image changes, fuses with its contrary,
> disengages itself, forms another image, and in the end returns to the starting point.
> Rhythm is the agent of change in this case. The key expressions of change are, as in
> poetry, metamorphosis and mask.[63]

Thus, the conclusion to the linear nihilism of the West is not a contin-
uous Hegelian dialectic finding an absolute Nietzschean superman, but a
mirrored, spiral dialectic in which the essence of conflict is absorbed and
transformed into the stream to be healed. The surface of the sacred river,
a thin membrane between worlds, is the zone of ambiguity, the zone of
poetry and mask, the mirror. The world is fragile, Silko's medicine man
tells us.[64] As she witnesses the emergence of Velma's awakening, Sophie
observes that it is a configuration of signs.[65] "Velma, rising on steady legs,
throws off the shawl that drops down on the stool a burst cocoon," and
another child bruised by the movement for human rights is healed.[66] We
are not admonished by the Rastas or by Betonie to be careful so much as
we are advised to be aware. The rest will follow. A new Jes Grew[67] will
come along to stir it up and get it going again: "Greetings from the
swinging HooDoo cloud; . . . the softest touch in Everything; doing a
dance they call 'The Our Turn' "[68]—the turn of the artist-necromancer-
griot to expose us to ourselves, to show us the mirror and disturb the false
equilibrium. New myths, new *loa*, must arise as phoenixes from ancient
memory. The nightmare is a purgation, a test of balance.

Notes

PREFACE

1. Joseph Campbell, ed., *The Portable Jung* (New York: Viking Press, 1971; New York: Penguin Books, 1976), p. xiii.

2. Harold Courlander, *A Treasury of Afro-American Folklore* (New York: Crown, 1976), p. 2.

3. Campbell, ed., *The Portable Jung*, p. xiii.

4. Ibid.

5. Ibid.

6. Ibid.

7. Ibid.

8. Ishmael Reed, *Mumbo Jumbo* (New York: Doubleday, 1972; New York: Avon Books, Bard Books, 1978), p. 241.

9. Toni Cade Bambara, *The Salt Eaters* (New York: Random House, 1980), p. 147.

10. Chester Himes, "Dilemma of the Negro Novelist in the U.S.A.," in *New Black Voices: An Anthology of Contemporary Afro-American Literature*, ed. Abraham Chapman (New York: New American Library, Mentor Books, 1972), p. 395.

11. Ishmael Reed, *Flight to Canada* (New York: Random House, 1976; New York: Avon Books, Bard Books, 1977), p. 40.

12. Maya Deren, *Divine Horsemen: The Voodoo Gods of Haiti* (New York: Chelsea House, 1970; New York: Dell, Delta Books, 1972), p. 138.

13.. Ibid., pp. 142–143.

14. Joseph Campbell, *Myths to Live By* (New York: Viking Press, 1972; New York: Bantam Books, 1973), p. 266.

15. Ibid., p. 13.

INTRODUCTION

1. Joseph Campbell, *The Hero with a Thousand Faces* (New York: Bollingen Foundation, 1949; New York: World Publishing, Meridian Books, 1956), p. 115.

2. Maya Deren, *Divine Horsemen: The Voodoo Gods of Haiti* (New York: Chelsea House, 1970; New York: Dell, Delta Books, 1972), pp. 27–28.

3. Ibid., p. 30.

4. John A. Williams, *The Man Who Cried I Am* (Boston: Little, Brown, 1967; New York: New American Library, Signet Books, 1968), p. 157.

5. Ibid., pp. 156–57.

6. Ibid., p. 281.

7. Ishmael Reed, "why i often allude to osiris," in *Conjure: Selected Poems, 1963–1970* (Amherst: University of Massachusetts Press, 1972), p. 43.

8. Ibid.

9. Toni Cade Bambara, *The Salt Eaters* (New York: Random House, 1980), p. 92.

10. Leslie Marmon Silko, *Ceremony* (New York: Viking Press, 1977; New York: New American Library, Signet Books, 1978), p. 37.

11. Bambara, *The Salt Eaters*, p. 92.

12. R. D. Laing, *The Politics of Experience* (New York: Pantheon Books, 1967; New York: Ballantine Books, 1968), p. 34.

13. Bambara, *The Salt Eaters*, p. 247.

14. Ibid., pp. 248–49.

15. Ibid., p. 18.

16. Ibid., p. 16.

17. Laing, *The Politics of Experience*, p. 13.

18. Alice Childress, *A Short Walk* (New York: Coward, McCann & Geoghegan, 1979; New York: Avon Books, Bard Books, 1981), p. 285.

19. Edgar Allan Poe, "The Philosophy of Composition," in *Selections from Poe's Literary Criticism*, ed. John Brooks Moore (New York: F. S. Crofts, 1926), pp. 34–38.

20. Alice Walker, *Meridian* (New York: Harcourt Brace Jovanovich, 1976; New York: Simon & Schuster, Pocket Books, Washington Square Press, 1977), p. 107.

CHAPTER 1

1. Erich Neumann, *The Great Mother: An Analysis of the Archetype*, trans. Ralph Manheim, Bollingen Series 47, 2nd ed. (Princeton, N.J.: Princeton University Press, 1972), p. 149.

2. Jean Toomer, "Portrait in Georgia," in *Cane* (New York: Liveright, 1975), p. 27.

3. Robert Graves, *The White Goddess*, amended and enlarged ed. (New York: Farrar, Straus & Giroux, 1966), p. 24.

4. Toomer, "Portrait in Georgia, p. 27.

5. Graves, *The White Goddess*, p. 24.

6. Alice Walker, *Meridian* (New York: Harcourt Brace Jovanovich, 1976; New York: Simon & Schuster, Pocket Books, Washington Square Press, 1977), p. 137.

7. Alwyn Rees and Brinley Rees, *Celtic Heritage: Ancient Tradition in Ireland and Wales* (London: Thames & Hudson, 1961), p. 45.

8. Ibid., p. 46.

9. Wendy Doniger O'Flaherty, *Women, Androgynes, and Other Mythical Beasts* (Chicago: University of Chicago Press, 1982), p. 154.

10. Ibid., p. 207.

11. Ibid., p. 237.

12. Robert Farris Thompson, *Black Gods and Kings: Yoruba Art at UCLA* (Bloomington: Indiana University Press, 1976), chap. 14, p. 3.

13. Ibid., chap. 11, p. 1.

14. Ibid., chap. 14, p. 3.

15. Ishmael Reed, *Flight to Canada* (New York: Random House, 1976; New York: Avon Books, Bard Books, 1977), p. 147.

16. "And is not the mercurial, shape-shifting, enigmatic magic which we have described the essence of all art?" Shape-shifting is the ability to transubstantiate. Rhiannon transformed herself into a horse or a bird. "Such correspondences are neither accidents nor inventions.... Their magic has delighted and sustained the spirit of man throughout the ages ... [with] the power to breach the constraining boundaries of the finite so that the light of eternity may transubstantiate that which is commonplace and fill it with mystery" (Rees and Rees, *Celtic Heritage*, p. 351).

17. Graves, *The White Goddess*, p. 24.

18. Edgar Allan Poe, "Annabel Lee," in *The Complete Poems of Edgar Allan Poe*, ed. J. H. Whitty, 3rd ed., rev. (New York: Houghton Mifflin, 1919), pp. 80–81.

19. Nor Hall, *The Moon and the Virgin: Reflections on the Archetypal Feminine* (New York: Harper & Row, 1980), p. 11.

20. According to Poe, "Beauty is the sole legitimate province of the poem; ... the *tone* of its highest manifestation ... is one of *sadness*.... When it most closely allies itself to *Beauty*; the death, then, of a beautiful woman is, unquestionably, the most poetical topic in the world" (Edgar Allan Poe, "The Philosophy of Composition," in *Selections from Poe's Literary Criticism*, ed. John Brooks Moore [New York: F. S. Crofts, 1926], pp. 34–38).

21. Hall, *The Moon and the Virgin*, p. 12.

22. Ibid., p. 11.

23. Ibid., p. 15.

24. Reed, *Flight to Canada*, p. 148.

25. Hall, *The Moon and the Virgin*, p. 18.

26. Edgar Allan Poe, "The Fall of the House of Usher," in *The Centenary Poe: Tales, Poems, Criticism, Marginalia and Eureka by Edgar Allan Poe*, ed. Montagu Slater (London: Bodley Head, 1949), p. 155.

27. Reed, *Flight to Canada*, pp. 18–19.

28. Ibid., p. 25.

29. Ibid., p. 19.

30. C. G. Jung, "Aion," in *Psyche and Symbol: A Selection from the Writings of C. G. Jung*, ed. Violet S. De Laszlo (New York: Doubleday, Anchor Books, 1958), p. 11.

31. Reed, *Flight to Canada*, p. 148.

32. Ralph Ellison, *Invisible Man* (New York: Random House, 1952; Vintage Books, 1972), p. 18.

33. Ibid., p. 19.

34. Ralph Ellison, "The Art of Fiction: An Interview," in *Shadow and Act* (New York: Random House, 1964), p. 174.

35. Leslie Marmon Silko, *Ceremony* (New York: Viking Press, 1977; New York: New American Library, Signet Books, 1978), p. 90.

36. O'Flaherty, *Women, Androgynes, and Other Mythical Beasts*, p. 199.

37. Chester Himes, *If He Hollers Let Him Go* (New York: New American Library, Signet Books, 1971), p. 136.

38. Ibid., p. 139.

39. Ibid., p. 138.

40. Ibid., p. 119.

41. Ibid., p. 118.

42. Ibid.

43. Ibid., p. 138.

44. Ibid., p. 21.

45. Ibid., p. 22.

46. Chester Himes, *The Primitive* (New York: New American Library, Signet Books, 1956), p. 82.

47. Ibid.

48. Ibid.

49. Ibid., p. 85.

50. Ibid., p. 49.

51. Ibid., p. 111.

52. Ibid., p. 112.

53. Ibid.

54. Ibid., pp. 115–16.

55. Ibid., p. 128.

56. Ibid., p. 130.

57. Ibid., pp. 5–6.

58. Ibid., p. 131.

59. Ibid., pp. 150–51.

60. Graves, *The White Goddess*, epigraph.

61. Himes, *The Primitive*, pp. 151–52.

62. Ishmael Reed, *Mumbo Jumbo* (New York: Doubleday, 1972; New York: Avon Books, Bard Books, 1978), p. 9.

63. Himes, *The Primitive*, p. 152.

64. Louis Phillips, "LeRoi Jones and Contemporary Black Drama," in *The Black American Writer: Vol. 2, Poetry and Drama*, ed. C.W.E. Bigsby (Deland, FL: Everett/Edwards, 1969; Baltimore: Penguin Books, Pelican Books, 1971), p. 207.

65. LeRoi Jones [Amiri Baraka, pseud.], *The Slave*, in Dutchman *and* The Slave: *Two Plays by LeRoi Jones* (New York: William Morrow, 1964), p. 73.

66. Phillips, "LeRoi Jones and Contemporary Black Drama," p. 208.

67. C.W.E. Bigsby, ed., "The Black American Writer," in *The Black American Writer: Vol. 1, Fiction* (Leland, FL: Everett/Edwards, 1969; Baltimore: Penguin Books, Pelican Books, 1971), p. 15.

68. Chester Himes, "Dilemma of the Negro Novelist in the U.S.A.," in *New Black Voices: An Anthology of Contemporary Afro-American Literature*, ed. Abraham Chapman (New York: New American Library, Mentor Books, 1972), pp. 395–97.

69. Ishmael Reed, "Introduction to *19 Necromancers From Now*," in *New Black Voices: An Anthology of Contemporary Afro-American Literature*, ed. Abraham Chapman (New York: New American Library, Mentor Books, 1972), p. 517.

70. Ibid.

71. LeRoi Jones [Amiri Baraka, pseud.], *Dutchman*, in Dutchman *and* The Slave: *Two Plays by LeRoi Jones* (New York: William Morrow, 1964), pp. 7–8.

72. Ibid., pp. 8–9.

73. Ibid., p. 19.

74. Himes, *If He Hollers Let Him Go*, p. 138.

75. Jones, *Dutchman*, pp. 17–18.

76. Ibid., p. 25.

77. Ibid., p. 29.

78. Shango is a Yoruba *orisha*, a mythic king who was above the law. His untamed magic destroyed an entire village and, although Shango killed himself in remorse, he was later elevated to the stature of the gods. The image of pure power, if controlled properly, can become the protective force of the community. In the New World, this Shango force found expression either in overt or covert resistance against oppression. (Thompson, *Black Gods and Kings*, chap. 12, pp. 1–3.)

79. Jones, *Dutchman*, p. 35.

80. Ibid., p. 35–36.

81. Ibid., p. 37.

82. C. G. Jung, ed., *Man and His Symbols* (New York: Dell, Laurel ed., 1968), p. 187.

83. Jones, *Dutchman*, pp. 26–27.

84. John A. Williams, *The Man Who Cried I Am* (Boston: Little, Brown, 1967; New York: New American Library, Signet Books, 1968), p. 16.

85. Ibid., p. 124.

86. James Baldwin, *Another Country* (New York: Dial Press, 1962; New York: Dell, Laurel ed., 1978), pp. 341–42.

87. Ibid., pp. 62–63.

88. Ibid., p. 63.

89. Ibid., p. 115.

90. Paule Marshall, *The Chosen Place, The Timeless People* (New York: Harcourt, Brace & World, 1969; New York: Random House, Vintage Books, 1984), p. 459.

91. Ibid., pp. 180–81.

92. Ibid., pp. 145–46.

93. Ibid., p. 178.

94. Ibid., p. 71.

95. Ibid., p. 329.

96. Ibid., p. 44.

97. Ibid., p. 437.

98. Jung, *Man and His Symbols*, p. 187.

99. Ibid., p. 202.

100. Jean Toomer, "Bona and Paul," in *Cane* (New York: Liveright, 1975), p. 77.

101. Ibid., p. 70.

102. Ibid., p. 73.

103. Ibid., p. 74.

104. Ibid., p. 77.

105. Joseph Campbell, ed., *The Portable Jung* (New York: Viking Press, 1971; New York: Penguin Books, 1976), p. xxii.

106. Jones, *Dutchman*, p. 15.

107. Ibid., p. 28.

108. Ibid., p. 27.

109. Hall, *The Moon and the Virgin*, p. 15.

110. Ibid.

111. Ibid., p. 241.

CHAPTER 2

1. Nor Hall, *The Moon and the Virgin: Reflections on the Archetypal Feminine* (New York: Harper & Row, 1980), p. 140.

2. Toni Morrison, *Beloved* (New York: Alfred A. Knopf, 1987), p. 33.

3. Ibid., p. 77.

4. Ibid., p. 90.

5. Jean Toomer, "Becky," in *Cane* (New York: Liveright, 1975), p. 5.

6. Ibid.

7. Ibid., p. 6.

8. Alice Walker, *Meridian* (New York: Harcourt Brace Jovanovich, 1976; New York: Simon & Schuster, Pocket Books, Washington Square Press, 1977), p. 130.

9. Ibid., p. 215.

10. James Baldwin, *Another Country* (New York: Dial Press, 1962; New York: Dell, Laurel ed., 1978), pp. 49–50.

11. Ibid., p. 50.

12. Ibid.

13. Robert D. Pelton, *The Trickster in West Africa: A Study of Mythic Irony and Sacred Delight* (Berkeley: University of California Press, 1980), p. 138.

14. Ibid., p. 76.

15. Ibid., p. 77.

16. Walker, *Meridian*, pp. 131–33.

17. Ibid., p. 133.

18. Ibid., p. 162.

19. Ibid., p. 157.

20. Ibid., p. 159.

21. Ibid., p. 164.

22. Ibid.

23. Baldwin, *Another Country*, p. 55.

24. Ibid., p. 31.

25. Ibid., p. 23.

26. Ibid., p. 14.

27. Ibid., pp. 23–24.

28. Ibid., p. 62.

29. Ibid., p. 48.

30. Ibid.

31. Richard Wright, *Native Son* (New York: Harper & Row, Perennial Classics, 1966), p. 362.

32. Ibid.

33. Ibid., p. 48.

34. Ibid., p. 121.

35. Ibid., p. 48.

36. Ibid., p. 84.

37. Erich Neumann, *The Great Mother: An Analysis of the Archetype*, trans. Ralph Manheim, Bollingen Series 47, 2nd ed. (Princeton, N.J.: Princeton University Press, 1972), p. 166.

38. Ibid., p. 168.

39. Ibid., p. 76.

40. Ibid., p. 74.

41. Ibid., p. 38.

42. Wright, *Native Son*, pp. 189–90.

43. Ibid., p. 190.

44. Ibid., p. 16.

45. Baldwin, *Another Country*, p. 32.

46. Ibid., p. 36.

47. Ibid., p. 32.

48. Ibid., p. 31.

49. Paule Marshall, *The Chosen Place, The Timeless People* (New York: Harcourt, Brace & World, 1969; New York: Random House, Vintage Books, 1984), p. 455.

50. Ibid., p. 456.

51. Ibid., p. 459.

52. Ibid.

53. Toni Morrison, *Song of Solomon* (New York: Alfred A. Knopf, 1977; New York: New American Library, Signet Books, 1978), p. 250.

54. Ibid., p. 249.

55. Ibid., p. 250.

56. "In the *Odyssey*, as in the mythology of Melanesia, the goddess who in her terrible aspect is the cannibal ogress of the Underworld was in her benign aspect the guide and guardian to that realm and, as such, the giver of immortal life" (Joseph Campbell, *The Masks of God: Occidental Mythology* [New York: Viking Press, Compass ed., 1970; New York: Penguin Books, 1976], p. 171).

57. Morrison, *Song of Solomon*, p. 251.

58. Ibid., p. 340.

59. Ibid., p. 241.

60. Ibid., p. 242.

61. Ishmael Reed, *Flight to Canada* (New York: Random House, 1976; New York: Avon Books, Bard Books, 1977), p. 147.

62. Ibid., p. 29.

63. Ibid., p. 36.

64. Ibid., p. 147.

65. John A. Williams, *The Man Who Cried I Am* (Boston: Little, Brown, 1967; New York: New American Library, Signet Books, 1968), pp. 136–37.

66. Toomer, "Becky," p. 6.

67. Ibid., p. 7.

68. Reed, *Flight to Canada*, p. 147.

69. Walker, *Meridian*, p. 220.

70. Morrison, *Beloved*, p. 42.

71. Neumann, *The Great Mother*, pp. 65–66.

72. Ibid., p. 67.

73. Ibid.

74. Ibid., p. 74.

75. Ibid., p. 76.

76. Ibid.

77. Ibid., p. 175.

78. Walker, *Meridian*, p. 107.

79. Baldwin, *Another Country*, p. 63.

80. Ibid., p. 64.

81. LeRoi Jones [Amiri Baraka, pseud.], *Dutchman*, in Dutchman *and* The Slave: *Two Plays by LeRoi Jones* (New York: William Morrow, 1964), p. 28.

82. Joseph Campbell, ed., *The Portable Jung* (New York: Viking Press, 1971; New York: Penguin Books, 1976), p. xxii.

83. C. G. Jung, *The Archetypes and the Collective Unconscious*, trans. R. F. C. Hull, Bollingen Series 20, 2nd ed., in *The Collected Works of C. G. Jung*, vol. 9, part 1, eds. Michael Fordham, Gerhard Adler, Sir Herbert Read, and William McGuire, senior editor (Princeton, N.J.: Princeton University Press, 1968), p. 85.

84. Baldwin, *Another Country*, p. 36.

85. Walker, *Meridian*, p. 107.

86. Williams, *The Man Who Cried I Am*, p. 147.

87. Charlotte Alexander, "The 'Stink' of Reality: Mothers and Whores in James Baldwin's Fiction," in *James Baldwin: A Collection of Critical Essays*, ed. Kenneth Kinnamon (Englewood Cliffs, N.J.: Prentice-Hall, 1974), pp. 89–90.

88. Neumann, *The Great Mother*, p. 296.

89. Ibid., p. 299.

90. Ibid., p. 33.

91. Ralph Ellison, *The Invisible Man* (New York: Random House, 1952; Vintage Book, 1972), p. 19.

92. Williams, *The Man Who Cried I Am*, p. 75.

93. Cecil Brown, *The Life and Loves of Mr. Jiveass Nigger* (New York: Farrar, Straus & Giroux, 1969), pp. 9–10.

94. Williams, *The Man Who Cried I Am*, p. 273.

95. Ibid., p. 281.

96. William Irwin Thompson, *The Time Falling Bodies Take to Light: Mythology, Sexuality, and the Origins of Culture* (New York: St. Martin's Press, Lindisfarne Series, 1981), p. 187.

97. Ibid., p. 184.

98. Maya Deren, *Divine Horsemen: The Voodoo Gods of Haiti* (New York: Chelsea House, 1970; New York: Dell, Delta Books, 1972), p. 184.

99. Ibid., p. 187.

100. Toni Cade Bambara, *The Salt Eaters* (New York: Random House, 1980), p. 12.

101. Deren, *Divine Horsemen*, p. 36.

102. Hall, *The Moon and the Virgin*, pp. 11–12.

103. Aphrodite is also a "half-caste" (Alfred Metraux, *Voodoo in Haiti*, trans. Hugo Charteris [New York: Schocken Books, 1972], p. 110).

104. Deren, *Divine Horsemen*, p. 143.

105. Ibid.

106. Gatsby associated the green light with his dream of Daisy, a shallow woman, who nevertheless represents his White Goddess. Like the New World was to the "Dutch sailors' eyes," Daisy was the promise of a new enchanted world, "commensurate to his capacity for wonder." Gatsby believed in the future, and though his dreams would prove empty, he had only to "run faster, [to] stretch out [his] arms farther" to capture it. Thus the tragedy inherent in the American dream is personified in an empty white woman. Daisy is a mannequin much like the "Miss Anne" of African-American fiction. (F. Scott Fitzgerald, *The Great Gatsby* [New York: Charles Scribner's Sons, 1925], p. 182.)

107. Walt Whitman, "Edgar Poe's Significance," in *The Recognition of Edgar Allan Poe: Selected Criticism Since 1829*, ed. Eric W. Carlson (Ann Arbor: University of Michigan Press, 1966), p. 75.

108. Jung, *The Archetypes and the Collective Unconscious*, p. 85.

109. Baldwin, *Another Country*, p. 78.

110. Blind Willie Johnson, "Motherless Child," Columbia Records, 14343-D, 1927.

CHAPTER 3

1. *Webster's Ninth New Collegiate Dictionary* (Springfield, Mass.: Merriam-Webster, 1984), p. 1156.

2. Nor Hall, *The Moon and the Virgin: Reflections on the Archetypal Feminine* (New York: Harper & Row, 1980), p. 33.

3. Alain Daniélou, *Shiva and Dionysus*, trans. K. F. Hurry (London: East-West Publications, 1982), p. 80.

4. Ishmael Reed, *Mumbo Jumbo* (New York: Doubleday, 1972; New York: Avon Books, Bard Books, 1978), p. 241.

5. Ibid., p. 110.

6. Ishmael Reed, "why i often allude to osiris," in *Conjure: Selected Poems, 1963–1970* (Amherst: University of Massachusetts Press, 1972), p. 43.

7. Reed, *Mumbo Jumbo*, p. 110.

8. Ibid., p. 56.

9. Ibid.

10. Ibid., p. 38.

11. Maya Deren, *Divine Horsemen: The Voodoo Gods of Haiti* (New York: Chelsea House, 1970; New York: Dell, Delta Books, 1972), p. 62.

12. Robert Farris Thompson, *Black Gods and Kings: Yoruba Art at UCLA* (Bloomington: Indiana University Press, 1976), chap. 6, p. 1.

13. Ibid.

14. Robert D. Pelton, *The Trickster in West Africa: A Study of Mythic Irony and Sacred Delight* (Berkeley: University of California Press, 1980), p. 88.

15. Ibid., p. 89.

16. Daniélou, *Shiva and Dionysus*, p. 76.

17. Ibid., p. 77.

18. Pelton, *The Trickster in West Africa*, p. 88.

19. Ibid., p. 94.

20. Ibid., p. 83.

21. Ibid., p. 89.

22. Robert Blauner, *Racial Oppression in America* (New York: Harper & Row, 1972), p. 41.

23. Hall, *The Moon and the Virgin*, p. 33.

24. Ibid., p. 34.

25. William Ryan, *Blaming the Victim* (New York: Random House, Vintage Books, 1972), p. 7.

26. Ibid., p. 4.

27. Ibid., p. 286.

28. Ibid., p. 5.

29. Toni Morrison, *Song of Solomon* (New York: Alfred A. Knopf, 1977; New York: New American Library, Signet Books, 1978), p. 194.

30. Ishmael Reed, *Reckless Eyeballing* (New York: St. Martin's Press, 1986), p. 59.

31. Ibid., p. 20.

32. Ibid., p. 17.

33. Eldridge Cleaver, "The Primeval Mitosis" in *Soul on Ice* (New York: McGraw-Hill, 1968; New York: Dell, Laurel ed., 1978), p. 165.

34. Ibid., p. 167.

35. Ibid., p. 168.

36. Ibid., p. 170.

37. Alice Walker, *Meridian* (New York: Harcourt Brace Jovanovich, 1976; New York: Simon & Schuster, Pocket Books, Washington Square Press, 1977), p. 116.

38. Alice Childress, *A Short Walk* (New York: Coward, McCann & Geoghegan, 1979; New York: Avon Books, Bard Books, 1981), p. 305.

39. Reed, *Reckless Eyeballing*, p. 119.

40. Ibid., p. 120.

41. Ibid., p. 140.

42. Cleaver, *Soul on Ice*, p. 149.

43. Reed, *Reckless Eyeballing*, p. 120.

44. Ibid., p. 128.

45. Ibid., p. 140.

46. Calvin C. Hernton, *Sex and Racism in America* (New York: Grove Press, 1978), p. 147.

47. Ibid.

48. Walker, *Meridian*, pp. 107–8.

49. Ishmael Reed, *Flight to Canada* (New York: Random House, 1976; New York: Avon Books, Bard Books, 1977), p. 62.

50. Al Young, *Who Is Angelina?* (New York: Holt, Rinehart & Winston, 1975), p. 261.

51. Toni Cade Bambara, *The Salt Eaters* (New York: Random House, 1980), p. 94.

52. Ibid.

53. Paul Green and Richard Wright, *Native Son: The Biography of a Young American*, rev. ed. (New York: Samuel French, 1980), p. 98.

54. Daniélou, *Shiva and Dionysus*, p. 77.

55. Ibid., p. 76.

56. Blauner, *Racial Oppression in America*, pp. 41–42.

57. Toni Morrison, *Sula* (New York: Alfred A. Knopf, 1973; New York: New American Library, Plume Books, 1982), p. 4.

58. Ibid., p. 15.

59. James Baldwin, *Another Country* (New York: Dial Press, 1962; New York: Dell, Laurel ed., 1978), pp. 25–26.

60. James Baldwin, *Blues For Mister Charlie* (New York: Dial Press, 1964; New York: Dell, Laurel ed., 1976), p. 6.

61. Bambara, *The Salt Eaters*, p. 84.

62. Ibid.

63. Reed, *Flight to Canada*, p. 35.

64. Hernton, *Sex and Racism in America*, p. 19.

65. Ibid., p. 46.

66. Ibid., p. 44.

67. Ibid.

68. Ibid., p. 78.

69. Baldwin, *Blues For Mister Charlie*, pp. 45–46.

70. Hernton, *Sex and Racism in America*, p. 79.

71. Ibid., p. 24.

72. Reed, *Reckless Eyeballing*, p. 103.

73. Ibid., p. 142.

74. Ibid., p. 94.

75. Ibid., p. 103.

76. Hernton, *Sex and Racism in America*, p. 26.

77. Ibid.

78. Young, *Who Is Angelina?*, p. 198.

79. Ibid.

80. Ibid., p. 202.

81. Ibid., p. 203.

82. Ibid., p. 216.

83. Ibid., p. 217.

84. Ibid.

85. Hernton, *Sex and Racism in America*, p. 45.

86. Ibid.

87. Young, *Who Is Angelina?*, pp. 145–46.

88. Ibid., p. 148.

89. Morrison, *Song of Solomon*, p. 193.

90. Hernton, *Sex and Racism in America*, p. 42.

91. Chester Himes, *Pinktoes* (New York: G. P. Putnam's Sons/Stein & Day, 1961), pp. 109–10.

92. Ralph Ellison, *The Invisible Man* (New York: Random House, 1952; Vintage Books, 1972), p. 399.

93. Ibid., pp. 402–3.

94. Ibid., p. 404.

95. Ibid., p. 406.

96. Ibid., p. 510.

97. Ibid., p. 513.

98. Ibid., p. 504.

99. Ibid., p. 506.

100. Ibid., p. 507.

101. Ibid., p. 509.

102. Ibid., p. 511.

103. Ibid., pp. 543–44.

104. Hernton, *Sex and Racism in America*, p. 47.

105. Ibid., p. 48.

106. Ibid., p. 49.

107. Ibid., p. 46.

108. Childress, *A Short Walk*, pp. 35–36.

109. Ibid., p. 37.

110. Ibid.

111. Morrison, *Song of Solomon*, p. 291.

112. Ibid., p. 293.

113. Young, *Who Is Angelina?*, p. 199.

114. Hernton, *Sex and Racism in America*, p. 44.

115. Ibid., p. 47.

116. John A. Williams, *The Man Who Cried I Am* (Boston: Little, Brown, 1967; New York: New American Library, Signet Books, 1968), p. 17.

117. Ibid., p. 65.

118. Hernton, *Sex and Racism in America*, p. 34.

119. Ibid., p. 36.

120. Ibid.

121. Childress, *A Short Walk*, p. 161.

122. Ibid., p. 160.

123. Walker, *Meridian*, p. 152.

124. Ibid., p. 155.

125. Ibid.

126. Childress, *A Short Walk*, p. 161.

127. Williams, *The Man Who Cried I Am*, p. 58.

128. Ibid., p. 104.

129. Ibid., p. 55.

130. Ibid., p. 57.

131. Ibid., p. 230.

132. Ibid., p. 231.

133. Ibid., p. 232.

134. Ibid., p. 283.

135. Ibid., p. 295.

136. Ibid., p. 296.

137. Hernton, *Sex and Racism in America*, p. 52.

138. Young, *Who Is Angelina?*, p. 26.

139. Ibid., p. 25.

140. Ibid., p. 263.

141. Hernton, *Sex and Racism in America*, p. 15.

142. Ibid., p. 16.

143. Ibid., p. 17.

144. Ibid., p. 20.

145. Alice Walker, *The Color Purple* (New York: Simon & Schuster, Pocket Books, Washington Square Press, 1983), p. 86.

146. Ibid., p. 87.

147. Ibid., pp. 102–3.

148. Ibid., p. 232.

149. Ibid., p. 234.

150. Cecil Brown, *The Life and Loves of Mr. Jiveass Nigger* (New York: Farrar, Straus & Giroux, 1969), pp. 52–53.

151. Ibid., p. 52.

152. Eldridge Cleaver, "To A White Girl," in *Soul on Ice* (New York: McGraw-Hill, 1968; New York: Dell, Laurel ed., 1978), pp. 25–26.

153. Chester Himes, *The Primitive* (New York: New American Library, Signet Books, 1956), p. 130. Himes also refers to white women as fish in *Pinktoes*, p. 196.

154. Hernton, *Sex and Racism in America*, p. 19.

155. Young, *Who Is Angelina?*, p. 147.

156. Ibid., p. 203.

157. Ibid., p. 201.

158. Hernton, *Sex and Racism in America*, p. 45.

159. Ibid., p. 85.

160. Ibid., p. 84.

161. Ibid., p. 66.

162. Leslie Marmon Silko, *Ceremony* (New York: Viking Press, 1977; New York: New American Library, Signet Books, 1978), p. 42.

163. John Okada, *No-No Boy* (Rutherford, Vt.: Charles E. Tuttle, 1957; Seattle: Asian American Resources Project and the University of Washington Press, 1976), p. 164.

164. Ibid.

165. Jean Toomer, "Box Seat," in *Cane* (New York: Liveright, 1975), p. 57.

166. Ibid.

167. Walker, *Meridian*, p. 108.

168. Paule Marshall, *The Chosen Place, The Timeless People* (New York: Harcourt, Brace & World, 1969; New York: Random House, Vintage Books, 1984), p. 23.

169. Ibid., pp. 5, 33.

170. Brown, *The Life and Loves of Mr. Jiveass Nigger*, pp. 35–36.

171. Ibid., p. 39.

CHAPTER 4

1. Erich Neumann, *The Great Mother: An Analysis of the Archetype*, trans. Ralph Manheim, Bollingen Series 47, 2nd ed. (Princeton, N.J.: Princeton University Press, 1972), p. 330.

2. Ibid., p. 331.

3. Ibid., p. 330.

4. Ibid., p. 336.

5. Joseph Campbell, ed., *The Portable Jung* (New York: Viking Press, 1971; New York: Penguin Books, 1976), p. 278.

6. Ibid., p. 288.

7. Ibid., p. 289.

8. Ibid., p. 300.

9. James Baldwin, *Another Country* (New York: Dial Press, 1962; New York: Dell, Laurel ed., 1978), p. 70.

10. Ibid., p. 431.

11. Ishmael Reed, *Hell Hath No Fury* (title later changed to *Mother Hubbard*), unpublished ts., Ishmael Reed Papers, University of Delaware Library, 1980, pp. 3–4.

12. Ibid., p. 11.

13. Baldwin, *Another Country*, p. 71.

14. Ibid.

15. Ibid., p. 242.

16. Ibid., p. 244.

17. Ibid., p. 305.

18. Ibid., p. 247.

19. Ibid., p. 309.

20. Ibid., p. 36.

21. Ibid., p. 94.

22. Ibid., p. 95.

23. Neumann, *The Great Mother*, p. 331.

24. Baldwin, *Another Country*, p. 341.

25. Ibid.

26. T. Lidz, *The Family and Human Adaptation* (London: Hogarth Press, 1964), p.

54; also appears in R. D. Laing, *The Politics of Experience* (New York: Pantheon Books, 1967; Ballantine Books, 1968), p. 64.

    27. Laing, *The Politics of Experience*, p. 28.

    28. Alice Childress, *A Short Walk* (New York: Coward, McCann & Geoghegan, 1979; New York: Avon Books, Bard Books, 1981), p. 159.

    29. Ibid., p. 160.

    30. Ibid., p. 161.

    31. Ibid., p. 186.

    32. Ibid., p. 222.

    33. Ibid., p. 223.

    34. Ibid., pp. 284–85.

    35. Ibid., p. 286.

    36. Al Young, *Who Is Angelina?* (New York: Holt, Rinehart & Winston, 1975), p. 22.

    37. Ibid., p. 23.

    38. Ibid., p. 29.

    39. Ibid., p. 159.

    40. Ibid., p. 261.

    41. Ibid., p. 26.

    42. Baldwin, *Another Country*, p. 36.

    43. John A. Williams, *The Man Who Cried I Am* (Boston: Little, Brown, 1967; New York: New American Library, Signet Books, 1968), p. 12.

    44. Ibid., p. 11.

    45. Ibid., p. 234.

    46. Ibid., p. 280.

    47. Ibid., p. 281.

    48. Ibid., p. 280.

    49. Ibid., p. 295.

    50. Ibid., p. 291.

    51. Ibid., pp. 290–91.

    52. Ibid., p. 295.

    53. Ibid., p. 334.

    54. Ibid., p. 34.

CHAPTER 5

    1. Alice Walker, *Meridian* (New York: Harcourt Brace Jovanovich, 1976; New York: Simon & Schuster, Pocket Books, Washington Square Press, 1977), p. 137.

    2. Al Young, *Who Is Angelina?* (New York: Holt, Rinehart & Winston, 1975), p. 261.

    3. Toni Cade Bambara, *The Salt Eaters* (New York: Random House, 1980), p. 84.

    4. Henry John Drewel and Margaret Thompson Drewel, *Gelede: Art and Female Power Among the Yoruba* (Bloomington: Indiana University Press, 1983), p. 73.

    5. Ibid., p. 39.

    6. Leslie Marmon Silko, *Ceremony* (New York: Viking Press, 1977; New York: New American Library, Signet Books, 1978), p. 36.

    7. Drewel and Drewel, *Gelede*, p. 39.

    8. Ibid., p. 103.

9. Ibid., p. 82.

10. Ibid., p. 74.

11. Ibid., p. 73.

12. Ibid., p. 102.

13. Robert Farris Thompson, *Flash of the Spirit: African and Afro-American Art and Philosophy* (New York: Random House, 1983; Vintage Books, 1984), p. 16.

14. Ibid., p. 19.

15. Robert D. Pelton, *The Trickster in West Africa: A Study of Mythic Irony and Sacred Delight* (Berkeley: University of California Press, 1980), p. 135.

16. Robert Farris Thompson, *Black Gods and Kings: Yoruba Art at UCLA* (Bloomington: Indiana University Press, 1976), chap. 4, p. 1.

17. Ishmael Reed, "Neo-HooDoo Manifesto," in *Conjure: Selected Poems, 1963–1970* (Amherst: University of Massachusetts Press, 1972), p. 21.

18. LeRoi Jones [Amiri Baraka, pseud.], *The Slave*, in Dutchman *and* The Slave: *Two Plays by LeRoi Jones* (New York: William Morrow, 1964), p. 73.

19. Ishmael Reed, "introducing a new loa," in *Conjure: Selected Poems, 1963–1970* (Amherst: University of Massachusetts Press, 1972), p. 83.

20. Ishmael Reed, "Can A Metronome Know the Thunder or Summon a God?", in *The Black Aesthetic*, ed. Addison Gayle, Jr. (New York: Doubleday, Anchor Books, 1972), p. 381.

21. Plato, *Phaedrus*, trans. W. C. Helmhold and W. G. Rabinowitz (New York: Bobbs-Merrill, Liberal Arts Press, 1956), p. 381.

22. C. G. Jung, "The Conjunction *Mysterium Coniunctionis*," in *The Essential Jung*, selected and introduced by Anthony Storr (Princeton, N.J.: Princeton University Press, 1983), p. 293.

23. Bambara, *The Salt Eaters*, p. 245.

24. Ibid., p. 248.

25. Ibid., p. 249.

26. Ibid., p. 251.

27. Ibid., p. 273.

28. Ibid., p. 276.

29. Ibid., p. 279.

30. Ibid., p. 278.

31. Pelton, *The Trickster in West Africa*, p. 151.

32. Ibid., p. 150.

33. Ibid., p. 218.

34. Ibid., p. 222.

35. Ibid., p. 232.

36. Ibid., p. 243.

37. G.W.F. Hegel, *The Phenomenology of the Mind*, trans. J. B. Baillie (New York: Humanities Press; New York: Harper & Row, Harper Torchbooks, 1967), p. 229.

38. Ibid., p. 679.

39. I borrowed this analogy from Ken Westhaver, artist and clinical psychologist.

40. Pelton, *The Trickster in West Africa*, p. 185.

41. Robert Farris Thompson, *Flash of the Spirit*, p. 114.

42. Ibid., p. 19.

43. C. G. Jung, *The Archetypes and the Collective Unconscious*, Trans. R.F.C. Hull, Bollingen Series 20, 2nd ed., in *The Collected Works of C. G. Jung*, vol. 9, part 1, eds. William McGuire et al. (Princeton, N.J.: Princeton University Press, 1968), p. 288.

44. Pelton, *The Trickster in West Africa*, p. 72.

45. Ibid., p. 73.

46. C. G. Jung, "Aion," in *Psyche and Symbol: A Selection from the Writings of C. G. Jung*, ed. Violet S. De Laszlo (New York: Doubleday, Anchor Books, 1958), p. 11.

47. Jung, *The Archetypes and the Collective Unconscious*, p. 82.

48. Chester Himes, "Dilemma of the Negro Novelist in the U.S.A.," in *New Black Voices: An Anthology of Contemporary Afro-American Literature*, ed. Abraham Chapman (New York: New American Library, Mentor Books, 1972), p. 396.

49. Reed, "why i often allude to osiris" and "introducing a new loa," pp. 43, 83.

50. LeRoi Jones [Amiri Baraka, pseud.], *Dutchman*, in Dutchman *and* The Slave: *Two Plays by LeRoi Jones* (New York: William Morrow, 1964), p. 19.

51. Himes, "Dilemma of the Negro Novelist," p. 397.

52. Jones, *Dutchman*, p. 37.

53. LeRoi Jones [Amiri Baraka, pseud.], *The Slave*, in Dutchman *and* The Slave: *Two Plays by LeRoi Jones* (New York: William Morrow, 1964), p. 81.

54. Himes, "Dilemma of the Negro Novelist," p. 395.

55. Ibid., p. 399.

56. Ibid., p. 401.

57. Ibid., pp. 400–401.

58. Ibid., p. 396.

59. Joseph Campbell, ed., *The Portable Jung* (New York: Viking Press, 1971; New York: Penguin Books, 1976), p. 286.

60. Ibid., p. 287.

61. Russell Banks, *The Book of Jamaica* (New York: Random House, Ballantine Books, 1986), p. 5.

62. Octavio Paz, "Laughter and Penitence," Epigraph in Banks, *The Book of Jamaica*.

63. Ibid.

64. When Betonie describes the world as "fragile" the word he chooses is "filled with the intricacies of a continuing process . . . with a strength inherent in spider webs . . . entangl[ing]" the sun. Each word is chosen carefully and must "be explained with a story about why it must be said this certain way." The stories and the healing are part of "the responsibility that [goes along] with being human" (Silko, *Ceremony*, pp. 36–37).

65. Bambara, *The Salt Eaters*, pp. 292–95.

66. Ibid., p. 295.

67. "Jes Grew was an anti-plague" which "enlivened the host. . . . Jes Grew is the delight of the gods . . . characterized by ebullience and ecstasy" (Ishmael Reed, *Mumbo Jumbo* [New York: Doubleday, 1972; New York: Avon Books, Bard Books, 1978], p. 9).

68. Reed, "introducing a new loa," p. 83.

Bibliography

AFRICAN AND AFRICAN-AMERICAN RELIGION AND PHILOSOPHY

Courlander, Harold. *A Treasury of Afro-American Folklore*. New York: Crown, 1976.

Deren, Maya. *Divine Horsemen: The Voodoo Gods of Haiti*. New York: Chelsea House, 1970; New York: Dell, Delta Books, 1972.

Drewel, Henry John, and Margaret Thompson Drewel. *Gelede: Art and Female Power Among the Yoruba*. Bloomington: Indiana University Press, 1983.

Metraux, Alfred. *Voodoo in Haiti. Trans. Hugo Charteris*. New York: Schocken Books, 1972.

Pelton, Robert D. *The Trickster in West Africa: A Study of Mythic Irony and Sacred Delight*. Berkeley: University of California Press, 1980.

Thompson, Robert Farris. *Black Gods and Kings: Yoruba Art at UCLA*. Bloomington: Indiana University Press, 1976.

———. *Flash of the Spirit: African and Afro-American Art and Philosophy*. New York: Random House, 1983; Vintage Books, 1984.

FICTION

Baldwin, James. *Another Country*. New York: Dial Press, 1962; New York: Dell, Laurel ed., 1978.

———. *Blues For Mister Charlie*. New York: Dial Press, 1964; New York: Dell, Laurel ed., 1976.

Bambara, Toni Cade. *The Salt Eaters*. New York: Random House, 1980.

Banks, Russell. *The Book of Jamaica*. New York, Random House, Ballantine Books, 1986.

Brown, Cecil. *The Life and Loves of Mr. Jiveass Nigger*. New York: Farrar, Straus & Giroux, 1969.

Childress, Alice. *A Short Walk*. New York: Coward, McCann & Geoghegan, 1979; New York: Avon Books, Bard Books, 1981.

Cleaver, Eldridge. *Soul on Ice*. New York: McGraw-Hill, 1968; New York: Dell, Laurel ed., 1978.

Ellison, Ralph. *Invisible Man*. New York: Random House, 1952; Vintage Books, 1972.

Fitzgerald, F. Scott. *The Great Gatsby*. New York: Charles Scribner's Sons, 1925.

Green, Paul, and Richard Wright. *Native Son: The Biography of a Young American*. Rev. ed. New York: Samuel French, 1980.

Himes, Chester. *If He Hollers Let Him Go*. New York: New American Library, Signet Books, 1971.

———. *Pinktoes*. New York. G. P. Putnam's Sons/Stein & Day, 1961.

———. *The Primitive*. New York: New American Library, Signet Books, 1956.

Jones, LeRoi [Amiri Baraka, pseud.]. Dutchman *and* The Slave: *Two Plays by LeRoi Jones*. New York: William Morrow, 1964.

Marshall, Paule. *The Chosen Place, The Timeless People*. New York: Harcourt, Brace & World, 1969; New York: Random House, Vintage Books, 1984.

Morrison, Toni. *Beloved*. New York: Alfred A. Knopf, 1987.

———. *Song of Solomon*. New York: Alfred A. Knopf, 1977; New York: New American Library, Signet Books, 1978.

———. *Sula*. New York: Alfred A. Knopf, 1973; New York: New American Library, Plume Books, 1982.

Okada, John. *No-No Boy*. Rutherford, Vt.: Charles E. Tuttle, 1957; Seattle: Asian American Resources Project and the University of Washington Press, 1976.

Poe, Edgar Allan. "Annabel Lee." In *The Complete Poems of Edgar Allan Poe*. Ed. J. H. Whitty. 3rd ed., rev. New York: Houghton Mifflin, 1919.

———. "The Fall of the House of Usher." In *The Centenary Poe: Tales, Poems, Criticism, Marginalia and Eureka by Edgar Allan Poe*. Ed. Montagu Slater. London: Bodley Head, 1949.

Reed, Ishmael. *Conjure: Selected Poems, 1963–1970*. Amherst: University of Massachusetts Press, 1972.

———. *Flight to Canada*. New York: Random House, 1976; New York: Avon Books, Bard Books, 1977.

———. *Hell Hath No Fury* (title later changed to *Mother Hubbard*). Unpublished ts., Ishmael Reed Papers, University of Delaware Library, 1980.

———. *Mumbo Jumbo*. New York: Doubleday, 1972; New York: Avon Books, Bard Books, 1978.

———. *Reckless Eyeballing*. New York: St. Martin's, 1986.

Silko, Leslie Marmon. *Ceremony*. New York: Viking Press, 1977; New York: New American Library, Signet Books, 1978.

Toomer, Jean. *Cane*. New York: Liveright, 1975.

Walker, Alice. *The Color Purple*. New York: Simon & Schuster, Pocket Books, Washington Square Press, 1983.

———. *Meridian*. New York: Harcourt Brace Jovanovich, 1976; New York: Simon & Schuster, Pocket Books, Washington Square Press, 1977.

Williams, John A. *The Man Who Cried I Am*. Boston: Little, Brown, 1967; New York: New American Library, Signet Books, 1968.

Wright, Richard. *Native Son*. New York: Harper & Row, Perennial Classics, 1966.

Young, Al. *Who Is Angelina?* New York: Holt, Rinehart & Winston, 1975.

LITERARY CRITICISM

Alexander, Charlotte. "The 'Stink' of Reality: Mothers and Whores in James Baldwin's Fiction." In *James Baldwin: A Collection of Critical Essays*. Ed. Kenneth Kinnamon. Englewood Cliffs, New Jersey: Prentice-Hall, 1974.

Bigsby, C.W.E., ed. "The Black American Writer." In *The Black American Writer: Vol. 1, Fiction*. Deland, FL: Everett/Edwards, 1969. Reprint. Baltimore: Penguin Books, Pelican Books, 1971.

Ellison, Ralph. "The Art of Fiction: An Interview." In *Shadow and Act*. New York: Random House, 1964.

Himes, Chester. "Dilemma of the Negro Novelist in the U.S.A." In *New Black Voices: An Anthology of Contemporary Afro-American Literature*. Ed. Abraham Chapman. New York: New American Library, Mentor Books, 1972.

Phillips, Louis. "LeRoi Jones and Contemporary Black Drama." In *The Black American Writer: Vol. 2, Poetry and Drama*. Ed. C.W.E. Bigsby. Deland, FL: Everett/Edwards, 1969; Baltimore: Penguin Books, Pelican Books, 1971.

Poe, Edgar Allan. "The Philosophy of Composition." In *Selections from Poe's Literary Criticism*. Ed. John Brooks Moore. New York: F. S. Crofts, 1926.

Reed, Ishmael. "Can a Metronome Know the Thunder or Summon a God?" In *The Black Aesthetic*. Ed. Addison Gayle, Jr. New York: Doubleday, Anchor Books, 1972.

———. "Introduction to *19 Necromancers From Now*." In *New Black Voices: An Anthology of Contemporary Afro-American Literature*. Ed. Abraham Chapman. New York: New American Library, Mentor Books, 1972.

Whitman, Walt. "Edgar Poe's Significance." In *The Recognition of Edgar Allan Poe: Selected Criticism Since 1829*. Ed. Eric W. Carlson. Ann Arbor: University of Michigan Press, 1966.

MYTHOLOGY, ARCHETYPES AND JUNGIAN PSYCHOLOGY

Campbell, Joseph. *The Hero with a Thousand Faces*. New York: Bollingen Foundation, 1949; New York: World Publishing, Meridian Books, 1956.

———. *"The Masks of God" : Occidental Mythology*. New York: Viking Press, Compass ed., 1970; New York: Penguin Books, 1976.

———. *Myths to Live By*. New York: Viking Press, 1972; New York: Bantam Books, 1973.

———, ed. *The Portable Jung*. New York: Viking Press, 1971; New York: Penguin Books, 1976.

Daniélou. Alain. *Shiva and Dionysus*. Trans. K. F. Hurry. London: East-West Publications, 1982.

Graves, Robert. *The White Goddess*. Amended and enlarged ed. New York: Farrar, Straus & Giroux, 1966.

Hall, Nor. *The Moon and the Virgin: Reflections on the Archetypal Feminine*. New York: Harper & Row, 1980.

Jung, C. G. "Aion." In *Psyche and Symbol: A Selection from the Writings of C. G. Jung*. Ed. Violet S. De Laszlo. New York: Doubleday, Anchor Books, 1958.

———. *The Archetypes and the Collective Unconscious*. Trans. R.F.C. Hull. Bollingen Series 20. 2nd ed. In *The Collected Works of C. G. Jung*, vol. 9, pt. 1. Eds. William McGuire et al. Princeton, N.J.: Princeton University Press, 1968.

———. "The Conjunction *Mysterium Coniunctionis*." In *The Essential Jung*. Selected and introduced by Anthony Storr. Princeton, N.J.: Princeton University Press, 1983.

———, ed. *Man and His Symbols*. New York: Dell, Laurel ed., 1968.

Neumann, Erich. *The Great Mother: An Analysis of the Archetype*. Trans. Ralph Manheim. Bollingen Series 47. 2nd ed. Princeton, N.J.: Princeton University Press, 1972.

O'Flaherty, Wendy Doniger. *Women, Androgynes, and Other Mythical Beasts*. Chicago: University of Chicago Press, 1982.

Rees, Alwyn, and Brinley Rees. *Celtic Heritage: Ancient Tradition in Ireland and Wales*. London: Thames & Hudson, 1961.

Thompson, William Irwin. *The Time Falling Bodies Take to Light: Mythology, Sexuality, and the Origins of Culture*. New York: St. Martin's Press, Lindisfarne Series, 1981.

PHILOSOPHY

Hegel, G.W.F. *The Phenomenology of the Mind*. Trans. J. B. Baillie. New York: Humanities Press; New York: Harper & Row, Harper Torchbooks, 1967.

Laing, R. D. *The Politics of Experience*. New York: Pantheon Books, 1967; New York: Ballantine Books, 1968.

Lidz, T. *The Family and Human Adaptation*. London: Hogarth Press, 1964. In R. D. Laing, *The Politics of Experience*. New York: Pantheon Books, 1967; New York: Ballantine Books, 1968.

Paz, Octavio. "Laughter and Penitence." Epigraph in Russell Banks, *The Book of Jamaica*. New York: Ballantine, 1986.

Plato. *Phaedrus*. Trans. W. C. Helmhold and W. G. Rabinowitz. New York: Bobbs-Merrill, Liberal Arts Press, 1956.

SOCIOLOGY

Blauner, Robert. *Racial Oppression in America*. New York: Harper & Row, 1972.

Hernton, Calvin C. *Sex and Racism in America*. New York: Grove Press, 1978.

Ryan, William. *Blaming the Victim*. New York: Random House, Vintage Books, 1972.

Index

Abyss, 1, 50, 53; and ritual reclamation, 57; and underworld, 54, 99

Aje, 1, 75, 77, 95

Ambivalence, 18–19, 81, 86–87; Bigger (*Native Son*), 45; Bona and Paul (*Cane*), 34; Femme Fatale, 50; Ian Ball (*Reckless Eyeballing*), 82; Invisible Man, 18, 86; Kriss and Jesse (*The Primitive*), 26; Leona and Rufus (*Another Country*), 40, 42, 78, 80; Madge and Robert (*If He Hollers Let Him Go*), 19, 26, 45, 80, 109; mother, 14, 35; Seductress, 58, 121; Well-Intentioned, 53

Analogy, 8, 67, 115, 124–25. *See also* Correspondence

Ancestors, 1–2, 110, 112; and divination, 116; Egungun, 26, 112

Anima, 7, 30, 34, 56, 73, 82; and feminine Archetypes, 66; conflict, 26; gloomy, 52, 60; initiation and, 57; integration of, 8, 74, 100, 118, 120, 122; mother-seeking, 17, 35, 52; as Muse, 54; positive, 33, 54, 103–4; and repulsive mates, 56

—negative, 38, 59, 68, 124; Aphrodite, the Lorelei, 54; in *Another Country*, 31–32, 52; in *The Chosen Place, The Timeless People*, 33; and devouring mother, 32, 61; in *Dutchman*, 27, 31, 54; in *Flight to Canada*, 17, 34–35; in *If He Hollers Let Him Go*, 27; in *Meridian*, 52, 90; and necrophilia, 17; in *The Primitive*, 8, 27; and suicide, 31, 52, 60; and Terrible Goddess, 122; and violence, 40–42

—projection, 8, 10, 68, 121, 124; in *Another Country*, 52; in *Dutchman*, 27, 31; in *Flight to Canada*, 17; in *If He Hollers Let Him Go*, 27; in *Meridian*, 52; in *Native Son*, 74; in *The Primitive*, 27

Animus, 26; and clinging behavior, 121; death, 31; integration of, 8, 74, 99–100, 114, 118, 120, 122, 124; mood, 32

—negative, 28; in *Dutchman*, 55; in "Fall of the House of Usher," 31; and Femme Fatale, 31, 59, 90; in *The Man Who Cried I Am*, 50, 89; and oppressive power structure, 120, 122; and outlaws, 34, 55; in *The Primitive*, 8, 23; projection, 8, 10, 43, 52, 99, 121; and rape fantasies, 19–20,

ABOUT THE AUTHOR

ANNA MARIA CHUPA is a teacher of studio art and art history in Wilmington, Delaware. She was previously a program development specialist for the Delaware Humanities Forum and Artist-in-Residence at the Delaware State Arts Council. Her article "Damballah and Erzulie as Major Loa in *Sula*, *Song of Solomon*, and *SaltEaters*: Continuity and Preservation" appeared in the collection *Quilt 4*.